To Sheila _ July, 1972

_ fo

with affection, Rose

THE
LEARNING
CHILD

THE
LEARNING
CHILD

. . .

Dorothy H. Cohen

PANTHEON BOOKS

A Division of Random House, New York

ISBN: 0-394-47112-1

Library of Congress Catalog Card Number: 79-184656

Grateful acknowledgment is extended to the following for permission to reprint copyrighted material:

Cambridge University Press: For excerpts from *Experiment in Education* by Sybil Marshall.

Design by Carol Halpert

Manufactured in the United States of America by The Colonial Press Inc., Clinton, Massachusetts

2 4 6 8 9 7 5 3

FIRST EDITION

Library of Congress Cataloging in Publication Data
Cohen, Dorothy H. The learning child.

Includes bibliographical references.
1. Education, Elementary. 2. Parent and child. 3. Child study. I. Title.
LB1555.C59   372'.01   79-184656   ISBN 0-394-47112-1

TO

Ben, Josh, Naomi,
and those they love in turn

Acknowledgments

. . .

No book comes to fruition without the help and support of many who contribute, sometimes knowingly, sometimes unwittingly, to the final outcome. The first sources for this book were my early teachers at the Bank Street College of Education, particularly Barbara Biber and Lucy Sprague Mitchell, who developed the outline of this essay long before I knew it would be written.

Since then, there have been my faculty colleagues at Bank Street, whose passionate concern for humanist education has spurred continuous thinking while giving me the heart for this work; the many teachers and student-teachers who have broadened my understanding of today's problems of teaching and learning; the parents whose concerns I shared at one-night stands in schools, in child study groups, and in individual consultations for more than two decades; and of course, the children, past and present, from whom I learned humility and for whom this book is an offering of hope. To all of them I owe a debt of empathy deeper than gratitude.

To my family, who lived tolerantly with yet another book, and especially to my husband, who endured my doubts and anxieties with stoic faith, I acknowledge a debt of love.

To Frances and Joan Clarke, who between them made the manuscript a physical reality, I owe special gratitude for the devotion and concern that are themselves the mark of the humanist.

To Clara Balter, Dorothy Bloomfield, Dorothy Bradbury, Peggy Cole, Ethel Horn, and Lois Wolf, I owe thanks for reading and reacting to parts of this manuscript as teachers and parents.

To André Schiffrin and Verne Moberg of Pantheon Books, my thanks for their patience and forbearance and for allowing me the latitude I needed to say what I thought needed saying. For its incompleteness I alone am responsible.

Dorothy H. Cohen
Bank Street College of Education
New York City

December 15, 1971

Contents

· · ·

Introduction

. . .

It is a truism that ours is a time of transition. The colonialism of centuries is in the last throes of dissolution; empire-building has ceased for Europeans, but has been taken over in a new form by Americans. It is a time when the race of man waits to be born out of the struggle of minorities for common equality, yet minorities of race and religion still snarl at each other. It is a time when the planet's population must no longer grow in uncontrolled fashion, yet ancient moralities still resist the necessity of control. Extraordinary contradictions exist between the outdated primitivism of war, hot and cold, and the pious profession of morality and love for fellow man, between the technological brilliance that makes a good life possible for all and the greed of those who hold power, between the enlarging vistas of comfort held open to all mankind and the social irresponsibility that is causing the destruction of the basic necessities for human survival—air, soil, and water.

Still, even in a time of turmoil and change, babies are born and grow; they enter first grade and go on to high school and college. Parents still try to bring up their children as though the values learned in their childhood will continue into their children's generation. As always, parents want "the best" for their children. They want them to be healthy, to have a happy childhood, to do well at school, and to grow up to be successful and happy adults.

But, for today's child, it is a far cry from the world in which seven-year-old Alice walked with Lewis Carroll in a mood of trust and love that led to his present of a fantasy world for her pleasure.

Today a seven-year-old points to his luncheon companions at school and taunts, "You're eating chemicals." Today an eight-year-old confides in her teacher, "Do you know what I dreamed last night? I dreamed that the Hudson River was not polluted any more." Today nine-year-olds look to their future with the skepticism of the disillusioned; they are not sure the world will last. A fourth-grade child celebrated Earth Day 1970 by writing of this fear:

> In 1985 the days got older, the sun got darker and was old. The people were dying little by little. The clouds were dark. I was scared to death. One day I started to cough and cough. Then I died.

In today's America are emerging eleven- and twelve-year-old children who cannot reconcile their moral and religious beliefs with allegiance to the American flag. A boy of thirteen expresses anger at his society in unbelievably strong terms:

> We strain to move aside the dead weight of authority blocking our path, but are either overcome by the bureaucracy or forced to use violent means.[1]

The American child, glued to the television screen, is informed with dispassionate objectivity that his earth is being despoiled, his air fouled, animal species threatened, and the survival of man himself is in doubt. He is shown graphically how

[1] Ernest Dunbar, "Trouble: The High School Radicals," *Look Magazine*, March 24, 1970, p. 73.

soldiers of his country burn, bomb, and destroy a faraway country whose name is well known to him: Vietnam. Each morning of his life he listens to the news about the numbers of Americans killed and the numbers Americans have killed. He hears of deaths by drugs, deaths by accidents, deaths of civil rights leaders, bombing of banks and other buildings, and hijacking of civilian planes at gun point. Through it all drums the monotonously steady build-up of weapons of destruction by his government and the protests of those for whom war is an anachronism.

Too young to remember the assassination of a president, children of elementary school age are dimly aware that the children of that president are of their time and generation. Of their time and generation also are the children of Martin Luther King and the younger children of Robert Kennedy. The echoes of these acts of violence, which grown-ups remember all too well, resound for the children in the anger and protest of the generation just ahead of them, of the young people, black and white, whose frustration with their country has often led to violence, even as they were themselves seeking to abort the violence and destruction they despise.

The white child and the black child growing up in America both face serious problems of identification as Americans, although the historical paths to this point of convergence have been different for each. The black child is caught in the crosscurrents of the drama played out over his head, and he has no way of knowing that separatism and hate are inevitable stages in the growing emergence of his people as men and women of dignity. For the white child, the contradictions between what he is taught and what he sees and hears confuse him, at the least, and leave him bitter at the other extreme.

In such a time, childhood stability is hard-won and can be a matter of illusion more than reality. A non-Jewish college professor, who was a child in Nazi Germany, recalled to this writer how she and her brother agreed not to tell their parents what they knew of the horrors going on around them. With the sixth sense that children possess, they knew that their parents preferred to believe that their children were safely unaware of the evils of the adult world and they did nothing to disabuse their parents of their illusion. But that was before the era of television and mass air travel dispensed with such illusions forever.

To the present generation of children, Europe is a mere six hours away, the Orient a skip and a hop across the Pacific. No place is far, the world is clearly one, and Americans hold a special place in it. Arnold Toynbee sees the United States as "the leader of a world-wide anti-revolutionary movement in defense of vested interests." [2] Noam Chomsky suggests that because of our position in the world, "the level of culture that can be achieved in the United States is a life-and-death matter for large masses of suffering humanity." [3] As we focus on the problem of rearing and educating today's children, we must ask with new seriousness: What are our children going to inherit? What kind of relevance must their education have to their adult lives in a world that is so small, so interdependent, and so full of contradictions?

The opportunism, the pragmatism, the let-the-chips-fall-where-they-may attitudes have run their course. There is no frontier to conquer, no South Sea islands to run away to, no escape from the stupidity and selfishness of man himself. Yet, looking to our children's future, we must recognize that, despite the ugliness and fear, this happens also to be the century of the common man. The surge upward into autonomy and independence of people who have been proverbially at the bottom is completely consonant with our own democratic heritage. More important, for the first time in man's history, there is a technological base from which the possibility of a life free from hunger and want is a potential reality for all mankind.

[2] Arnold J. Toynbee, *America and the World Revolution* (New York and London: Oxford University Press, 1962), p. 92.
[3] Noam Chomsky, "Some Thoughts on Intellectuals and the Schools," *Harvard Educational Review,* Vol. 36, Fall 1966, pp. 484–491.

For the first time, too, the world is small enough so that the vision of a brotherhood of man can begin to make practical sense. Alternatives are still open, and we can and must make choices for our children which will lead to a hopeful destiny for them.

In times of stress, adults tend to focus on their children with extraordinary intensity, as though their anxiety were easier to bear if they could at least feel that their children's future was guaranteed. A long-ago period of anxiety similar to ours about America's future is described by Bernard Wishy in *The Child of the Republic*.[4] Fifty years after the American Revolution, people worried about a growing contradiction they saw between the morality and ethics of the Revolution on the one hand and the drive for material success on the other. That time of anxiety, like ours, also saw a mushrooming of interest in child-rearing and childhood education and was the background from which emerged both the liberal and the organizational ideas about schooling that are in contradiction with each other today. Are we perhaps at the critical end of that contradiction in purposes that worried Americans enough 150 years ago to cause them to place great stress on their children's education? As Americans today struggle with their conscience and their fears, is it possible that intense interest in children and their education today also incorporates a frantic search for a toe-hold on a future which we otherwise feel is uncertain? Is this why there is such adult pressure on children to achieve earlier and earlier, even at the cost of their childhood and youth? And why so many young adults protest against *any* kind of pressure or even structure? Is it the anxiety of adults that is creating such emotionally charged antagonisms over the education of children?

There are many Americans who accept the fact that we are at a turning point in our national life and that our children must be directed toward life in an open, plural society, where people have priority over things. But large objectives of this

---

[4] Bernard Wishy, *The Child of the Republic* (Philadelphia: University of Pennsylvania Press, 1968).

kind need to be translated into manageable goals and practices in child-rearing and schooling. As we examine the current educational scene and its ferment, it is apparent that today's schools, no less than today's parents, are enmeshed in a system which is altering values in every aspect of living, yet the directions we can take are contradictory.

Four views seem to be competing for the schools and our children's future. The first is the traditional view of elementary education, which seeks to perpetuate itself with some slight modifications but no essential redirection. Perceiving the child as dependent on schooling for knowledge, the traditional view sees its task as substantially that of passing on to children the heritage of the past. In the elementary years, this means teaching the basic skills during the first years of schooling in order to lead children toward some peripheral involvement in the heritage during the later years of the elementary school. True involvement must wait until the secondary years and later. The traditional view shows little awareness of what is happening to children themselves during their middle years. Even less does traditional education project a changing world.

A second view looks with respectful awe upon our technology. Children are seen as the recipients of technological benefits and as the potential participants in technological advancement. As future men and women, they may have to be prepared to spend years in a capsule traveling to distant planets. They must be geared in all ways to sustain their existence under such conditions, the likes of which man has never known. In this view, it is technology that guides and steers the person's destiny and must perforce control and guide children's education. The earlier the technical education begins, the better.

A third view springs from a disavowal of the first two. It seeks to turn its back on contemporary society and return to a simple, rural life, to find a true humanity and restore the underlying communion between man and the earth. Men and women must learn again to rely upon their own energies for survival; the reality of feeling must take precedence over the contribution of the intellect. Present-oriented, this view gives little consideration to the probability that parents will not be able to guarantee their children a non-technical society for their adulthood and makes little preparation for the children's adaptation to its existence when they grow up.

A fourth view sees men and women as the determiners of their destiny. Recognizing that machines were built in the image of the person, it asserts that persons must not be made into the image of the machine. It acknowledges that freedom from hunger and want on a world scale is not possible without technological skill, giving to technology a position of vital importance. But it asserts firmly that this knowledge without social responsibility or emotional commitment to human life and dignity is what has led us to the brink of disaster, even to the possibility of the destruction of humanity itself.

It is this last view that is developed in this book, a view that assesses our children's future from accumulated human experience and not only from simple support or rejection of traditional educational patterns. Life itself is bigger than school, and in this time of pressure, we have tended to forget that.

Social, intellectual, and emotional maturity in adulthood is long in developing and depends upon the fulfillment of life's tasks at each stage prior to adulthood. Since the content of a full life is not the same at every age, the education of young children must be strongly rooted in the developmental growth processes of childhood, even while adults look toward far-reaching goals of a social character for them. This means that we must tackle the problem of educating toward uncertainty without destroying children's sense of safety in their present; of encouraging complexity without denying the basic characteristics of childhood, which lean toward simplicity and literalness; of supporting tolerance for ambiguity, while surrounding children with order at the time in their lives when they need it; of developing social responsibility with commitment as great as the social indifference that surrounds them.

In short, we must make the effort to give children growing up in a society that worships the mechanical a full measure of childhood devoted to a visceral sense of being, to depth of feeling, to critical thinking, and to realistic coping. Surely, at all stages of life and in confrontation with all kinds of problems that we cannot now foresee, a sense of being, the capacity for critical thinking, depth of feeling, and reality in coping will be useful assets. Our children need skills, but they need even more the wisdom to use skills in ways that do not violate total human needs.

The education of children must deal with man himself, with his nature, his potentialities, his aspirations, his responsibilities for himself and for others. It must face realistically man's unbelievable capacity to improve his life or destroy his planet. It is from this position that I am examining children's education, with consideration for the special growth needs of the child and with full recognition that the choices we make will be political and social as well as narrowly educational. I shall point to schooling that takes into account several levels of psychological functioning at once and departs once and for all from a conception of childhood education as lessons in carefully organized sequences of facts and skills to be memorized, drilled, tested, and scored.

I am addressing this book primarily to parents, but hope that teachers, too, will find it worth their while. I discuss at length the styles of growth and learning that seem characteristic of large numbers of children who grow up under reasonably good home conditions, children of that vast middle America whose great numbers are due to America's extraordinary growth in technology and whose members include neither the very rich nor the very poor. Within that group, I know, are black and other minority children, for whom there are special problems associated with membership in a dominant, non-accepting society. I hesitate to deal with these here; we must all wait for writers from within the minority groups to themselves explicate their particular experience. To the extent, however, that any parent of any ethnic or racial background is concerned about the dilemmas involved in rearing flesh-and-blood children of this moment against a projected image of a future in which the robot looms larger than the person, this book is for all.

I have chosen three stages of the early school years for scrutiny. Each stage approximates a reasonably definable period in childhood growth which presents its own critical home and school problems, an inclusive approach not generally made available to parents or to teachers. Discussed first are the five-year-olds and the contemporary confusion about beginning reading. Second are the six- and seven-year-olds and the need during the primary years for an intellectually stimulating life which the current three Rs curriculum does not by itself satisfy. And third is the period from eight to eleven, in which the first major identification with the values of the adult world creates serious questions as to how school and home learning can support moral growth and personal integrity, particularly in an amoral, dehumanized time.

For each age and stage, I discuss in detail the most important aspects of child growth and learning that influence adult relations with children. These cluster around certain themes that appear and reappear in ever new form throughout the processes of growth. One is the emergence and enhancement of the whole person in the child in its complexity and uniqueness. Another is the establishment of the child as a being separate from others, including separation from the parents he loves. A third is the testing and strengthening of the self in a variety of physical, social, and intellectual endeavors. A fourth has to do with the socialization of the child, including the limitations on the self that follow from the needs of others, the slow learning of responsibility to and for others, of right and wrong, of conscience, and a system of ethics. A fifth has to do with formal learning.

Although I include implications for school curricula, I am not offering ideal models to follow. I have, rather, attempted to clarify the reasons behind procedures, while stressing mental health principles that pertain in many aspects of living and learning. In this way, I have left latitude for individual adaptation by groups of parents and teachers to serve their own children and communities best.

Each generation, each decade, must shape its education in the light of new and old findings about children, learning, and the evolving demands of society. In our time of alienation and anxiety, enlightened parents can work with their children's teachers to help shape their children's education in ways that will not lead to destruction of themselves or their society. I am convinced that only through such an alliance will the schools change, and I have tried consequently to break unrealistic public images of teachers, whether sentimental or pejorative, and to seek out the person underneath. Parents and teachers need each other as allies if they are to succeed in the task that is needed: inculcating in children the open minds and warm hearts that, coupled with skills and information, will surely be of value to them in the troubled, changing world they must face and help to change. It may be a matter of their survival that we succeed.

THE
LEARNING
CHILD

What Does Innovative Mean?

. . .

Innovation. Change. Charged words hurled at the educational establishment by critics outside the schools. Key words at educational conferences and in educational publications all over the country. Hard-sell advertising words of business firms milking the lucrative educational market. Words picked up excitedly by the mass media to publicize any hint of anything different in the educational world—in explanations sufficiently oversimplified for the average citizen. Charged everywhere with a sense of righteousness, the words "innovation" and "change" have inevitably come to be associated in the public mind with significant progress in education.

In actual fact, our national habit of building images and grabbing at panaceas has played havoc with a serious and thoughtful effort to assess our children's education for its meaning during their childhood and into their adulthood. Words and phrases have become slogans under whose banners very different, even contradictory, programs are put into operation. Whether the slogans are "Basic Foundation," "Open Classroom," "Non-graded Primary," "British Infant School," "Individualized Instruction," "Montessori Method," "Self-pacing," "Perceptual Training" or whatever, there appears to be little effort to assess them on more than one dimension, and that, generally, an obvious one. Any relation between the concepts underlying the various changes offered as innovative, or their impact on children on more than one dimension, is a rarity. As a result, interpretations of any program's meaning flow freely among parents, and applications of programs in classrooms are contradictory and confused. Two illustrations of how quite different programs, the British Infant School and programmed instruction, can be equally distorted, should make this point clear.

The British Infant School approach is based on the combined theoretical insights of Piaget, Susan Isaacs, and Montessori, each of whom contributed to recognition of stages of development (intellectual and social-emotional), the dynamics of emotional and social growth that affect and influence learning, and the value of a prepared environment for children. The first two authors also wrote fully on the value of play in childhood learning. In practice, the British Infant School is run on the conviction that children can be trusted to learn, that play is a natural road to learning, and that raw materials must be made fully available for their use. Time schedules for achievement are long-range and muted; chronological age is not considered as crucial to learning as individual readiness. There is considerable support of a child's efforts, but there is neither haste nor anxiety about immediate results, and testing is therefore minimal. Children are expected to learn to read and write, but an infant classroom, which is for children five to seven, gives no special status to the three Rs over other areas of learning. Despite the great value placed on reading and writing as a cultural necessity (a value most evident in the extensive numbers of story books available to the children), a young child who builds a wagon out of wood, who paints a picture, or dresses up to give a play, is not considered any less productive than the child who copies his letters or reads a book.

Interpretations in the United States, however, swing from

one unlikely extreme to another. At one end is the expectation on the part of some school administrators and parents that the British Infant School approach will be the answer to raising reading and math scores within the lockstep schedule of our elementary schools by a simple change of room arrangements and the addition of new materials. At the other end is the assumption by some teachers and parents that all children will ask in time to be taught essential skills as they perceive the need for them; that the teacher plays little part in stimulating or inspiring their desire; and that the teacher waits for the children to approach her. Neither view is true to the intent, spirit, or practice of the British Infant School. Both are unrealistic, and both can be expected to fall short in their objectives. As has happened many times before, the "model" will prove disillusioning, it will be rejected in disrepute, and a new one will be sought with equal superficiality in an endless search for panaceas.

The second innovation—programmed instruction and mechanical aids—has been presented to parents and teachers as the most advanced answer to educational problems yet, and even hailed as revolutionary. The rationale behind this approach is that individualized learning is not possible in the present self-contained classroom, because no one teacher can deal with such variety as exists among children. It can be managed, however, by providing the class with lessons at many levels of competency, pre-planned and prepared by experts outside the schoolroom. The lessons are reinforced by machines or workbooks which have corrective devices built into them and allow the children to differentiate right from wrong answers. It is argued in this approach that old-fashioned teaching of a single lesson was directed toward the "average" child. By this newer method each child supposedly learns at his own pace, because the full range of capacity from the brightest to the slowest can be fitted with a precise match in carefully developed materials. Children have only to absorb the lessons with smoothness and ease once the match is made.

This progressive-sounding, humanist slogan turns out on

careful examination to be something quite different. Regard the following example. A school in a suburban school system devoted to the principle that each child should learn at his own pace looked for ways of implementing the goal of individualizing instruction, and a system of programmed instruction in reading was introduced. There were many books and workbooks at varying levels of difficulty, so that each child could, and did, go from level to level at his own speed.

A visiting educator, captivated by the principal's enthusiastic report of the individualization in his school, was invited to observe a second-grade class. The room was pleasant and peaceful, and all the children were busy working. The visitor was seated near a little girl whose reading book lay open in her lap, while her eyes and hands were obviously engaged with a rubber band on the table. The visitor edged closer and noted that the illustration on the page of the book was of a ballet dancer on her toes. "Are you reading about a dancer?" she asked the little girl. The child brought her book up onto the table and nodded. "I would like to know about the dancer," continued the visitor. "Would you read to me about her?" The little girl hesitated, then began compliantly: "The ballet dancer earns her living by dancing. She whirls and twirls. Her dress is made of lace." As the little girl reached the bottom of the page, the visitor asked, "What does 'earning a living' mean?" The child shrugged her shoulders and looked blank. "How does your daddy earn his living?" the visitor persisted, in an effort to aid clarification. "I don't know," the child replied. Dropping this, the visitor went on: "What does 'whirl' mean?" The child's eyes brightened, and she stretched her arms wide. "Oh, that means the world," she said cheerfully. "And the lace?" the visitor asked. "Do you know what lace is? Do you have lace on *your* dress?" (She did.) The child shook her head, and when the visitor said with a smile, "You do," the child began to examine her dress. With a question in her eyes she touched the lace trimming on her yoke and sought confirmation. What could that reading selection, carefully "individualized" on the level of mechanical aptitude, have meant to a child who did not understand so many important words and concepts? Is differentiation of children on the single measure of mechanical skill really individualization? Yet the personnel of that school was seriously convinced that the graded material was changing the school experience of children in basic ways.

Mechanical aids and programming may indeed have their place in a classroom, but the claim to individualization and self-pacing must be set into a total context of how children learn. Neither understanding, feeling, motivation, concepts, imagination, nor aesthetic response can be systematized or taught in objectively efficient fashion. The programs and machines, when used as the only change under the guise of being innovative, actually work to strengthen the traditional emphasis on the factual, the unambiguous, and the measurable, so long associated with teaching for conformity. The claim to individualization of the mechanical approach turns out to be no more than an extension to individuals, instead of to the whole class at once, of the question-and-answer method of textbook learning, a method which limits children to the right answers within the narrow band of learning facts and skills. In view of the unhappy reality that elementary schools have not as yet moved too far away from this restricted view of education for young children, the mechanization and systematization must be seen for what they are—greater technical efficiency applied to a completely traditional and outmoded goal of education. Used in a proper context, mechanical aids can offer a teacher a helping hand in certain limited aspects of learning. They are hardly revolutionizing education, unless downgrading the role of human interaction in children's learning could be called revolutionary.

Societal Values and School Approaches

School and society serve each other, and the search for quick solutions is endemic to our culture. As a nation, we have come to repudiate arduous human effort on the assumption that technology can provide solutions for just about everything. We have believed that technology would open up a better life for all and, indeed, it has done much for our material standard of living. But we are seeing unexpected and unplanned-for by-products of our technology in every sphere of life, and our hitherto unshakeable faith in technical answers is beginning to waver. Despite this sobering development, as a result of which we must question the uses to which technology is put, there are those in our schools and outside of them who offer more and better technology as the answer to children's education. The present zest for systematization via programming and hardware, to the exclusion of emotional, social, and aesthetic experience, has the quality of a crusade: Children will be the saviors of America if we but turn them into better and better technicians. The drive is toward efficiency in materials, efficiency in teacher use, and efficiency in grouping for learning, as though externally imposed administrative efficiency under a good management agency could train children to learn and grow.

To people who perceive efficiency in terms of money made or squandered, an educational system is evaluated in terms of its money's worth. Measuring results allows the dollar-minded to evaluate the dollar's worth. Since time is money, schedules of learning progress are important too. From such a base, far removed from children, has come many an innovative program.

Rote learning and memorization can be measured. There is one answer, and a child is either right or wrong. It is therefore not accidental that memorization, repetition, and drill are the backbone of the efficiency thrust. Coincidentally, a dollar can also be made in this kind of educational approach, as is obvious from the number of business firms, never before interested in schools, who are deeply involved in preparing materials and teaching aids for this market now. Since only a human teacher can respond to and assess children's slowly and unevenly developing capacity to think and feel about ideas and issues, the new crop of materials being pushed so hard exert a very definite, if subtle, influence on children's schooling in the direction of non-thinking and non-feeling. At some points the emphasis on efficiency takes on an almost sinister quality, as contracts are let to business firms to engineer children's education. Yet this kind of "progress" is the logical outcome of changes introduced into schools at the turn of the century, as pointed out by Robert Callahan in *Education and the Cult of Efficiency*, when efficiency supposedly in the interest of mass literacy meant copying methods of manufacture, and superintendents of schools were selected for managerial and business skill rather than for educational vision.

Much of what is happening today can be clarified by a review of the way our elementary schools did change over the decades. The one-room schoolhouse of the early days gathered all the children of a community eligible for schooling and brought them together with a teacher. The first major break in this natural grouping was the sorting of children by age instead of by reading level—an innovation for its time. This change was caused by the logical enough assumption that large-scale teaching would be practical and more effective if the children were all at a particular stage of experience and readiness when the lesson was taught. No one then suspected how wide a range existed among children of the same chronological age. The practice within the one-room schoolhouse of preparing lessons throughout the day for small groups or individuals according to an orderly progression of subject matter gave way to single-lesson teaching of very large groups of supposedly alike, same-age children. Although it turned out that in the single-age classroom there were always children who were ahead of the class and others who could not keep up, these differences in ability were considered a natural law of life that complicated teaching efficiency, but had little relation to facilitating learning. The single prescribed lesson for all was not questioned, and children were rewarded or punished as they succeeded or failed within a tight progression of skills and facts.

When the era of standardized testing set in after World War I, a more narrowly organized homogeneity for mass teaching than age alone seemed tantalizingly possible. I.Q.

scores were used to "separate the sheep from the goats" among children of the same age. All "bright" children were placed in one class, all who were "average" in another, and all who were "slow" in still another. Despite the promise of easier teaching offered by greater homogeneity, it turned out that in almost every I.Q. grouping a high, middle, and low sub-group emerged. And the slower the class, the more varied were the problems encountered. At the same time, because arbitrary levels of accomplishment for specific ages and grades remained unquestioned, the grouping of children by I.Q. for skill learning was peculiarly liable to the creation of an elite, something which troubled many educators and parents alike. An elite among children was recognized to be bad for the non-elites because their attitude toward themselves was considerably affected by the failure to achieve the status accorded to high achievers. But it was bad for the elite as well, because they ended up either valuing themselves and other children from a wholly one-sided point of view, or they grew overly anxious about keeping up the pace.

As a result, whenever the negative effects of homogeneity got to be too oppressive, heterogeneous grouping was reintroduced into the schools. But the large classes remained, as did the one-lesson approach. The curriculum continued to deal mainly with standardized levels of achievement in skills and facts; rewards and punishments were built into the system of marks. Heterogeneous grouping without the incorporation of multiple levels of lessons and small group organization made the teacher's life a nightmare. Consequently, shifts occurred over the years in alternating patterns of heterogeneous-homogeneous grouping. Each was reintroduced as something innovative, until, finally, a new organization was conceived which merged the two. This was the plan for ability grouping across a grade instead of within one class. Under this system, currently in operation in many schools, grouping of home classes remains heterogeneous, allowing for social diversity; but all the fast readers or apt mathematicians in the grade go to one teacher, and slow ones go to another for their hour of reading or math.

In a further effort to increase the efficiency of teaching, teams of teachers with special strengths in different academic areas were introduced to offer their special strengths in rotating order. The science specialist handled the science for the entire grade, the math specialist all the math, the art teacher all the art, and so on, bringing the subject matter compartmentalization of the secondary schools down into the elementary grades at lower and lower ages. Thus, in the earliest innovations of an administrative, managerial kind, *children* were grouped for efficiency teaching. In a later development, the *teachers* were organized for efficiency along with the children. The current emphasis, still geared to facts and skills teaching for the most part, is on the structuring of *materials* along with children and teachers. Programmed instruction is simply an attempt to break down a specific sequence in a content area or skill into small segments for easier memorization and drill, thus allowing individual children to be on different parts of the identical material at different times, supposedly without status values.

During the period of these changes, the eight-year elementary school was replaced with loud fanfare by the six-three pattern that accommodated the junior high school, only to be currently replaced by the five-four or five-three patterns of the intermediate school. But old-style relationships and old-style learning are harder to change. It is easier to put up new buildings, to effect liaison between services, and provide efficient distribution of materials and equipment; easier to group and regroup children around I.Q., socio-economic class, sex, and achievement; easier to put teachers into teams or give them aides than to cut through to meaningful content, methods, and materials in ways that affect children's total growth, their relationships with adults and other children, and their feelings about themselves. This is not to deprecate the value of good buildings, mechanical aids, human aides, or fresh approaches to grouping children and teachers. It is rather to make clear that external, structural, administrative types of change which are touted as the latest in education seldom produce basic, internal change at all.

The old question-answer approach to school learning, when carried out between a machine and a child instead of a teacher and a child still limits the range within which a child's mind may roam. Testing, which long ago was found to lead to excessive anxiety, has been increased, if anything, in the mechanically based "innovation," and tests are still interpreted by the children as acts of hostile judgment, not as diagnostic aids to teacher and child. Children carry out their homework assignments with the same unthinking obedience as always, reassuring the parent who asks, "But what does the assignment mean?" with a bland, "I'm doing what the teacher said." The search for meaning and understanding, the right to speculate and ponder, and the pursuit of inquiry which is the basis of all genuine learning, are no more a part of the innovations of hardware, software, and reorganization plans than they ever were in the most traditional-looking classrooms.

It is these truths that make the sterility of mechanized teaching and rote learning a poor augury for a future in which democratic principles can continue to exist only if they are safeguarded by a thinking, questioning, and caring citizenry. Schools must provide a deepening of social and emotional experience and the tools of critical thought along with the skills necessary to life in a technological age. They must begin as children require them to begin, with a child and a teacher, with a child and vital content. And the democratic process must be embodied in the interaction among the three. This is the heart of the education crisis.

The Roots of Conflict

Looking to contemporary historical necessity for cues to educational purpose, we can see great urgency in the widening gap between concern for human life and dignity and the force of technological development. Unheeding of human values, technology is capable of destroying human life itself, let alone human worth. The present adult world is primitive and immature in coping with the problems of man's relation to man, problems which technology has not only heightened, but to which it could make the solutions easier if the need were seen more clearly. We do not give high priority at school to the learning necessary for social responsibility and problems of human interaction, although it is known that the shaping of attitudes toward people begins early, and emotions take a long time to mature. School and society are deeply interrelated, and in our clearly transitional period, the purposes of school must be re-examined, not so much with passion as with thought. Contemporary approaches to the education of children, from open school to programmed instruction, reflect a basic schism in our society's values. The open classroom and the mechanized classroom both offer guides to the shape and direction of society's future.

This polarization in school, as in society, has roots in two very different philosophical-psychological conceptions that go back centuries. Each reflects an assessment of humanity and, by inference, of its children. Each has been in the ascendancy at different periods of socio-political-religious development, and they confront each other in the approaches to children's learning today. One is the belief in human beings as spontaneous, active, self-directed, and inner-motivated; the other is a perception of human beings as helpless, passive, and dependent upon a higher or stronger power for direction. Socrates lost his life for teaching from the first view; the second underlies educational practice in countries all over the world.

Complicating the existence of a polarity in the attitude toward children is the history of elementary education in our country. Growing out of a social vision that for its time was progressive and innovative in a true sense, elementary education has become inevitably intertwined with the concepts of efficiency and mechanization inherent in our expanding industrial society. As a result, it is not always easy today to separate the many different aspects of positive and negative contribution that the elementary school system has made to individuals and to society as a whole. Nevertheless, faced with new problems of living, inundated by a vast increase in knowledge of all kinds, the schools as now constituted do not serve our children or our transitional society well. Yet the reasons for the lags must be related to any proposed changes, and schools must be seen in the light of historical development as well as historical necessity.

The History of Elementary Curriculum

When the nation was illiterate, the goal of the elementary school was to teach all citizens basic skills—reading, writing, and arithmetic. Life was simple, and the basic skills carried people far enough. Despite the fact that few went beyond the elementary school, far-reaching outcomes were anticipated from schooling. Those who first introduced compulsory education into American life knew exactly why children should go to school and learn to read: to save their souls. The preamble to the Massachusetts Law of 1647 says it:

> It being one chief point of that old Deluder, Satan, to keep man from knowledge of the Scriptures, as in former times, by keeping them in an unknown tongue, so in these latter times . . . it is therefore ordered that every township in this jurisdiction, after the Lord has increased them to the number of fifty householders, shall then forthwith appoint one within their town to teach all such children as shall resort to him to read and write.

Consistent with this goal, the first book written and printed for children in America was titled *Spiritual Milk for Boston Babes in either England, drawn from the Breasts of both Testaments for their Souls' Nourishment. The New England Primer,* first recorded in 1683, impressed children with the dangers of hell and the devil in passages such as the following:

Praise to God for Learning to Read

The praises of my tongue
I offer to the Lord
That I was taught and learnt so young
To read His holy Word.

That I was brought to know
The danger I was in
By nature and practice too
A wretched slave to sin.

That I was *lead* to see
I can do nothing well;
And whither shall a sinner flee
To save himself from Hell.

But times change, and little more than a hundred years later the reason for going to school was a different one. Social revolution demanded that all citizens be trained to understand the duties and problems of citizenship and be responsible as independent individuals for their own worldly transactions. A citizen's salvation became his own problem, not the state's. Thus, after the Revolution, distinctly American histories appeared for the first time, and these, along with textbooks on arithmetic, spelling, and geography became a major portion of the reading literature for children. The elementary school curriculum was expanded to include history and geography. Still later, in a growing America, art and music were added as acknowledgments of the value of the aesthetic, even in the lives of the children of the plain people.

Such was the picture for many decades, until the 1920's and 1930's, the era of progressive education. Attempts to change the approach to content resulted in an important departure in the handling of subject matter in a number of independent experimental schools. Aside from the kindlier attitude and joy in children that permeated those schools, a conviction arose that children must be helped to see facts in relationship to each other and that concepts emerging from interrelated aspects of a subject are essential to genuine understanding of the subject's meaning.

An early report by Lucy Sprague Mitchell describes her search for a method that would facilitate what she came to call "relationship thinking." Experimenting with maps made on cellophane in order to make visible at a glance the different factors affecting man's use of his environment, she wrote:

> We decided to try the experiment of superimposing a current plan, such as Secretary Wallace's farm plan, upon various outstanding physical characteristics of the United States.
>
> How much of the past history of the land was necessary in order to understand and judge a present-day plan? The answer to this particular query we sought through a study of a few transparent cellophane maps. Inadequate as they were, through them familiar old facts took on new meanings. The heroic settlers of New England turned out to have chosen marginal or submarginal land for farms, where soil is thin and modern farming methods can seldom be applied. Their location was an historic accident rather than a geographic choice. Back to the native forests or to the new "recreational industry" must go the land of the Puritans! The western pioneers had chosen good land, but abused it. The map of erosion coincided faithfully with the stretch where native forests had been cut down or where the thick native sod had been ploughed and left for rains to wash away. The map of exhausted soil marked the path of the tobacco and cotton growers as they pushed west to fresh land. It also marked the site of tenant farming and, in part, of Negro population. This was suggestive. Once again I vowed to work for tool maps and an atlas which should show trends, social as well as physical, instead of the usual static picture . . . tools to help in discovering relationships between natural environment and the regional cultures which develop within them.[1]

[1] From *69 Bank Street* (The mimeographed house newsletter of the Cooperative School for Teachers—now known as the Bank Street College of Education), Vol. 1, No. 1, 1934.

The attack on memorization of facts in isolation from each other, as in the case of historical dates and events, names of capital cities and regional products, names of parts of plants, or mechanical coupling of titles of books and their authors, had an effect. Throughout the country school systems altered their elementary curricula to acknowledge the relatedness of hitherto separated areas of knowledge. The new Social Studies grouped together the old history, geography, and civics; the new Language-Arts curriculum included reading, writing, oral language, and literature; art and music were used to support and deepen the intellectual content.

This particular revolution in the approach to the elementary school curriculum was not as thoroughly assimilated by the elementary schools as a superficial glance at courses of study might have one assume, largely because its underlying conceptualization was not understood. Habit dies hard, and, typically, teachers have continued to apply conventional rote-learning approaches to the new groupings that were meant to help children strengthen conceptual understanding. Newly trained teachers continue to come out of college classes where both their education professors and their teachers of academic subjects were themselves exemplifying the old ways of learning by rote even while preaching the new. Such relationships of facts to each other as are incorporated into the newer materials tend to be predigested and to assume the arbitrary character of fact instead of the dynamic search for new relationships that fosters fresh thinking. Children are still expected to learn by rote the concepts they should be grasping through experiences in which their own thinking is stretched and deepened.

The emphasis on the administrative format of schooling carried over from a search for efficient ways of disseminating literacy plagues us to this day in every aspect of school life. It has come to final fruition in the impersonality and irrelevance of our education. Edgar Friedenberg, writing about a classroom in Evergreen, Colorado, criticizes the efficiency approach as it operates in the teaching of social studies, the area Lucy Mitchell struggled so hard to make alive and meaningful.

The walls of Chris Samples' five-sided classroom are cluttered with photographs, maps and cut-outs. On the floor stands a plaster and wood replica of an Iraqui village. . . . The tables are covered with models of Iraqui huts which the children have made with clay, water and straw, and with materials for making more. . . . The subject is social studies, an experimental unit developed by Educational Services, Inc., which has assembled the photographs on the wall, the clay and straw and the other material that the children use; all of it was shipped to Evergreen from Boston. . . . This approach to Social Science education is foolproof. There is little possibility of either confusion or controversy, for even those materials that might violate local sentiment will be too "official" to be easily challenged, and, in any case, they will *not* violate it on heated local issues. And it is no small achievement to improve the intellectual quality of the public schools' materials of instruction without making them too hot for teachers to handle.

But the price, especially in Social Studies, is to confirm officially that education consists in the application of the tools of cognition to units of material, the content of which is as impersonally prescribed as a T.V. dinner.[2]

What Is Innovative?

Pre-packaging and mass distribution of study units are not education. Parents concerned with their children's schooling must bring the skeptical eye of the consumer to bear on the many claims to innovation and change that are suggested for their children's education. The "commercials" need to be checked against performance. And parents must learn to ask the right questions about any program. To what end is change being offered? Are the goals of the new program narrow or broad? What exactly in a new program is different from what is being rejected? Is the difference significant? What in a new

[2] Edgar Friedenberg, "Recess," *New York Review of Books*, July 7, 1966, p. 22.

program is the same as in previous programs? Why are similar features kept? How are the differences between the old and the new expressed in action?

Basic change is clearly called for in the elementary schools and on more than the single dimension of technical achievement. The movement toward what is called the "open school" recognizes this. Socially conscious citizens, parents, teachers, and would-be teachers have turned their backs on their own educational experience to embrace a vision of something more meaningful for the next generation. The exhilaration of discovery and hope attendant on dreams of a new schooling merge with deeply-felt anger at the "system" which betrayed them. Much heat about schools has been generated, and much subjective recall of repression, inadequacy, and punishment has come to light. Yet this first step—repudiation of a personal educational past—slips too easily into a general mistrust of the entire educational past, so that rich lodes of educational thought and practice are closed off, instead of being selectively mined for contemporary application.

The continuity of human thought that places today's advocate of the open school on a spiral of human aspiration to which earlier pioneers have already made contributions is overlooked in the excitement of personal discovery. The findings of similar efforts remain buried in the literature or in the memories of a handful of elder statesmen of the educational world. Disheartening and unnecessary stumbling and fumbling go on, as the results of earlier trials of the same kind and toward the same goals are ignored, and the errors wastefully duplicated. It is not by chance that a group of American educators on a trip to British Infant Schools were asked in surprise by the headmasters they were interviewing, "Don't you Americans read your own books?" Or that sophisticated educators return from England saying, "There is nothing in the British Infant Schools that we have not seen in one or another of our own independent schools at home!" The works of Dewey, Caroline Pratt, Lucy Mitchell, and others reveal exciting and genuine educational innovations of the first four decades of the century that have yet to be applied on a large scale. They are surprisingly fresh today, because men and women who struggled as we are now struggling with the problems of applying a humanist philosophy to children's learning have to some extent already explored, tested, altered, and deepened many of the ideas that seem completely innovative to a fresh generation of educational pioneers. The big problem for the anti-traditionalists of the past was exactly the same as for those of the present: how to transmit humanist philosophy, goals, and values in life-size application to children of different ages, stages, and backgrounds. The question remains: "How do you make it work?" In immediate terms, this means asking what the current, popular parental outcry, "I want my child to be free," means in actual practice both at home and in school. Does freedom owe anything to necessity? to group need? to inner turmoil? Does it have the same relation to ethics as it has to materials or to sociality and friendship? Do all parents, or all teachers, agree on how freedom for children should be enacted? Or on the price that must be paid for freedom?

Let us not assume that ready-made answers and good models lie buried in the past. The search for models in the past is no less subject to analysis and question than are the bandwagons of the present. But it is possible to learn from others who have been there before. In connection with such a search it may be useful to examine the very word "model," so popular among contemporary innovators.

Coming out of an engineering approach to inanimate phenomena, "a model" is actually something of a misnomer when applied to education. To adopt models of schooling is to deny the uniqueness and the individuality of each teacher, each child, each group. It is an anti-humanist position which suppresses the infinite variabilities of teacher-child encounters, of child-child encounters, and of child-environment encounters. It denies equally the historical development and contemporary need of any given group at any given time for its special solutions. Rather than speak of models, an analogy to family life is better drawn. Many kinds of families satisfy the basic needs of their members, yet no two do so in precisely the same way. Where family life is not satisfactory, whether on a commune or in a nuclear family, the problem far more frequently goes back to people than to form. Schools, no less than families, are intricate networks of human interaction, and no two need be alike.

Given the nature of childhood, the knowledge of the learning process, and the social convictions about where we want to go, there are, however, general principles affecting specific practice which can be helpful. Only through understanding at this level can parents, teachers, and the general community make choices concerning schooling that will carry out their chosen objectives in their individual ways and within their individual situations. Unfortunately, parents seeking to make an impact on their children's schooling often waver between a cautious timidity that suggests they cannot possibly understand what is good or bad for their children and a brash oversimplification that there is nothing to the whole thing, but that educators are too stupid or too ambitious to know it. Neither attitude makes sense nor supports needed change. Parents can, and should, be knowledgeable about schools, can, and should, work closely with school personnel in thinking deeply about goals and objectives for children. At the same time, they can, and should, recognize the specialization that is called for in the teacher's role, a specialization that in no way denies the importance of the parents.

It is one of the shameful heritages of the whole elementary school system that, even though teachers are the ones in constant contact with the children and held responsible for the children's performance, they are rarely involved in the development of the curriculum, but are instead expected to carry out instructions developed by others. Granted the role of the consultant, the "expert," and the more experienced, there is no excuse for the assumption that good teaching can be carried out mechanically by the administrative distribution of materials and methods that may call forth neither personal investment nor understanding on the part of teachers who are to apply them. It is ironic that the most passionate attacks on the schools have included a pattern long familiar to the establishment, which perhaps more than anything else is responsible for poor schooling, namely the attitude of contempt for teachers. It must be recognized that the repressive and sterile climate of so many of our schools grows out of a long dual tradition—on the one hand of treating children as potential scores, and on the other of treating teachers as incompetent members of society who would not teach if they could do something better. Since most elementary school teachers are women, it is entirely possible that the societal stereotype that gives them secondary roles has been operating here, too. Educational administrators and the supporting textbook publishers who follow school guides (largely men, it must be said) have tended to plan for curriculum and develop materials apparently convinced that children are unwilling learners and that teachers cannot be counted on to know how to teach. Taking their cue from the manufacture of cars, which are made to be mechanically simple enough for citizens of below average intelligence to handle, an efficient, "foolproof" system of manuals and directions inundates teachers, as though teaching and learning were also mechanical skills. Who can teach creatively from a manual which opens with the suggestion to start the day by saying, "Good morning, children" to the class?

Protests against our schools have mounted on behalf of the children, and rightly so. But few protestors have recognized the experience or the commitment of the many potentially fine teachers who have been trapped by a system in which their humanity and intelligence have been endlessly denied and their experience and insight endlessly rejected. As parents and other members of the community have demanded changes in their schools, there are those who have slipped with as much ease as the most reactionary superintendent into the glib assumption that teachers can produce on demand a program to which they have not been asked to contribute, which they might not understand, with which they might disagree, are afraid of, feel threatened by, or for other reasons cannot feel committed to. It is valuable to note in this connection that one of the important components in the spread of the informal British Infant School in Great Britain has been its adoption by voluntary participation of the teachers. It is also important to note that the uniqueness of each British school stems from the fact that headmasters and headmistresses are given a great deal of latitude to develop *with their staff* practices that are consistent with an agreed-upon body of theory and principles. There is no Infant School "model" in Great Britain, and teachers are not expected to change and grow without moral support as well as practical help.

Our educational system will not change until both teachers and children are perceived as human beings. Only a self-respecting, accepted, autonomous teacher, proud of her professional integrity, can relate to children in ways that will give children self-respect, acceptance, autonomy, and pride in their accomplishments.

The heart of any educational experience lies in the interaction of people with each other and with their total environment, be that environment concrete or abstract, immediate or past. Education is more than rote dispensing or rote-learning of important skills and basic facts. There are effects on children other than grades that result from the interaction which takes place in the service of their lessons. These effects have either not been taken seriously or else have been ignored. Here is the recall of a young teacher-to-be, a Bank Street College graduate student, as she assessed certain side effects of her own schooling:

> I understood at an early age what was expected of me in school and I gave to the teacher only what she wanted to know. I never answered unless I was sure of the answer, never went through a process of discovery out loud with the teacher, because I knew the final fact was what was important to her. Because I wanted to be successful within that framework, I gradually abandoned many of my own interests outside of school. School became my real source of motivation, but it was a bad source, because it em-

phasized fact-learning rather than process and because its specific demands destroyed my individual searching out in other directions. Luckily, I was able to go to a university, which re-emphasized process and autonomous thought. But I can't help thinking how terrible it would have been had I not been reguided. Once outside the school environment, I would have had to start completely over to discover what really interested me, how I really felt about certain things. I can imagine that, with such a monumental task, many people might never begin to cope with it.

We are sufficiently aware of the complexity of child growth and learning today to face up to what actually does happen under the guise of reading, writing, and arithmetic. Parents must be the first to extend their concept of school to include more than the obviously academic.

A Bank Street College research team studying the effects of school on behavior related to mental health as well as to learning came to the conclusion that educational goals and methods must be conceived on two different dimensions simultaneously: one, the effect of school on a child's mastery of knowledge and skills of a varied kind; and the other, the associated effects on the broader modes of dealing with experience, such as docility, autonomy, tolerance for ambiguity, and openness to learning. The impact of school on the children's self-image and interpersonal relations, as well as on their styles of thinking and mastery of knowledge, was uncovered in their study of fourth-grade children of similar middle-class backgrounds who attended "good," representative schools of both traditional and modern type.[3] (*Modern and traditional* were defined in terms of the school's tendency to incorporate knowledge about child development and learning into its educational policies and practices.)

It was found that schools do influence attitudes, for example, the way children perceive adults and the way they assess cer-

[3] Patricia Minuchin, *et al., The Psychological Impact of School Experiences* (New York: Basic Books, 1969).

tain values having to do with living and learning. Thus, the traditionally educated children in the study accepted without question the role of school adults as disciplinarians and respected the conventional stereotypes of male and female expectations for themselves. On the other hand, children educated in more informal schools saw rules as *socially* necessary, not something the teacher wanted, and their attitudes toward male and female activities were considerably less codified. The children's feelings about learning and competing for grades differed, too, with the type of school. Those who attended a modern, independent school loved their school the most and were the most involved in their learning. But the wholly noncompetitive stress on intrinsic meaning unrelated to tests and grades seemed to produce an interesting, unexpected effect on their response to formal tests. The children who cared most about what they learned, yet were the least motivated to do well in conventional terms, scored lower on I.Q. tests than children of the same socio-economic level in the more traditional schools. In describing themselves, the children in the modern schools dealt with a more varied spectrum of feelings and behavior than did those from the traditional schools. The latter wrote in better form, but were more limited in what they had to say when describing themselves. While most of the children from both types of schools felt they had a good life and most were satisfied with their own sex, on important attitudes affecting their lives, such as pleasure in learning, or male/female interests and activities, they were clearly different as a result of their schooling.

Children are passing harder tests today than they ever did and spending longer hours at homework than their parents did at their age. From first grade to sixth, they are "covering more ground" and apparently showing more sophistication. But, at the same time, increasing numbers of bright graduates of prestigious colleges are giving up their degrees and their status for the simple satisfactions of making things with their hands and living direct, face-to-face relationships with flesh-and-blood people. Many more are turning off the words of their professors and listening to their inner selves instead. Is this saying something we may not ignore with safety? Sensitive teachers and psychologists who observe children closely note that it is far easier to overcome the academic inadequacies created by a mediocre school than it is to eradicate the unhappiness with self as a learner, the guilt and feelings of inadequacy among achievers and under-achievers alike which are inevitable in schools that have not yet broken with traditional views and practices.

What is worse is that in schools dominated by arbitrariness of content and status associated with marks, it is all too easy for still dependent children to assume that it is *they* who are at fault when they are confused and uncomprehending, or perhaps bored, that somehow they are expected to come out on top of the system no matter what and that their imagination, curiosity, and interest in people are to blame if they do not conform. Many learn to beat the system, learning in the process how to fake, cheat, beguile, pretend, and otherwise play the game so they will not be touched. But while, from a mental health point of view, this may be called coping, the cynicism it leads to about school and learning leaves an ugly scar. The many honest or naïve children who do not play the game suffer for a long time.

What should be our purposes for sending children to school today? To insure college admission? To guarantee a better livelihood? To survive in the technological world of our time? To find a haven for childhood values in a world falling apart? Would anyone say "to strengthen mental health"?

Schools must be seen to have significance far beyond the traditional transmitting of culture or the imparting of facts and skills. Real changes call for working with people and helping them grow. It is much simpler and faster to preserve the traditional in a new form than to accomplish a basic shift in the nature of school purposes and goals. Yet nothing short of a basic shift will do.

What Changes Do We Need?

• • •

Everyone associated with schools—teachers, parents, administrators, psychologists, philosophers—all agree that children should learn to read, to write, and to do mathematics. But there is little agreement on what else might be important in the early years of school. Views differ according to whether children's learning is understood to be simple or complex; whether children's involvement in their own education is considered essential or irrelevant; whether early learning is seen as organically or mechanically related to later learning. There is controversy on how the 3 Rs can be taught most effectively to each child and wide differences of opinion exist as to how other areas of learning relate to success in skill-learning. The effort to tie knowledge of child development into curriculum design has barely begun. And the big question of the effect of school on children's mental health is one we have only recently become sophisticated enough to ask. Underlying the values stressed in all these areas is the clarity or bias with which historical reality is perceived as giving new perspectives to man's existence.

Yet when the problem of schooling is approached with concern for children's total growth, meaning mental health as well as intellectual attainment, it becomes clear that the conditions indicated for optimal learning cut into the very fabric of school life as we know it. The size and structure of the school, the nature of the teacher-child relationship, the way in which content is developed and offered, the availability and use of which kinds of materials—all must be reassessed in order to create a school environment in which genuine learning can proceed.

Schools Must Be Social Units

Let us begin with the size and structure of the school itself. The administrative planning that followed the trend of industry toward bigger and bigger amalgamations has been a disaster when applied to children's schools. There are no doubt ways in which the central administration of school units can, and should, effect economies. But the laws of efficient management hardly take into account the laws by which children learn and grow. The contradiction between the two is a major factor contributing to the plight of children in our time. The problem confronting the children goes beyond the immediate school experience and is actually their general isolation from the adult world. But the size and structure of schools is a reinforcement of that isolation from adult reality which we can, and must, change.

In former times and in less complex societies, children could find their way into the adult world by watching workers and perhaps giving them a hand; by lingering at the general store long enough to chat with, and overhear conversations of, adults; by taking on small jobs; by sharing and participating in the tasks of family and community that were necessary to survival. They were in, and of, the adult world while yet sensing themselves apart as children. Going to school was a separate child experience, but schools existed in a total setting of adult life and work, from which children did not feel themselves excluded. School may have been a chore and a bore, but the important realities of adult existence were not lost upon them.

By contrast, the children of an advanced technological society find it increasingly difficult to understand their society or to find a meaningful place for themselves within it—a condition that persists long past adolescence. The alienation bemoaned by adults starts early—for most children, the day they enter the large, impersonal plant known as the elementary school. Before they have had the chance to find out fully who and what they are or how they can hook into the adult stream, they become puppets in an organization ostensibly developed for them, but whose rules for conformity actually grow out of necessity related to problems of large-scale management and control. Little attention is given to children's requirements for growth in their own management and control, either in the construction or the organization of large schools.

The physical structure and internal organization of a school can, and should, be a vehicle through which children can strengthen themselves as individuals while learning the meaning of social involvement. A school plant and its organization should lend themselves to the emergence of a cultural entity that has an honest relationship to the adult world of work and interdependence, but which children can feel is their own. Relationships between physical structure and cultural mode are more easily found in earlier periods of American life than at present. For example, when a small community built its town hall to accommodate all its members, the very existence of the building allowed for the mutual thinking and decision-making that gave the town its democratic character and meaning. In present-day urbanized society, the town hall is a vast repository of records, and decision-making is by means of examination of recorded evidence. This may be the only efficient way in a large city, but it robs the individual of his sense of participation in the direction of his life, and society itself of a certain reality.

The magnitude of our industrial civilization has in fact had the effect of curtailing inter-personal relationships and inter-environmental experiencing on many levels of the adult world, although it has spread the range of possible contacts to the entire globe. We decry the loss of the small neighborhood grocer, who personalized our order, although we appreciate the efficiency of the supermarket. We deplore the unfriendliness of the big city bus driver, although we acknowledge the frustration inherent in his job of driving and collecting tolls in heavy vehicles through congested streets. We feel lonely in crowds, and we protest the computerization that reduces us to numbers in coded files. But, being adults, we fall back upon the relationships we have already made with some people, some things, and some processes, and, although we might like a closer sense of relatedness to more people, more things, and more processes, we begrudgingly accept the inevitability of size and impersonality as the price of comfort at a material level. With chosen friends, perhaps at jobs, and certainly in recreational activity, we try to implement the intimacy we feel we need.

But children are not yet completely formed. The range and span of their close relationships have of necessity been limited, and primarily to the family. As they enter school, they are developmentally at a point where they must make a shift away from the old intimacy of the family, based as it is on babyhood relationships. But they still require close and intimate contacts with adults for their continued growth and learning. They start their elementary schooling with very little perspective beyond their immediate experience and cannot easily find a place for themselves within too large and impersonal an enterprise. And the society in which American children are growing up is a very large enterprise! School is a halfway step into the adult world. Schools too big to be graspable leave young children psychologically stranded, and the condition will not be improved by the impersonality of the adult society they will eventually enter.

Ours is a time when individualization is giving way to standardization at an unbelievable pace, and responsibility to others is hardly a value at all. Yet the early school years are the very ones when children must strengthen their identities as individuals, while learning to function as participants in small groups and in society itself. Character and values take final shape during this period, so that society's failure to fulfill young children's needs for genuine involvement in a larger social orbit than the family can lead to something more serious than a mild sense of loss. There must once again be a public setting for children in which they can achieve important and responsible interaction with a variety of adults other than parents and with children other than siblings in order to satisfy their growing sense of self as independent of their families. There is no recourse, in the face of contemporary pressures, but for schools to become the allies of parents in the difficult task of strengthening individual and social identity.

School buildings and separate wings of large buildings must be small units of interdependency in which every individual child has the opportunity to be, and to feel himself to be, a participating member of a functioning community; where a child can work out for himself and with others the hard realities that exist whenever people live and work in close communion with each other; where a child is known by name to many more than his one classroom teacher. Schools must be of such a size and so organized that every child can grasp the school's wholeness as a community in a reasonably short time and live comfortably in it with a sense of belonging.

Children Need to Understand
the Reality of Social Effort

The elementary school must also fill the vacuum in children's lives created by the mechanized and impersonal organization of society, as a result of which children can nowhere identify with a stable community of working adults or make their own socially necessary contribution. The aura of magic must be taken out of technology by giving children concrete and direct involvement with materials, varied processes of work, and standards of workmanship. Only in this way will they understand and relate better to the out-of-home world, even if it is so much a push-button world.

It was Dewey who first recognized that the elementary school would have to play such a role in the face of the changes industry was making in society. He saw that children were being cut off from the roots of life and from responsible participation in it and he saw this during a time when most educators were borrowing formulas from industry to make the schooling of the masses more efficient. We are at the point now where the threat of alienation to our children can no longer be ignored. In the responses of the young adults who avidly seek to *feel* and resist analyzing experience, who weave and bake and grow organic foods, who repudiate image-making and search for the real, especially in human relations, there is a message to be taken seriously. Children cannot grow into full maturity unless they are tuned in to a world of work and responsibility which is real for them.

Sporadic efforts to do this have been made in some independent schools. Carolyn Pratt [1] conceived of the still functioning City and Country School around World War I. Sensitive to the fact that a changing society was robbing children of the opportunity to fulfill their growth needs for work and responsible social participation, she established a school in which every child during the middle years can consciously and conscientiously become a part of the school's working life. The grouping of the children does not reflect a singleminded categorization by academic level. Each class is known by its dominant age and its name appears in bold roman numerals on each classroom door as VIs, VIIs, and so on up to the XIIs.

From age eight on, each class in this school is responsible for some necessary aspect of the school's total functioning. The VIIIs run the school post office, which handles all intra-school communication of a written character. Absence cards and trip slips are picked up and delivered to the appropriate adult each

---

[1] Carolyn Pratt, *I Learn From Children* (New York: Cornerstone Library, 1970).

day; special delivery notices, by means of which any child or teacher can be given an urgent message from within or outside the school, and round robins, by which necessary messages intended for every teacher or every class can be communicated, are also the responsibility of the VIIIs, who each year design a series of inner school stamps for the school mail. In addition, they sell string, brown paper, and U.S. postage stamps. What makes the program work for the VIIIs is the reality that, in order to assist the administrative functioning of the school, every class is required to mail an absence card to the nurse regularly in the school mailbox stamped with school postage. The administration uses the same postal service for its communication needs within the school.

The IXs run the school store, which sells a wide variety of classroom supplies, as well as supplies for individuals. This works because every class from the three-year-olds up to the thirteens is allotted a budget for school supplies. Three- to six-year-olds shop for newsprint, manila paper, construction paper, tempera, brushes, crayons, scratch pads for the teacher, scissors, safety pins, and tissues. As the needs of the older children are affected by their curriculum, the shopping at the school store is for notepaper, school binders, rulers, pencils, compasses, plasticine, and sewing equipment.

The Xs manage the school's hand-printing needs. They are responsible for the luncheon menus, signs in the building giving directions and rules for traffic behavior, the signs on each classroom door, and other needs of this type as they arise through the year. The XIs run the school's printing press. It is they who print the stamps designed by the VIIIs, as well as the absence cards the VIIIs collect and return to the nurse. The XIIs are responsible for working with the four-year-old group as teacher helpers, a task both boys and girls find immensely rewarding.

The City and Country School developed its entire social studies program around the jobs held by the children, but neither that nor the actual format of their work program is necessarily the only way in which children can participate in the processes by which a school community survives.

In describing the Malting House school which existed in Cambridge, England, in the 1920s, Susan Isaacs gave a clue to the kind of reality that lends meaning to children's participation. In that school, whose stimulating intellectual program is still a thing of wonder, children were asked to plan their luncheon menus so they could be served the food they enjoyed.

> . . . the children took turns at selecting the items for each meal from a list of possible dishes which we gave them. The cook told them that, if they wanted this right of choice, they would need to give her the list well beforehand as she had to order the goods, and they had to be delivered in good time for cooking on the particular day. We therefore got the children to make out a list of the week's menus at the beginning of each week. If they did not do this, they had to have the dishes which the cook had time to prepare at short notice. . . .
>
> A further instance of educational demands is that we made each child responsible for the cleansing of his own dinner crockery, etc. after the meal. . . . We asked each to wash his own utensils, every day, and made it clear that no one else would do it if he did not, and that we would not serve the next day's meal on a dirty plate. This plan worked very well indeed, probably because the responsibility was perfectly specific and clear. . . . Once or twice there were rebellious souls who asked impatiently, "*Why* do we have to wash our own things?" My reply was simply, "Why not?" which sometimes led to a discussion of the various things people did for each other and for themselves.[2]

There are many ways to satisfy the needs of children for growth in social responsibility. But that which is necessary and effective in one setting may not work at all in another and should not be copied slavishly. What matters is that every elementary school unit should be sufficiently small and its working processes sufficiently clear, so that children who are ready,

[2] Susan Isaacs, *Intellectual Growth in Young Children* (London: Routledge & Sons, 1944), pp. 24 and 26.

and in fact need, to feel responsible to units beyond the family can become so in a realistic situation and not a contrived one. The monitor system of the traditional schools in no way satisfies this need. The work of the monitor is done in servility to adult-perceived duties. Monitors are "good" children, often favored, "reliable" children, or else difficult, disturbing children who are being bribed to be good. Monitors are given a position of superiority and power over their peers which they do not earn and which can be destructive of their evaluation of themselves and of others. Children all need to make the kind of contribution to the school community that affects the lives of all, children and adults, because without that contribution, all would suffer in some way. Within their level of capacity and awareness, that contribution which children make, can, and must, be real. And children must so understand it.

Schools Must Involve Children Fully As Individuals

School must be a place where children are not only involved in responsible work, but are encouraged and helped to understand and order their world through the full use of their senses, their feelings, and their intellects. A wide range of materials and equipment is needed to provide the opportunities and appropriate supervision for all kinds of creative and constructive activities—a library, stage, art room; places for activities as different as cooking and bookbinding, gardening or building a rocket; maps, charts, blueprints, and models of things made and in the making. The strong need during the elementary years to develop individual taste and aptitude makes it desirable that different activities go on simultaneously in classrooms conceived as workshops, studios, research, and reference areas. Work space can easily be differentiated on many surfaces and by shelving, but of special importance is space for quiet and reflection, for the ebb and flow of pairs and small groups, for movement and physical activities, for noisy and messy activities, for the study of animals and plants. Implicit in this kind of setting is the assumption that good craftsmanship is valued, whether in dramatics, dance, music, poetry, woodwork, clay, or in writing, math, and science. Implicit also is the recognition that children are individuals and will pursue individual schedules of learning. The child who lags behind his peers for developmental reasons must obviously be protected from humiliation and shame as surely as the child who leaps into new understanding must be supported in his forward growth.

Individual and Group Needs Are Equally Important

Within such a working community children can function as individuals and as members of groups in a variety of structures. While the pursuit of individual learning is axiomatic, especially in the skills and to satisfy individual taste, it is also true that the group life and interaction so dear to children of the middle years can accommodate more than the purely social. Group intellectual and creative endeavor should therefore also be incorporated into the life style of children's schooling as a response to developmental need. Informal rather than formal schooling is obviously better suited to helping children express and work through the spontaneous, shifting, exploratory interpersonal reactions so vital to them in the many aspects of learning that are possible at this stage.

From a socio-political point of view, it is a necessity that children be grouped heterogeneously, so that all classes, colors, and creeds will share at least part of a common childhood experience. From the point of view of childhood need for interaction, groups must be set up so that they are not seriously unbalanced as to numbers of boys or girls, or numbers of children with severe emotional and learning problems in proportion to the numbers who fall within the normal range. Groups must be large enough for every child to have sufficient choices for friendship and work companions; they must be small enough for the teachers to get to know each individual well and have contact with each on a regular basis.

Grouping at school can be across ages or within one age. Either has advantages. Since no group is ever really homogeneous, no matter on what criteria it is put together, age alone does not guarantee sameness of emotional and social maturity any more than it does the same levels of intellectual capacity. Crossing ages introduces greater diversity for the teacher, but at the same time offers children the benefit of a family-style relationship in which older help younger, and the younger feel they have more resources than a teacher alone to turn to. Yet, in a group of children of one age, children can learn to be helpful to each other, too, if the teacher sets the tone for mutual trust and kindness instead of for cutthroat competition for her favor and/or for the highest marks.

The seriousness with which children respond to the challenges of group life causes them to grow quickly conscious of the internal hierarchical structure of their groups. Adults need to know that the relative prestige assigned to a child by the peer group becomes a fairly powerful influence on his behavior and that, even though on the whole the adult role is to provide opportunities for children to develop meaningful interaction with each other, they must be ready at times to protect children from each other.

The group can serve everyone's learning in a number of ways. Perceived as a working society, it can establish common goals and cope with the processes of communication and group decision-making involved in close living. Children can, and should, struggle with the evolution of suitable social organizations and order for themselves, deciding together what behavior they will and will not tolerate for the betterment of the group. At another level, the group can serve as a forum for opening up issues, expressing differences, pooling information and planning strategies for solving problems of various kinds. In small, and sometimes larger units, children can learn to think together in a mutual pursuit of knowledge. Experiences must be planned for and with children as a search for meaning within a context that matters to individuals and/or groups; not all children can be expected to be equally invested in all areas at all times. Problems for study need to be developed in a way that allows children to make their own closures and not merely copy predigested results.

Content Must Be Meaningful

The problems that concern children cover so wide a range that no teacher could hope to help them learn all they want and need to know in any one school year. For example, on the wall of a second-grade classroom there were the following questions asked by the children:

What makes your eyes open and close?
How did the world start?
What is the world made of?
How do we grow?
What is air pollution?
What is multiplication?
How do planets stay in space?
What are brains made of?
What is it like under the ground?
What are worms made of?
How was the very first person made?

And in a fourth-grade class studying Eskimos, the children asked:

How did Eskimos come to be Eskimos?
How do they eat frozen fish?
Do Eskimos get married?
When Eskimos die, do they celebrate?
Are the Eskimos related to black Africans?
Do the Eskimos ever have happiness?
If an Eskimo met a New Yorker, would the Eskimo think
    the New Yorker was strange?

Young children do not learn in compartmentalized, tidy packages of test items, and the content of their minds seldom adds up to the syllabus-like order of the pedagogic mind. They may get to know a great deal about a topic, but this knowledge is likely to be quite unevenly weighted, even in the specific areas that interest them most. Like adults, their learning is influenced by their tastes and feelings. Whatever children are newly interested in spills over into whatever they already know or what they want to know. They mix science, math, poetry, body movement, and feelings with total ease in the examination of problems that concern them.

Children are integrated and of a piece; their learning proceeds in integrated fashion. They assimilate and adapt in their own way and in their own time the experiences they pursue independently or the ones they choose from directions offered them by a parent or a teacher. While they are gaining in knowledge, they can learn also the art and skill of reasoning, of problem-solving, of acquiring and ordering the information that is meaningful to them. An adult must consciously encourage them to record their experience, to predict in experimentation, to make inferences, and to formulate hypotheses and establish operational definitions.

Recognition of how children function and the necessity for guiding them toward increasing maturity on several levels at once means that teachers must be prepared to cope simultaneously with a variety of possibilities for learning. Such a function is markedly different in outlook and skill from that of the traditional teacher for whom restricted, predetermined content and method established a formal, limited working mode of subordinate-superior relationships along a question-and-answer axis. A modern teacher listens to and observes children so that she can adapt her resources to what she sees and hears from them. She recognizes that boys and girls may have different as well as overlapping interests. She is constantly alert to cues and clues, and ready to react and respond to the extent she is able. She takes into account such factors within the children's stage of development as their degree of dependency on concrete examples rather than words, their ability to deal with symbols rather than the real thing, the weight of their fantasy, and the depth and limits of their objectivity in thinking. She is more concerned with the process of learning than the product. She wants her children to be learners, not encyclopedic store-houses.

Boundaries for Choices Are Necessary

Making choices of their own is a major experience for children in genuinely educational situations. Yet, though the choices are the children's to make, the range and possibilities must be bounded by the teacher's knowledge of the children, her understanding of what they need, and her acquaintance with the potentials of the materials and problems. Guiding children in their choice-making, while encouraging independent decisions at the same time, calls for maturity and perspective in the teacher, absolutely indispensable assets in an informal school. Nothing, for example, is more cruel than to allow children, in the name of freedom, to choose to do what is fraught with the probability of failure for reasons beyond their control. Yet this happens when adults committed to free choice on principle do not recognize their responsibility to protect children as well as to free them.

Children need the opportunity to figure things out, to be challenged, and to solve hard problems. But hard is relative to the reasonableness of the chance for success, and this calls for a teacher's best judgment about each individual in each situation. Choices have consequences, and sometimes alternative consequences have to be considered before true choices can be made. Teachers must help children to be clear about these. Choices involve judgment, and often children do not have the judgment for particular choices, such as those involving psychological needs, as when they exercise judgment over other children's work and behavior.

Many facets of informal, reality-based learning call for on-the-spot weighing of evidence by adults who must know where the children are as well as where they need, or want, to go. The judgments demanded of a teacher in an informal school are as often as not of a kind that are unfamiliar to more conventional perceptions of educational need. For example, although the delicate balance between the rights and needs of the individual and the rights and needs of others is recognized in traditional schools, it is not expected that children themselves will face or resolve this kind of problem at school. The teaching about it is consequently confined to preachment and command and has no meaning. But in a school committed to total growth, the children's own struggles with balancing individual-group responsibilities form an integral part of the learning situation, if only because children are permitted activities which involve people and materials in minimally restrictive and therefore unpredictable situations. Out of the realistic encounters and resolutions that inevitably occur in such openness of interaction can come a living appreciation of the complexities inherent in relationships, whether they be with people or materials.

But, for consistent deepening, most of the opportunities to experience must come within the purview of adult guidance. When children are granted the right to participate in the direction of their schooling, they may come to know where they would like to go, but an adult must help them to get there. While there is much that children can, and should, discover for themselves as learners in life, there is no reason why they should recreate all the world's accumulated wisdom over again. Adults can help children interpret their experience, understand it, and learn from it without in any way destroying their initiative to try for themselves. This is not an easy balance to achieve. Unless adults are as cognizant of children's limitations as they are of children's strengths and potential, an open situation intended to encourage minds to roam and feelings to be freely expressed can lead to chaos and mutual destruction as easily as to fulfillment.

Teachers Are Crucial

Beyond the structure and organization of materials, beyond space and opportunity, is the critical role of the teacher in the success of the open school. As in any schooling anywhere, the teacher, not the method or the materials, is the key to children's learning. The values and goals of the newer projections of a humanist education are broader, deeper, and more complex than those of traditional education or the simplistic offering of programmed instruction. In a free situation, the role of the teacher is more, not less, important; and more, not less, difficult to achieve. It is also more satisfying and professionally fulfilling, when it is understood, than the traditional teacher's role could ever be. If we are to move into increasingly free schooling, the role of the teacher in a non-traditional setting must be clarified.

The traditional school has had its share of excellent teachers who modified and adapted the restricted structures within which they found themselves. But the system as a whole was, and is, severely limited, because the relationship between teacher and pupil revolves around a presentation and feedback of foregone conclusions to and from more or less docile children. Charles Dickens satirized these limitations long ago in the opening speech of the headmaster in the novel *Hard Times*.

> Now what I want is facts. Teach these boys and girls nothing but facts. Facts alone are wanted in life. Plant nothing else and root out everything else. You can only form the minds of reasoning animals upon Facts: nothing else will ever be of any service to them.

The aura of sacrosanct piety that surrounded the rote learning of facts and skills was, and is, a threat to children's willingness to ask questions or take chances. Inevitably, in such a climate, the teacher's role incorporates elements of compulsion and judgment, while the child's holds elements of conformity and fear. The respect for children's minds that follows from attention to their questions does not develop, and the natural ease of a shared experience does not exist. Yet both respect and sharing appear when teachers delight more in their children's discoveries than in their own presentations; when they are aware of the strengths to be gained by children who meet and conquer challenges they accept as their own, who resolve conflicts and live up to realistic standards because they seek satisfaction in mastery.

The modern teacher must begin with the children and radiate out to content. This in no way implies a denial of the importance of subject matter or of intellectual development. But it does take into account a much larger field of possibilities for study, comprising both what adults consider suitable and children find desirable. It recognizes that values associated with scholarship and good living "take" better when teachers do not isolate intellectual standards from a conscious awareness of the struggles children undergo to meet those standards. And it respects the style in which children learn, so as not to force them into Procrustean beds.

In a program committed to children's self-propelled learning, the relationship between teacher and child must be built on premises quite different from the traditional ones. It is true that children of the middle years are still dependent enough on adults for their interaction with teachers to be important to them. But these are also the years when they step up the struggle to free themselves of adult control, and teachers need to accept the children's growing distance from themselves and respect the loyalties and allegiances children give each other. The infantile relationship to authority, in which the adult knows best and children must obey, is thus no longer necessary or appropriate, except in emergencies and special circumstances beyond children's experience and judgment. Yet the relationship between teacher and children can grow rich. But it must do so out of the struggles and victories embodied in a common search for learning.

The children's readiness for changing criteria of control is apparent in the fact that at the start of formal schooling, children are at a stage where they quite spontaneously establish rules for themselves, and rules, if one examines them analytically, fall halfway between uncritical acquiescence to a parent or teacher and the recognition of the necessity of law. As children's thinking grows in the power to be objective and impersonal, they can accept a rational authority structure at school in which the content itself and the necessities of social living set the limitations on work habits and social behavior.

There is one paradox. While the content and issues children can study grow more objective as the children mature, they themselves continue to a large degree to react subjectively all through their elementary years. Thus, neither the impersonal, pay-attention efficiency of the old "school marm" nor the comforting, protective lap of the teacher of pre-school children will now do. Children in the middle years of childhood need human, not womanly, qualities in teachers, male and female, who relate to boys and girls with equal attention to the differing tastes and styles of the sexes as well as of individuals within the sexes. They need teachers who take into account where each child is developmentally and what personal life experience has led him or her to expect of school.

Teaching children of the elementary years as feeling, thinking individuals who are also members of groups is an integrative task beyond the mere knowledge of subject matter. Without professional expertise in the areas of child development and group dynamics, there is unlikely to be good teaching on the early childhood and elementary level no matter what the academic preparation. This places a special demand on teachers of children which few within the profession and fewer still outside it have fully recognized.

The concept of integrative teaching, as against a single-subject orientation is remote from the traditional academic view, the upper reaches of which have influenced all schooling below. In the academic world, teachers are considered well prepared when and if they are thoroughly knowledgeable in a specific, necessarily limited area—that is, they are authorities in American history from 1812 to the Reconstruction period, they are mathematicians, biologists and chemists, or they know psychology or English literature. The capacity to specialize in this way has its usefulness at the adult level of learning, although many a college student wishes his professor had a better grasp of interrelated disciplines and a better knowledge of the people he teaches. But it is not desirable for children at the beginning of their organized schooling to approach learning from the stance of narrow specialization. Nor should their teachers be prepared as if this were so.

The traditional, academic concept of teaching and teacher-preparation finds an integrative approach to learning utterly incomprehensible and interprets any departure from conventional academic standards as intellectually shallow. Yet, when we recognize that a child is far more complex than his capacity to memorize, we must realize that integrative teaching means inter-disciplinary preparation in which the intellectual and emotional requisites are far broader than any perceived by the narrowly academic approach. The role may be fulfilled equally well by a man or a woman if it is understood. For the sake of smooth reading, we will refer to the teacher in the customary sex of present practice, i.e. female, although it is our conviction that at all ages children should be taught by both sexes.

A teacher of children under twelve must be broadly educated. But she need not necessarily be a master of any one subject, unless personal interest directs her into such a course. She should be a person whose learning has sparked her to be a learner all her life and certainly someone who cares about matters of the intellect. As an adult, she has interests of her own; as a teacher, she is willing to learn more about what interests children, even if the topical areas that attract them are not prime interests of her own. But she is more like the family doctor of another era in her integrative role than the highly specialized dermatologist or neurosurgeon of today.

The elementary teacher need not be an expert on the resources of a foreign country, but she must be sensitive to ecological relationships; she may not have studied calculus, but she must be aware of the beauty of mathematical logic and ordering; she may not be able to quote the Elizabethan poets, but she must love and value literature; she may have forgotten the names of minerals, yet be tuned in to scientific principles. And her knowledge of history should have strengthened her sense of multiple cause-and-effect relationships. Her general education and her specific training for teaching should alert her to possibilities in many fields and imbue her with the excitement of learning, so that when questions come at her for which she has no preparation in detail, she will not be afraid to say to children, "I can find out" or "We will go to someone who knows." She grows increasingly educated as she continues to study, with the children, areas and topics spurred by them or herself in the pursuit of honest inquiry.

The development of teachers who can function in an integrative way does not occur through the simple accretion of courses. It is not easy for teachers or students of teaching who have been brought up in controlling, subject-matter approaches to learning to make the transition to a non-authoritarian relationship with children in which content is shared and yet the authority of the adult as an adult is neither abdicated nor abused. It is not easy to establish and maintain a structure for children's independent learning. When the teacher leaves her status-laden position at the desk to move freely among children who may not all be seated at *their* desks, she may risk losing her class as an entity. Feelings about children, about herself as an authority, about her expectations of the teaching role must all be submitted to scrutiny as part of her preparation in order that the adult-child relationship can be non-humiliating, non-exploitive and non-threatening to children and teachers alike. Knowledge of childhood stages and modes of learning must be in her bones. Attitudes needed for work with children must be internalized so that they can be spontaneous and genuine. They cannot be put on without the children's knowing it.

Teachers of children have special demands placed upon them.

Teachers, alone among the professions, spend all their working lives in continuous contact with immature human beings. They are therefore peculiarly liable to experience deep reverberations in their own personalities, set in motion by the infantile and immature emotions and behavior of their charges. Childish behavior is a constant challenge and stimulus to the child which exists within every adult. The well-adjusted teacher is therefore one who has come to terms with the child in himself and is capable of reacting to immature behavior with mature attitudes.[3]

A teacher must be a person whose own emotional house is in order. Exposed to children's adoration, hostility, ambivalence, ambition, and impulse, she must be sufficiently able to differentiate between their needs and hers, so that she can deal with theirs with good sense. Aware of children's deep, impassioned feelings, she must neither take personally their expressions of hostility when she limits them nor exaggerate their admiration when she yields to them. She must deal consciously with her own biases, fears, and anxieties to keep them from interfering with her good judgment about what is objectively the best procedure to follow with a child.

Because the children are still young, teachers may also have to relate to parents (and in some cases to the baby-sitter). They must interact with other adults at the school with whom they share the responsibility for the children. Dealing with content in a complex inter-personal network in a social setting is a much harder job than staying within one limited subject-

[3] Ben Morris, "Mental Health in the Classroom: The Teacher's Personality and Problems of Children's Adjustment," in Studies in Education: *Bearing of Recent Advances in Psychology on Educational Problems* (London: University of London Institute of Education, 1955), p. 94.

matter area which never fights back! There are few academics who have either the breadth or the flexibility needed to support the variegated learning of children in their early school years. Unfortunately, our national teacher corps is not quite at this complex level of professionalization either.

The shift that is necessary in the orientation of teachers and of those who train them is related to the perception of education itself and will not be an easy one to make. The traditional academic bias, which puts those most thoroughly educated in one narrow dimension of learning at the top of the hierarchy, is so pervasive that when Conant, for years the president of Harvard University, wrote *The Education of American Teachers*[4] and unleashed a storm of attack on teacher training institutions, he not only argued for subject-matter and fact-retention learning as appropriate for elementary as well as secondary students (where it is also questionable), but in his suggestions for the training of elementary teachers was not at all embarrassed to reveal his general lack of knowledge of children and the learning process in childhood. The book was much touted, and because of Conant's prestige, it influenced the certification requirements of many states in the direction of deflecting the training of teachers from important requirements of the preschool and elementary years into the more conventional image of knowledgeableness at the upper levels of schooling. This same attitude supports a long held assumption that children of the elementary years and their teachers are of minor consequence intellectually. How much of this is related to the secondary position of women, who have been the mainstay of elementary education, is anyone's guess. Certainly, for long years, the salary schedules, training, prestige, and status of elementary teachers were at the bottom of the hierarchy. Although preparation and salaries are improving, recognition of the complexity of young children's requirements has yet to

[4] James Conant, *The Education of American Teachers* (New York: McGraw-Hill Book Company, 1963).

come. Parents may be no less conservative than educators in this regard.

School changes of the kind indicated may be difficult for many parents to accept, because the paraphernalia of familiar signposts, of schooling from stars to grades, from report cards to white shirt and tie, from homework to "good" behavior, from subject matter to daily schedules, will have to be discarded in favor of new signposts that still indicate that work is in progress but not in the same way.

To adults who judge children in adult terms, children will often seem to be bypassing much that has value, as they flounder in apparently uneconomical use of energy and time. But true learning cannot be made to happen on schedule or by decree. It will be easier for adults to make the shift from the old expectation by admitting that feelings exist in childhood, and that the process of learning is at least as important as the product during these formative years. The errors children make, as well as their unwise choices, are as much a part of a learning curriculum for them as the ultimate mastery of information and skill.

The growth of a child is not steady and even, as every parent knows. Yet, in the school learning of a child, even the most accepting parents have an expectation of steady and even progress that must be reassessed.

So let us turn now to a closer look at the stages of childhood that concern us and to a more detailed explication of possibilities in school curricula related to each of the stages.

Developmental Aspects of Five-Year-Olds Including Learning Style

· · ·

Five is the beginning of the end—the end of the pot belly, the end of the cuddly lap hug, the end of the lisp, and the end of the unquestioned faith in adult omnipotence. Five is the end of babyhood, a time parents find both satisfying and unsettling—satisfying because one can reason with a five-year-old, unsettling because fives are so unpredictable.

Parents look at their bright-eyed five-year-olds with nostalgic remembrance of when they were babies, but the children do not believe they ever were babies at all. To parents, five is at last the age when reason and dialogue promise the long-awaited civilized behavior that is close to the adults' own; to the children, five is power and strength, to be tested and expressed with as full a measure of autonomy as they dare take.

Very different perceptions—and the beginning of the generation gap!

A five-year-old is likely to feel quite certain he knows how to handle his affairs, with or without the good judgment that his parents consider a prerequisite, as the following anecdote well illustrates. Two little girls who attended a private kindergarten were suddenly nowhere in the schoolyard when their teacher and her assistant rounded up the class at 1:10 one Monday afternoon. Over an hour later, while teacher and assistant were still hunting under staircases and in all the bathrooms for them, the father of one of the girls telephoned the principal in somewhat of a rage. He had come home early that afternoon to find both girls sitting on their haunches in front of the door to his apartment. The story they gave him was quite unbelievable, but it had to be true, because at 2:30 on a Monday afternoon they were literally in that hallway and not at school. The two had slipped quietly out of the school playground (which was fenced), when both teachers were occupied with other children, and fled to the corner. There they boarded a local bus (no one ever found out whether they got on free or had money) and rode for about twenty minutes to a stop where one of them lived. They crossed a major traffic artery, got to the apartment building, and took the self-service elevator to the fifth floor. At that point, their plans went awry —Barbara did not have a house key! So they sat down to wait. Barbara's mother would have come home from her teaching job shortly after 3:00, but Barbara's father had decided to cut short his own day as a salesman and unexpectedly arrived at 2:30, hoping for a short nap before the rest of the family got back. Instead, he was greeted by two smugly self-confident five-year-olds on his doorstep.

There is an avant-garde among the fives who are like these girls. They are no longer dependable about holding a parent's hand or reliable about observing established limitations that challenge their feeling of "I bet I can do that myself." (Other children reach this self-view at about six.) They are on the threshold of the push into independent, autonomous boy and girl behavior associated with the middle years of childhood, when the spell of child society draws them away from the taken-for-granted security of the family. Fives are nowhere near the ambivalence in allegiance to parents that will come some years later, but the signs indicating the direction they will travel are all there.

The Roots of Confidence

If one looks back at the long distance children have already come in five short years, one can understand the cocky sense of self-importance five-year-olds so often display. From a state of complete physical dependency at birth, when any movement or satisfaction of need called for a mother's good grace and willing arms, they have arrived at sufficient agility and bodily control to allow them far more latititude than they need just for getting about. Fives are so pleased with themselves over their powers that they often set up physical obstacles to conquer just so they can enjoy their bodily competency all the better. They go up the steps of the slide in rhythmic patterns and go down the slide backwards or head first. They time the bumps on the see-saw so that the smooth up-and-down rhythm will have drama and suspense built into it. They ride their bikes at breakneck speeds, unless grown-ups stop them. They stand at the top of the jungle gym with arms outstretched and crow.

They not only move with wonderful ease and freedom, but also have learned, in their first five years, all kinds of difficult feats of coordination that society has demanded of them. They eat with utensils (unless they choose not to), they know about toileting (although they often just make it when absorbed in play), and they can do a superb job of washing their hands. (They rarely have enough time, however.) They can blow their noses and wipe their own backsides, put on their clothing (in their own fashion, it is true, but it's on), and turn lights on and off without thinking about how it is done. And they can talk in long sentences. In a word, they are pretty much indoctrinated in the culture of their society, and their bodies are obedient to *their* wills, not their parents'. Both sexes are pretty independent about handling their physical selves, unless they have been badly corrupted by over-solicitous parents; girls are often a bit more docile in accepting the restrictions of social living than the boys.

Fives like to do, to build, and to make things. They are active, often boisterously and noisily so, and, most significantly, they have not lived long enough for the outside world to have seriously impinged on their very personal, egocentric view of what is important.

Such feelings of competency as they have are based on solid achievement of a physical character, gained by trial and error, but ending in a sense of mastery which they can identify as their own.

Many parents at this stage inadvertently deprive their children of genuine feelings of competency and importance, because their immediate standards are not geared to the nature of childhood growth and learning. The parental goals are justifiably future-oriented, but, unfortunately, adult and societal standards related to social status, such as appearance, manners, and verbal behavior, offer children little inner strength as they move out of babyhood to face the realities of people and things by themselves. Parents would not knowingly give their children undependable sources of strength with which to cope with the inevitable problems and challenges of growing up, but it is easy to understand why they do.

The unevenness of development characteristic of all childhood is easily obscured in five-year-olds because of the children's so recently realized, remarkable facility with language. Adults understandably assume that the level of verbal proficiency a five-year-old displays represents his level of proficiency in all areas of functioning—if he *talks* like an adult, he must *think* and *feel* like one. However, five-year-olds, despite fine vocabularies, are known to cry with loud wails and heartbreaking sobs when they are disappointed or frustrated; and immediately after impressing an adult with their knowledgeableness in a stream of verbal power, can smack or kick another child with completely non-verbal gusto and "moral" justification. Again and again, they belie the promise of adult-like behavior with their childlike, impulsive actions.

5 THE LEARNING CHILD

They come up with endless variations of error on supposedly understood themes, and make more mistakes out of sheer ignorance than one could imagine possible. Contradictory behavior is commonplace at five and continues to exasperate parents for many years after five. But fives are so dramatically competent with words (in comparison with the toddler period they have only just left) and so close to formal school age at the same time that they are peculiarly vulnerable to adult expectations and demands which are out of keeping with their own concerns and need for competency, even though these are closely related to the adults' own.

Contradictions in Growth

The contemporary pressure for reading and writing in the kindergarten is a case in point; it is far more related to parental concern about college entry a dozen years away than to five-year-old need, style of learning, or even the reality of college admission. The pressure is rationalized by the speculative theory that present-day five-year-olds are actually better developed and more "advanced" than those of an earlier era, because mass media and global transportation have broadened the children's horizons considerably. But careful observations by seasoned kindergarten teachers reveal the sophistication to be skin-deep. How really "advanced," for example, is the following conversation among five-year-olds?

> *Jay* (to Robert): Did you see *The Wizard of Oz?*
> *Robert:* Oh, yeah, Tin Man chopping a tree in the rain, and he got rusty and needed oil . . . I don't watch Lucy. That's a girl's picture. I watch *The Green Hornet.*
> *Bill:* I'm going to chop my father's head off.
> *Robert:* You're not supposed to chop your father's head off 'cause "Up There" is going to punish you. He pointed a finger waveringly at Bill.
> *Bill:* Then I'll chop off "Up There's" head.

Robert: Then the Devil will get you and make you sick and go to the doctor and get a needle, so you better not.

Convinced, Bill put his head on the table and looked at Robert sullenly.

Are Young Children More Advanced?

Children talk more freely to adults than they once did, a consequence of the progressive elimination of fear from the modern adult-child relationship. They share their observations and comments, ask good and even unanswerable questions, and one can marvel at their growth in understanding in so brief a span of time. Many children have an impressive accretion of detailed information about all kinds of things, which is certainly a sign of good intelligence, but is hardly even or consistent. As one reads the accounts of children of educated parents in other times, one is forced to wonder whether today's children are significantly more knowing for their era than former children were for theirs. In any case, how can we assess such a thing? If one is to judge by the percentage of children with learning problems, which has remained fairly constant over decades, then the children of the uneducated, on whom the educational world has at last focused its attention, have certainly not made the dramatic leap that is sometimes claimed for the children of the middle classes. Are children at the same stage of life so differently capable that the mass media can seriously change some and hardly touch others?

Nevertheless, even assuming the possibility of greater knowledge among responsive young children of a mass media age, it is questionable whether an increase in verbal knowledge and expression has much effect on the capacity for understanding in depth or on the style of behavior of children with no more than five years of living and growing behind them. What could the five-year-old block-builder making a ship to carry food to Biafra have possibly understood of the phrase he was repeating with solemnity to his age mates, "The most important thing in life is life itself." Or examine the unexpected interchange between two boys who announced loudly that they were dinosaurs. Down on all fours (a piece of five-year-old behavior unchanged over centuries), the two were hissing at each other and making clawing, scratching movements, until one of the children suddenly stopped short and peered somewhat anxiously at his fellow dinosaur. "Then you'll change back to yourself, O.K.?" he queried. Or listen to the five-year-old whose mother read a storybook account of a battle between *Tyrannosaurus Rex* and *Brontosaurus*. He heard the sentence, "And his breath came in gasps" and promptly interpreted, "That means all the gas came out of it."

Does the substitution of dinosaur for tiger or lion represent real change in the children? Or is it possible that adults, who first learned at an older age what has become commonplace in their children's time, assume precocity when in reality every generation picks up the pulse of its time and the advance in general knowledge with an ease that impresses willing-to-be impressed parents?

Childhood Under Pressure

The drawings of contemporary fives are no more complex, the capacity for judgment no sharper, the feelings of helplessness when they get sick or into trouble no less painful than they have ever been, as far as we know. Young children play boat on the floor singing "The Yellow Submarine" instead of "Chug, Chug, Chug, I'm a Little Tug"; they imitate the flight of a jet with the same simple, swooping gesture with which they once undoubtedly imitated the flight of an arrow. Five-year-old girls are more likely to build with blocks than they once were, and five-year-old boys are less ashamed to play house, but that is true principally among children of sophisticated parents. Children of conventional parents play out society's sex roles with complete faithfulness to conventional ideals.

If children are to feel competent deep inside themselves, it is

essential that parents look at the emerging strengths and potential assets of every stage of growth with the perspectives of
both past and future in mind. One must see realistically the
limitations imposed by age and inexperience as well as the
promise of a growing person. There is good reason to try to
gauge this as honestly as one can. When children strive prematurely, and therefore too hard, to achieve what will come much
more easily only a little later, there can be side effects as a result of the inner pressure that are not worth the gains. A generation ago this became clear to psychologists, pediatricians,
and parents in connection with the pressure to toilet train as
early as possible. For one thing, the training broke down under
stress involved in illness, moving, or a new baby, all commonplace experiences in children's lives. For another, the relationship between parent and child was much colored by the existence of this *bête-noire* in their lives together. The ensuing
relaxation about toilet training characteristic of the 1960s
would be incomprehensible to parents of the 1940s. By the
same token, earlier parents would find strange the excessive
anxiety about reading so common to parents today.

Human Competency in an Age of Technology

Perhaps the technological and sociological changes which are
tending to make it increasingly difficult for the individual man
to feel that he alone can control the course of his life demand a
new quality of concern about feelings of competency. For
example, it may be of special necessity that today's children
develop in their very sinews and by their bodily efforts firm
conviction about their capacity to cope with the environment.
Such conviction has its roots in experiences during the early
years of childhood. At that time the sensory style of learning
natural to that stage of life lends itself to mastery of a changing
environment in concrete, physical ways that children can
themselves recognize and feel good about. Such inner feelings
about one's ability to cope are far more likely to be carried for-

ward into adulthood in a useful way than the early verbal glibness which satisfies adult vanity but fails to strengthen children's sense of power over the external environment, except
possibly in terms of manipulating people.

Words Are Deceivers

Children of educated families all too often use words to conceal
their ignorance, because they have learned that words please
their parents, and the desire to please comes to outweigh the
desire to know. Or they will use words to conceal their feelings, since some parents make it clear that strong early childhood feeling is not appropriate in a household of controlled
adults. Or they will ask questions, sometimes the same ones
over and over again, not as an honest search for information,
but as a means of engaging an adult whose generosity in responding to a child is likely to occur only in the cognitive
areas.

Children are shrewd about assessing their parents' over-
weighted concerns, and they behave accordingly. An educa-
tor-mother, whose daughter grew up during the era when giving children accurate sex information was a major concern of
enlightened adults, told the following story at a parent's meeting on sex education. "I don't remember how I told you about
babies being born," she recalled confiding to her young adult
daughter. "Do you?" "Of course I remember," the young
woman answered with a trace of mischievousness. "I was almost five, and I was in bed supposed to be asleep, but I was not
asleep. You were in the kitchen baking a cake, so I called out,
'Mommy, where do babies come from?' You got very serious
and said, 'Come, I will tell you.' And I got to stay up late and I
licked the batter in the bowl."

Mental Health Begins in the Body

Despite their flow of language, five-year-olds are still subject to
the style of behavior typical of the entire period of early child-

hood: the demands of the body for movement and the impelling motivation of emotions carry greater force than do the mind and its logic. Five-year-old children are capable of good, sound thinking; they are responsive to ideas and reason. But the locus of a young child's confidence is not in his thinking, although he enjoys being clever and knowledgeable. It is in his solar plexus, in his sense of himself as a physically active, feeling, coping being.

Fives grow competent by using fingers and toes, eyes, ears, and nose to find out what they want to know and to act upon the knowledge they have. They are in the process of learning how to substitute words for hands and feet to express strongly felt wants. They are gaining in controls of all kinds, from buttoning buttons to holding back tears. But they still prefer to run, not walk, to climb, not sit, to do, not watch. Action response takes precedence over the sedentary, and it will be many years before these inclinations are reversed.

For young children to experience the fullness of being which is the underpinning of mental health, they must experience their bodies and bodily senses with competency and not be diverted to the more adult modes of sitting and listening too soon. Even physically handicapped children must be encouraged to use their limited motoric resources to the utmost. Mastery of the body and its senses as tools for coping with the environment is too basic to selfhood to be ignored, too intertwined with learning in the early years to be bypassed without consequence. The feelings of adequacy and mastery gained in one's muscles and fingers are necessary reserves with which to face the increasingly difficult obstacles that children will need to cope with and conquer as they grow.

It is entirely reasonable for parents to look eagerly from the first for signs of a civilized being in their primitive children. It is understandable when they are proud and pleased at any evidence of mental alertness and social grace. But, while these are much to be valued and appreciated aspects of children's maturing, it is a mistake to underestimate the significance of sensory experience and bodily success, at least to age seven, if not beyond that. Nor, at the same time, ought one to minimize the task involved in learning to handle feelings, a matter of particularly serious challenge to young children.

Feeling and Friendship Grow Together

Fives are hungry for friends. Keeping a five-year-old at home on a rainy day or after an illness is, in some families, a disaster worse than a leak in the roof. The need for friendship at five represents a high peak in a developmental progression of social awareness that began with curiosity about children (and perhaps a bit of fear) at about two; grew into self-assertion and outright selfishness somewhere about three; veered toward comparison of self with others (to the others' disadvantage) at about four; and finally arrived at an honestly expressed need for children to play with (along with a real shortage of techniques) at about five. This is the stage when getting along with other people gets its first genuine trial in the field. Some children have more sophistication than others, learned perhaps from an older sibling or from ample experience in a well-populated apartment house or park playground. But most fives encounter pitfalls and challenges as they struggle for the satisfactions inherent in play with peers.

Just as the young child's need to stretch muscles, to touch and see for himself, is so often misinterpreted by adults, so the potential for growth in the social life of five-year-olds may get no more than a bow and a nod when it deserves considered attention.

With a seriousness which is almost an instinct for self-preservation, five-year-old children begin to tackle the hard realities involved in interacting with age mates whose feelings are as passionate as their own and whose social techniques are as crude. If they do not, there is a good chance that they will be at a disadvantage during the coming years of middle childhood and adolescence, when the weakening of emotional dependency upon parents must begin if progress in independence is to proceed. Peers support each other in this common task, which is not accomplished without its share of ambivalence and stress. The peer relationship during the middle years thus serves as a buffer against excessive anxiety as each child loosens his own silver cord and moves toward the wanted but feared transition from the dependency of babyhood to eventual self-reliance.

The frantic search of five-year-olds for friends can thus be seen to forecast the beginnings of a basic shift in the parent-child relationship, a shift which will occur gradually over many long years, and in which a child needs not only the support of child allies engaged in the same struggle but also the understanding of his parents. Nevertheless, few adults regard the child-to-child experience with anything like the seriousness with which they handle the children's relationships with themselves.

Social Applications of Right and Wrong

As an example of the difference in parental emphasis, let us look at the child's learning of right from wrong, an understanding which grows primarily out of the adult-child relationship, but which is stabilized in practice with peers. Few five-year-olds of reasonably optimal home environments are unfamiliar with the general concept that there is a right and a wrong, because adults are constantly on the alert to increase the depth, and define the details, of this comprehension. Watching full-faced as well as out of the corners of their eyes, parents take every opportunity to note and redirect any aberration from the moral code they value, and the children ultimately take on the values of their parents. By contrast, relationships among children can, and often do, go on without adult observation or supervision, as, to a major extent, they should. The autonomous working out of their own peer relations is a necessary aspect of children's growth, quite apart from the incidental boon this provides to busy mothers. But in the development of friendships, it often happens that beloved children of understanding families meet head-on the beloved children of other, equally understanding families, and the clashes of righteousness and frustration are dramatic signposts that progress in friendship is under way. It is not easy for children at this stage to share leadership, materials, ideas, or bosom companions, despite their desperate hunger for friends. It is at this point that parents scold "impartially," punish "equally," or else decide that the psychic energy called for in settling the quarrel is probably not worth the impermanent results.

What the children are struggling with has as much far reaching significance for them as the original learning of right and wrong, the application of which may even be the immediate cause of the difficulty as each child sees the morality of the issue from his own egocentric eyes. Children do need the chance to work things out for themselves; they need the struggle, the conflict, and the tears to value the pleasures that come with satisfactory solutions. Their fighting is not only not necessarily harmful, but can be of great value, since it is so frequently the only problem-solving technique children know. But they could use some insight into other people's rights and motivations as well as some short-cut social techniques that help. While they do not need, and ought not to have, adults hovering over them, they do need help in understanding that what their companions desire and fear may be as valid as, even if different from, their own feelings. And they need help in the kind of social techniques that, in the end, make it possible for them to achieve their goals. It is not at all axiomatic, unfortunately, that adulthood is always reached with full awareness of what goes into the sharing process, which includes both not taking advantage of others and not being taken advantage of oneself.

In families where there is great stress on the cognitive learning of the young child, and especially where the children are bright and gifted, it becomes all too easy to overlook that part of the child which involves the deepening of his feelings and the skills of socializing. No matter how brilliant a human being becomes, life is generally lived with people, in comradeship with the companions of one's chosen work, in the intimacy of marriage, and in the numerous interactions by which society survives. A sense of comfort or discomfort in human relationships flows out of attitudes learned early and out of accrued experience in the ways with which one deals with differences among people. If parents want children to have social attitudes which are neither destructive to the children themselves'nor to other children, if parents would like children to know how to manage healthily and with judgment the variety of interpersonal interactions all people must face, then the children must be guided toward such understanding within the crucible of their own awkward and painful efforts. Lecturing is not effective. In the living situation of conflict and stress, both the rights of one's own child and the rights of others can be acknowledged and managed, and alternative solutions offered. While this task may cause parents to feel they need the wisdom of Solomon to moderate the battle (especially when both sides are right!), and few parents feel as wise as Solomon, a little honest commitment to the problems children face will help parents find the ways of giving children the benefit of what they know without intruding unnecessarily on the children's right to make mistakes and solve their problems themselves. Obviously, the chance to try independently must come first, but when an adult does make a move, it can be a constructive one instead of the "plague on both your houses" technique by which social strife is so often stopped.

When children are helped by adults to recognize what is fair, reasonable, and manageable in relation to the needs of other children and the play situation, their link to reality, and therefore to mental health, is being strengthened in an important way. Five-year-olds find it hard to disentangle the convincing character of their own strong wants and fears from the objective reality of the external situation. If they are afraid of another child's taking a toy, they may act defensively and not in response to what the child is actually doing. If they are angry or frustrated, they will assume another child's guilt all too readily. If they want someone else's toy, they may become blind to the other child's feelings and simply help themselves.

Saying and Doing Are Not the Same

Although young children *verbalize* adult edicts, proscriptions, and morality, they behave more often as their feelings dictate. This apparent dichotomy is absolutely normal. According to Lauretta Bender,[1] emotionally disturbed children fail to verbalize adult proscriptions and standards, but simply act on impulse, whereas normal children predict future behavior by giving lip service to it first.

Feelings are powerful motivating forces at five. Wishes, fears, envy, and jealousy; ambition, trust, affection, compassion; rivalry and the desire for power rule children at one time or another with unabashed passion. It is this aspect of child life that grown-ups find so difficult to deal with, especially when the children are also highly verbal and even very bright. But the deepening of feeling and the know-how of social experiencing proceed in their own slow, zig-zag way during the early years, no matter how scintillating the brilliance or how sharp the memory of the five-year-old. It is rare, even among the most sophisticated and informed five-year-olds, to find one whose emotional and social development is as far above the average as his intellectual giftedness might lead one to predict. There is apparently little actual connection between the organic bases of intellect and those of emotion, or little relationship in the pace at which each develops.

Kindergarten teachers are well aware of this discrepancy. What they find most disturbing is the child whose intellectual brilliance is accompanied by such extreme emotional and social immaturity that he is readily victimized by other children, is too needful of adults to help him get by, and is generally a very sad creature. More often than not, the parents of such a child believe his difficulties come about because he is too bright for

[1] Lauretta Bender, *Aggression, Hostility and Anxiety in Children* (Springfield, Illinois: Charles C. Thomas, 1953).

the other children. It is more likely that they have stressed the precocity and played down the babyhood, so that the child could neither be nor grow in the way of young children.

Brightness is an adult criterion of acceptability. Children do intuitively seek out children of their own intellectual level because the interactions can develop better, but they are drawn or repelled by personality factors far more than by intellect. It happens to be easier to adapt to someone less knowledgeable, but friendly, than to someone hostile, mean, rivalrous, or helpless, even if bright. When children sense ineptness of physical or social functioning in another child, they fail to be impressed by the verbalizations which mean so much to adults. They can become unbearably cruel at worst, or indifferent at best, to this kind of peer.

Subjective versus Objective Reality

The way in which feeling colors perception at this stage of childhood reflects a certain confusion about inner and outer reality, a confusion which is evidenced in several ways. Dreams are very real to five-year-olds, and children are often sure that what they dreamed did happen. At the same time, on another level, five-year-olds enjoy a freedom from boundaries of time, accountability, adult values, and truth that, in a positive sense, allows them uninhibited flight into imaginative play. They can be all kinds of people in all kinds of situations with little more than a hat and a stick for props. In this latter context, the inner life is often referred to as the child's fantasy life, and includes not only the feelings described earlier, but misconceptions, misinterpretations, plans, plots, and uninhibited speculation, among other things. Whereas adults, unless they are mentally ill, know perfectly well that fantasy is fantasy, and older children know it, too, but enjoy pretending at times that they have forgotten, the five-year-old has a certain amount of honest uncertainty about which is which. He couldn't be so accepting of

all the Santa Clauses at Christmas time if he didn't shuttle easily between what he *wants* to be true and what *is* true, even if
he does know at another level not to eat a "pie" he has made
out of mud. The childhood confusion is the result of immaturity and inexperience, not distortion.

Five-year-olds are about ready to fit their longings and their
fears into the framework of what is really so, but they need
help. This does not mean that their imaginations need to be
curtailed or their pleasure in make-believe destroyed. Rather,
children must be helped to differentiate between the inner life
and the outer reality, so that while they enjoy either, they are
clear in their minds as to which is which. The child who pre-
tends he is a fireman putting out a fire does not need an adult
to build him a real blaze. Nor does the adult have to let a child
know he is not a fireman and to stop kidding himself. The urgency of a child's inner world of feeling needs to be avowed
and directed into acceptable social behavior. At the same time,
the free-flowing inner world of thought and imagination needs
to be encouraged, even though differentiated from wishes and
fears.

The style of functioning at five is physical, the emotions are
raw and strong, and the fantasy life is as real as reality itself. At
the same time, five-year-old psyches are stretching their social
and intellectual selves in the direction of greater maturity, even
though they are doing it in their own unsystematic way.

Active Minds

Five-year-olds are remarkable learners. Their interests cover
an amazingly broad scope, but fives seldom pursue an interest
in great depth or persist in it without interruption for extensive
periods of time. Almost everything is fair game for their curiosity and interest, but "almost everything" refers in the main
to that which is available to them through their eyes, ears, nose,
mouth, and fingers, or, if vicarious, can be conceived in concrete, sensory terms. Parents can remember with vividness the

rigors of marketing with their four-year-olds, who had to touch all the cans and boxes, had to poke their noses into the cash register, had to taste the contents of sealed packages, and were otherwise a great nuisance in the market. Most fives no longer do that—they have learned some controls. But the controls operate in adult-prescribed situations as part of their growing knowledge of what is right and wrong. When they themselves want to learn something, they continue to use their senses to examine and investigate. They pick up insects and stare at them intently; they crackle dry leaves and clap stones or blocks together to hear the sound; they smell empty perfume bottles and lick their ice cream sensuously. Their senses are out like antennae all the time, ready to draw back into themselves the myriad impressions which their minds then sort and classify.

Classification follows two major patterns. For one thing, children begin early to generalize from their repeated experiences with similar objects, events, and people: forks are to eat with, dogs bark, pressure on pencils leaves marks on paper, grandmothers give you anything you want. Generalizations are, in the main, based on their own concrete and sensory activity. Adults supply the important ingredient of words, which allow children to expand their understanding by stating, thereby objectifying, their generalizations. As factual detail continues to be added, generalizations deepen and change to more subtle classification. Having grasped the concept of "car" from much seeing, sitting, riding, and touching, details like 1963 Ford, Thunderbird, white-walled tires, or power steering are readily incorporated into the initial concept of car.

Something different is involved in the more abstract concepts. While these, too, grow out of sensory and concrete experience in early childhood, they do not develop as simple generalizations of objects, events, and people that have literal likeness. Instead, children come to perceive the non-obvious characteristics which objects may share, abstracting the concept of "softness" from a pillow, a rabbit, a toy cat, and a mother's bosom, all of which they have *touched*. They learn "above" from reaching up to high shelves, bumping their heads on the underside of the table, craning their necks, and lifting their heads, all *physical* experiences; they learn "noisy" and "quiet" from *hearing;* pink and yellow from *seeing;* bitter, sour, and sweet from *tasting.* Here, too, appropriate words offered by adults assist the growth of meaning; language and thinking grow together.

But the thinking process remains heavily dependent on the sensory base in early childhood, as the two youngsters below reveal:

> Karen is carefully molding a piece of clay into a flat pancake, while Donny sits with head on hand watching her. With great care, she uses a tongue depressor to cut away the four curves of her circular piece, making a square out of the original pancake. Donny asks her with great seriousness, "Karen, what's your recipe how you square that cake?" To which Karen replies with the assurance of the experienced, "You take your knife and you cut it all around."

And it is still tied to the literal, as in this next episode. A German child, Axel, visited a kindergarten class for a month. The children learned some German, and Axel learned much English. Some weeks after he had gone, a black child joined the class, which already had a light brown child in it. The children walked around the new child, sizing her up. Finally, one child asked, "Can you talk English?" Sarah spoke up, assuring everyone she could, and another child commented, "Oh, then you are *not* different."

Dramatization Supports Understanding

The natural world is especially exciting to five year olds. Everything that moves catches their eye, most often if it is at their feet or not too far above eye level. Bugs, ants, kittens, flies, spiders, and worms inevitably mobilize them to exploration and experimentation. Our industrial civilization excites them whenever they themselves can see some of the processes by which things happen—cement mixers, airplane flights and landings, traffic controlled and maneuvered, escalators endlessly running, boats docked and leaving, dump truck deliveries. People interest them mainly in terms of their action roles. The clue to what offers learning possibilities for them lies in the very style by which they learn. Fives are great imitators and use the information they gather about the world in their play. They set up pretend situations within which they play out roles, thereby pinning down what they understand. The activity they imitate must therefore have fairly obvious and clear relationships, and the meaningfulness of the activity must be seen in physical terms. They can imitate a pilot at his controls, but they cannot reproduce the machinery behind the knobs; they can imitate a snake slithering through the grass, but can do nothing with a hidden process that takes place at the push of a button; they can leap like a frog or sling cans like a garbage collector, but they do not know what to make of the work of an accountant, a lawyer, a stockbroker, publisher, or judge. They cannot imitate what they do not grasp as some kind of whole; yet their way of learning is dependent on the imitative process through which they focus on what they are learning about.

Their questions generally refer to the more literal and obvious aspects of what they see rather than to subtleties, even when they ask about birth and death. Many adults tend to deluge children with explanations they cannot really understand, although they can frequently repeat the explanation on request. Nevertheless, despite the apparent limitations of sensory orientation and style, the amount of information children are capable of absorbing can be startlingly impressive. When the spread of children's concerns actually serves as a base for answers to their questions, and opportunities are offered them to examine with their senses, there is no telling how much they can absorb. It is not in the *amount*, however, but in the *type* of learning that children's distinct style shows the sharpest differences from that of adults.

How Do Children Learn?

Among the many important figures of the twentieth century who have studied children in order to understand them better, the Swiss psychologist, Piaget, stands confirmed as the giant. Now an old man, he has spent all his life in concentrated, persistent investigation of children's growth in thinking and learning, and his work is being disseminated all over the world as guidelines to the education of children. Piaget is quoted widely in support of, and in opposition to, early training in symbols and abstract learning. Piaget's findings, however, have a kind of neutral quality, because he did not set out to prove anything, only to find out how children learn. He began and continued his studies by interviewing children, observing them, and offering them simple to complex tasks involving concepts of all kinds. The interviews and tasks were grouped around different areas of intellectual understanding, such as language, mathematical concepts, morality.

Piaget's careful study of children led to insights into certain universalities of childhood thinking and learning. The first of these discoveries is the existence of a developmental sequence in each important area of understanding, a sequence through which all children pass. The implication of this finding for education is that certain kinds of concepts cannot be understood by children before some degree of maturing has taken place, no matter how much we try to teach them. On the other hand, the exact time at which the stages or sequences begin and end varies with individual children. It is thought that the kind and amount of experience a child has affects his maturation and accounts in some degree for an earlier or later emergence of a given stage. Still, there are limits: no five-year-old is capable of thinking generally like a ten-year-old, although he may show a specific aptitude in one area—mathematics, for example. Appropriate experiences therefore seem to help children achieve the next stage of understanding earlier than if they simply "matured." But this is almost impossible to pin down. In reality, no one simply "matures," and no child just grows. Every child interacts with people and the environment for better or for worse, and growth ascribed to maturation is always a combination of genes and opportunity. Even in so clearly a maturational phenomenon as walking, malnutrition or fear can inhibit the maturational unfolding.

Five to Seven Is a Critical Period of Growth

Important to school learning is Piaget's discovery that among children between five and seven sequential development in the direction of abstract thinking occurs within a normal range, that is, some children begin at five, others at six, and most by seven, to handle abstraction. Although a normal range is typical of all phases of growth, the prestigiousness associated with school success blinds many parents to this fact.

Thus, the mother who boasts about the tooth that appeared "early," (maybe at four months) gets a little smile but not much more; and the mother who joyfully announces the tooth that appeared "late," (maybe at eleven months) gets a wide grin of appreciation. But neither performance is considered special enough for an award. They are both normal. Thought processes, according to Piaget, fall into a similar band of age range, some of it due to genetic differences like pace of growth, others due to opportunity to develop the innate ability every person has. Yet when Piaget's findings about thought processes eventually became widely known to psychologists, two common responses followed. Some looked at the evidence and asked thoughtfully, "What are the experiences that support maturation?" But others looked at the evidence and asked impatiently, "Can't maturation be hastened?" In these two subtly different questions lie a value system and a bias about achievement.

It is with this in mind that we look to the kindergarten, the five-year-old school experience.

Kindergarten: Underpinning for Academic Learning

· · ·

At one time kindergarten was the magic entry to the "big school," the gentle introduction before the real work began. In kindergarten one could play with blocks, draw pictures, sing, and dance—truly a children's garden. Not so for middle-class children in the United States since World War II. The nursery school movement has taken up the slack, and as children enter kindergarten after one or two years of nursery school experience with play, blocks, paints, song, and dance, parents are inclined to ask, "Isn't kindergarten more of the same? Won't they be bored? Shouldn't they be promoted to the real stuff—reading, writing, and arithmetic?"

On the surface it certainly looks that way. More blocks, more paint, more singing hardly seem like progress in the direction of school achievement. Yet closer examination uncovers a fallacy.

The criteria by which the kindergarten program and materials are thus negatively assessed come from the only remembered school experiences adults have, that is, sequentially prescribed, fact learning dependent on the ability to read. Implicit in this experience is the assumption that children learn little of value before they can read, and so the sooner they learn to read the better for their intellectual progress. In reality, children learn a great deal before they can read, and much of that is good, solid information. The fact that they learn it by seeing, hearing, touching, tasting, and smelling does not make the information less accurate, or the learning style less valid.

Very different modes of learning can enhance intellectual development, and all who have taken the trouble to study young children have found that the most significant intellectual learning at that stage occurs in action and through the senses. In adulthood, however, intellectual enhancement is more likely to occur through the written word. In the latter years of childhood, the two styles overlap, but children make the transition from a concrete to a more abstract style of learning in their own time and at their own uneven pace. To understand the way in which the play program of the kindergarten and its raw materials, blocks, paint, and clay, help children to utilize the knowledge gained through their senses, the very word *learning* must come in for fresh interpretation.

In the experience of most adults educated in subject-matter schools, easy reading words preceded hard ones, addition was learned before algebra, and French I obviously had to precede French II. The order of difficulty within the content itself logically determined its sequence and grade placement. But, as understanding of the learning process has deepened, the concept of difficulty in a given subject has changed to include its *psychological* difficulty, and this change affects both content and sequence.

An excellent example of the change from a logical to a psychological approach to learning exists in the contemporary approach to the teaching of mathematics. For generations children learned addition in the first grade, subtraction in the second, multiplication in the third, and division in the fourth—an order of difficulty that seemed logical at the time. But present first-graders add, subtract, multiply, and divide all in the same grade, and continue to do so for several grades thereafter.

This is not because today's first-graders are brighter, or the curriculum tougher than in the past. It is because earlier educators were unfamiliar with the learning characteristics of young children and were at the same time wedded to the logical pattern of sequential subject-matter that has come down to us from the Middle Ages. Since it never occurred to anyone to question the curriculum, the explanations for children's resistance were quite simple. Good children repeated what they were told. Children who did not learn were clearly bad or stupid.

Yet almost all first-graders were, and still are, capable of handling all four mathematical processes, *provided they are tackled in concrete form.* They can divide a candy bar, multiply the number of pencils three children will need if each uses one, subtract a given number of portions of ice cream from the lot, and tally large numbers of items to a total. But they may not be able to do any of these things *in writing* during most of first grade or well into second. It always was, and still is, hard for them to handle the *symbolic rendering* of these processes, and they are generally struggling with such symbolic rendition, even today, into the third grade.

This is the knowledge about young children's learning style which Piaget uncovered and which caused such a shift in mathematics education. Traditionally, only a limited portion of the content, such as addition in first grade, and subtraction in second, was isolated for teaching. Almost immediately, and quite prematurely, the mathematical transactions were translated into symbolic manipulation, that is, $1 + 1 = 2$, or $2 - 1 = 1$. The vertical pursuit of one aspect of the subject straight into its symbolic rendition was replaced in the new math by broad, horizontal experience with the several interrelated concepts simultaneously learned through *physical manipulation* of *concrete materials.* The manipulation of materials goes on for a long period before the symbols for the transactions are used. It should be clear that neither the content of mathematics nor the nature of children's capacity has changed radically. We simply know better how to bring children and content together, a talent in which schools are not as successful at the older levels as they are beginning to be at the younger ones.

The Different Requirements of Reading and Math

Because mathematical principles can be drawn so well from concrete, pliable materials—floor and table blocks, scales and weights, containers, and so on—mathematics learning is well suited to the kindergarten. The same cannot be said for reading, however. Reading differs from mathematics in ways significantly related to children's natural learning style. This difference is somewhat clarified by the following illustrations.

Imagine a child of five, six or seven standing before a balance scale trying to match a pound of toothpicks on one side with a pound of nails on the other. Out of his efforts, physical in character, he comes to recognize that there is no necessary relationship between volume and weight. This is sound mathematical thinking, which serves as the base for an *eventual* symbolic rendering of questions. Developed out of first-hand experience, it has far more meaning to a child than if he had learned it by rote.

But reading is a symbol system to begin with which must be learned before meaning can be abstracted. And the symbols bear no relationship to anything concrete and real as they do in math. Before a child can learn to use the symbols of reading, he must grasp the existence of symbol systems as such, and find a quality of reality in an abstraction. However, to "see" the meaning of reading, a child can do almost nothing by himself. Only as and if he listens while countless stories are read *to him*, countless labels interpreted *for him*, and countless signs explained *to him*, does the essential meaning of symbols in print become clear to him. Beginning from an awareness of this kind of reality, which is quite remote from the more literal and concrete understanding of reality more characteristic of this stage, a child must go on to deal with details of the reading process which continue to be abstract in concept, such as silent vowels or syllabication. It is true that children can be helped to memorize the letters of the alphabet by concrete approaches such as sandpaper letters or tracing of letters. But *recognizing* the basic tools is hardly the same as learning the principles which the skill supports. The fact is that when children were taught math by rote manipulation of the tools—numbers and signs—without any conceptualization of mathematical relationships, the "right answer" became a nightmare of anxiety to generations of children who did not know what they were doing or why. This is the background that explains why large sections of the adult population have resisted math in their further learning, and shudder when they think about it.

Another point of difference exists in the way in which the mechanics of math and reading can be used. The skill aspects of mathematics can be assigned to machines, for example, adding machines and computers, provided the conceptual understanding of the person handling the machine is clear. But the skills of reading can be given life only by the person. Only as the mind of a person understands how and why the skills can be applied do they become valuable to him. Ultimately, they will allow him to abstract a wide variety of content from print, but the content will be understood and used subjectively, quite dependent on what the reader brings to it. For mathematical proficiency to proceed, skills become the means of reinforcing concepts learned through the senses. For reading proficiency to proceed, a child's total life experience and especially his use of oral language are the indispensable support; without these, the mechanics of the skill are useless. Thus, learning in mathematics can proceed in both a concrete and symbolic form, a flexibility suitable to children's changing styles of learning as they go from younger to older. But the reading process at no time has such a relationship to anything concrete.

Reading is a symbol system for another symbol system, that is, print for oral language. While oral language initially rests on concrete experience (for example, the word "mother" stands for a living being), it can also grow far from it, as in the word "motherhood." Therefore, in the stages from five to seven, readiness for reading is quite a different matter from readiness for mathematics.

Abstract Learning During the Piagetian Stage of Concrete Operations

Children up to about seven are at a stage of life when reality has personal meaning. It is that which they can see, touch, smell, hear, taste. The content of mathematics, although conceptual in nature, is drawn from the discovery of universal laws that are clear *in action*. Five- to seven-year-olds can think in their own style and yet understand the relationships and principles embedded in mathematics. But the principles of reading are not embedded in the procedures. Treated as a subject to be learned, its content is the steps of a process; children cannot use reading to think with until they have first mastered an abstract symbol system—the direct reverse of what happens in mathematics. Research in the field of reading has not, up to the present, been as seriously concerned with these psychological aspects of learning to read as it has been with testing and arguing various approaches to how reading should be taught. Without full understanding of what learning to read demands of a child, it is not possible to make sensible decisions about methods and certainly not of timing. Hence, the place of reading in the curriculum for children from five to seven, which has become an issue in this age of pressure for achievement, has to be carefully evaluated in terms of its true suitability, given the general development of children at this stage and the variations in individual readiness.

A first serious question that must be raised is whether the skill of reading is actually equatable with intellectual development, since it is proposed for five-year-olds ostensibly to strengthen the intellectually barren kindergarten. Reading is indeed a tool to unlock the intellectual treasures of the past and the present, but one look at the vast numbers of people who have achieved the mechanical skills of reading, only to confine reading to the captions under pictures in the tabloids, should be enough to convince us that reading skill and intellectuality do not inevitably go hand-in-hand.

Intellectual development refers to a host of mental processes, hardly to the technical skill of decoding. It refers to conceptualization, to the relating of facts to concepts, to the ability to compare, analyze, synthesize. It refers to data-gathering, experimentation, hypothesis, and conjecture. Intellectual is of the mind, and the mind can grow deep and broad in intellectual strength without the ability to read at all. To an inquiring mind, the skill of reading is an open door; to a closed mind, it is a direction-finder on streets and avenues, and not much more. Reading is a skill that allows a symbol system to be decoded; after that, the message must be comprehended. One can decode and not get the message; one can decode and stretch one's mind as a consequence of the message; one can decode and be utterly bored by the message. Facility in decoding is not in itself intellectual, although a given level of intellectual maturity is required to comprehend the possibilities of the decoding process. As in all phases of learning, so in reading, too, grasping the idea of the action must precede the action itself. But there is a long road even between the conceptual grasp of reading as a process and the action of reading, because all the pieces of a child may not be ready for this push at the same time, and reading demands more than the understanding of its function.

What Makes for Reading Readiness

Differences in readiness for reading are clear enough to kindergarten teachers, whose appraisal of individual readiness compares very favorably with formal reading readiness tests. But the temper of the times is such that parents and educators unfamiliar with the stage of growth that coincides with the beginning school years find the differences in readiness a cause for anxiety or misplaced pride. While most parents become knowing about the variations in physical differences among children that all add up to normal, the same parents seldom know just what the boundaries of normal are in relation to readiness for a variety of intellectual experiences, because little attention has been paid to such insights by the schools.

This lack of knowledge is matched by the rigidity of society's expectation, also learned from the schools, that a specific level of achievement must be accomplished at a specific date, despite the fact that school timetables have never worked for all children. The notion that reading before a prescribed date is desirably precocious and reading after that is shameful, slow learning is a view that must give way to the recognition of the *normal* range of growth that exists in this as in other areas. Just as parents lovingly fit their children's shoes for perfect comfort (and within an age group there are several sizes), so they must take into account with equal conscientiousness the differences in pace and timing with which normal children arrive at the necessary levels for academic achievement. Unless this happens, we will continue to inculcate in our children the anxiety over achievement and the fear of failure that are so characteristic of far too many children, including those who objectively do well at school.

The notion that an I.Q. score is sufficient indication of readiness for learning to read is quite erroneous, as recent research and clinical experience indicate. Some of the factors involved may come as a surprise to parents—and teachers, too. Several studies strongly indicate a relationship between physical immaturity and reading. A little thought will show that general neurological development affecting various kinds of coordination is involved in the reading process. For example, the ability to read from left to right (or right to left or up and down) is dependent on a child's sense of direction. This in turn emerges only when he has an internal sense of his center of gravity and body balance, to which laterality can be related. This kind of maturing, which must be at a satisfactory level before a child can learn to read, takes place quietly, when no one is looking, sometime between the ages of four and eight, a normal range. Yet all children are assumed to be developing neurologically at exactly the same rate and are expected to begin reading at exactly the same time, despite the fact that schools have no procedures for diagnosing neurological developmental readiness.

In one of the studies that refute the premise that the I.Q. is a sole factor in readiness for reading the investigators followed a group of middle-class children from kindergarten to fifth grade. At the fifth grade they matched children who had similar I.Q. scores, but whose reading levels were different. In an effort to find the factor other than I.Q. that was at work, the investigators re-examined the Rorschach tests they had given the children in kindergarten. They discovered that the children who were slower in reading, despite comparable I.Q.s, had indeed shown a tendency on the Rorschach test that accounted for the difficulty.

One aspect of the Rorschach responses reveals the extent to which a child differentiates the parts of a whole from the whole, or tends to see the whole in undifferentiated fashion. That is, he either perceives the paws of the puppy at the same time he sees the puppy himself, or he fails to note the paws in his perception of the whole puppy. The children who did not make as much progress in reading by fifth grade were children whose kindergarten Rorschachs showed them to be less able to perceive differences, obviously a strong element in learning to read. The research which indicates physical maturation to be a factor in reading may explain other research showing that children of the same I.Q. who start school when they are well past six generally do better than those who enter first grade at six or earlier. The big question parents must ask is whether the side effects of continuous struggling to achieve beyond one's comfortable capacity of the moment and the attendant fear of failure or worry about displeasing adults is in the long run worth the apparent success of early reading.

Here are two observations of a child in a reading kindergarten made by a student-teacher assigned to the child's class for a term.

Robin attended a private school where reading was taught

via I.T.A.[1] to ease the process. He made the transition to the regular alphabet by himself. He was five years and nine months of age at the time of the record.

Robin

Academic Functioning

Robin is able and interested in academic work and seems to follow this interest independently, as seen in making a fan to demonstrate moving air for science, reading the writing in regular alphabet on a toy, reading a record cover in regular alphabet, seeing a mistake on a book title, writing "fascinated" in I.T.A. on board during freeplay, adding more sentences to writing paper and, according to his mother, changing to regular alphabet on his own. He reads very well and is advanced in reading in the class.

Robin appears in the academics to be quick and accurate. He made the fan quickly and explained it matter-of-factly. He quickly and correctly answered questions on numbers after asking the teacher a question when "stuck." Two writing papers were described as accurate, and he reads books to teachers quickly and perfectly. He writes about the play steadily, and it is accurate and original.

Worrying

Robin often appears worried, concerned and anxious about peers' and adults' reactions to a mistake he may have made. Several times he became afraid that the teacher would be mad at a mess he'd made once with a cookie and twice with crayons. Another time Robin was afraid Miss B. and his mother would be mad that he'd accepted Batman cards from a peer. Robin is worried when criticized by Bill for squeezing in line and by Miss B. for not buttoning his coat and also when his father suggests he hang leggings he's forgotten.

---

[1] Initial Teaching Alphabet. The twenty-six letters of the regular alphabet have more than twenty-six sounds (e.g., *g* has two sounds as in *George* and *gas,* or is silent as in *thought*). I.T.A. added new symbols for the extra sounds, making the relation between symbol and sound reliably phonetic and therefore easier to learn.

Several times Robin was anxious when something was out of his sight or grasp, such as a yesterday's painting that he can't find, when his father hasn't come to the roof yet, when Miss W. and Bill have a secret he hasn't heard and when a friend hasn't arrived at school yet. Also he worriedly tells me his parents may leave him for a weekend with his siblings, who tease him.

Three times in the observation period he worried if something was good or not—once he asked a peer if his painting was good and the teacher if he's good at anything in the play and still another time if his name is written well.

Robin's expression is often serious and intense as seen while making the fan; brows knit when reading letters on toy; intense with tongue-on-lip writing on board; tongue on lip while writing about play.

At these times Robin looks apprehensive, agitated, worried, anxious, upset and frowning, shivering all over, concerned, tears in eyes, his voice sad, brows knit, nervous, disoriented, shaky voice, distressed face and plaintive voice.

He worries quite often.

Do those who push for early reading stop to consider this kind of cost?

Reading Readiness Combines Many Facets of Growth

The high correlation between the evaluation of kindergarten teachers concerning children's readiness for reading and the results of reading readiness tests is not accidental. Teachers take into account a variety of factors that are obvious to them from their intimate knowledge of children. They are aware of the level of responsiveness and curiosity of a child from his questions and interests; they generally do not need I.Q. scores to know whether he is bright or not. But they are also familiar with, and take seriously, such aspects of a child's behavior as his patience with himself when he makes mistakes; his standards for himself which keep him from trying, or, on the contrary, make him try harder than ever; his attention span in physical and non-physical activities; his ability to follow directions; his ability to tell a story with coherence and sequence; the ease with which he is distracted by his friends or can ignore them when he is concentrating; his ability to start and finish work independently or his need for constant support and approval before he can complete either self-imposed or adult-imposed tasks; his compliance with, or resistance to, authority and the strength of his "I can do it myself" attitudes; his interest in books and his ability to follow stories read to him; his relationships with children from which reading may provide an escape rather than an entry to additional experience; the level of his vocabulary and general knowledge and his own motivation to read.

It is not a widely broadcast fact, but nevertheless supported by the research, that children who learn to read by themselves before first grade are mostly girls who prefer quiet, sitting activities, prefer to be alone rather than with other children, and when playing with other children, participate in quiet games. Does this description of the early reader give a clue to why, under present school practices, more boys than girls end up in reading clinics? How many little boys *or* girls at this stage prefer quiet activities, or prefer to be alone rather than with children? Knowing the five-year-olds' penchant for action and friendship, is it surprising that the percentage of children who learn to read on their own before school entry is very small? In Dolores Durkin's study[2] of 5,000 children, only forty-nine, or 1 per cent, were found to be readers before entering school. In a second study by Durkin, the percentage was only slightly higher. On the basis of such data, ought anyone to conclude that the best thing for five-year-old children is to be taught to read?

Nothing is really gained by an early start, and much can be

[2] Dolores Durkin, *Children Who Read Early* (New York: Teachers College Press, 1966).

lost of the experiences that support successful reading. Is it advisable to place children prematurely in the position of having to cope with formal, structured, orderly, and sequential learning of an abstract symbol system of communication? True, there are children who seem able to take this. But, as Durkin's study shows, they are fewer than most people think.

It is probably not accidental that, historically, the introduction to reading in many countries has coincided with common folk wisdom about the kind of growth that occurs in childhood at about seven. Piaget's studies that revealed a leap in thinking powers occurring among most children between five and seven support this folk wisdom. The leap involves a shift from dependency on concrete underpinning for symbols to the ability to deal with abstractions without the concrete support. That is, to the ability to cope with such symbols as the spoken *word* "house," a *picture* of a house, or a *block construction* of a house (because behind them all is the knowledge of a real, three-dimensional house) is added the beginning capacity to deal with a symbol for a symbol—the printed word "house" for the oral word "house," a step twice removed from the real thing. A few five-year-olds, more six-year-olds, and practically all seven-year-olds attain the capacity to manipulate written symbols naturally. But there is no way to force the leap by training, although many psychologists have tried. It has been possible to get children to *recognize* symbols, for example, the letters of the alphabet and even words and numbers. But no one seems able to get children to *think* with those same symbols before they are themselves ready.

As a result, rote learning of symbols often proves successful in beginning reading, but does not stand up reliably in long-term goals, such as zest for reading books. The British, who for decades introduced reading at five, always had about the same percentage of reading failures as the Americans, who have started their children reading at six. The British are now in the process of officially changing over to a totally non-graded approach in the early school years of five, six, and seven, encour-

aging children to begin reading individually as they are ready
—at five, or six, or seven. They have had encouraging success
in decreasing both their reading problems and school anxiety.[3]

Anxiety About Reading Is Exaggerated

Confusion about childhood learning is at the heart of the
pedagogic and public debates about early childhood curricula
which arise from time to time and are so bewildering to parents. The bewilderment is considerably compounded in our
day by the speed with which information is disseminated in the
press. Before most of the educational research has been tested
over time, and with much of it still contradictory, the mass
media create a frantic spur to action in a "before it is too late"
mood that has parents convinced a child's academic future is
jeopardized before he is hardly launched.

It happens that there are children whose futures are jeopardized early, and about whose learning capacities there is considerable concern. These are the children for whom parental malnutrition and inadequate prenatal care can lead to deficiencies
in the uterine environment which bear a relationship to intelligence;[4] or children for whom untreated pregnancy abnormal-
ity in the mother apparently affects the capacity to read years
later.[5] There are also the children who are born into relatively
barren, unstimulating environments that limit the variety and

[3] According to an unpublished speech by Mary Langmuir Fischer Essex,
Professor of Child Development, University of Cardiff, Wales, presented at
the annual meeting of the New York State Early Childhood Council, May,
1968.
[4] Benjamin Pasamanick and Hilda Knobloch, "Epidemiologic Studies on the
Complications of Pregnancy and the Birth Process" in Gerald Caplan, ed.,
Prevention of Mental Disorders in Children (New York: Basic Books, 1961).
[5] A. Kawi and B. Pasamanick, *The Association of Factors of Pregnancy with
the Development of Reading Disorders in Childhood*, monograph of the Society for Research in Child Development (Yellow Springs, Ohio: Child Development Publications, 1959).

kind of experiences available to them, and the children who receive inadequate attention as individuals. These are mainly the children of the very poor, whose "failings" as they enter kindergarten may include such generalized disabilities as absence of sustained curiosity, along with specific unfamiliarity with the letters of the alphabet. But such "failings" occur far less frequently among children who have had reasonably good conditions for development.

The knowledge that suitable biological conditions, stimulating environment, and loving, individualized attention are indispensable to the growth of intelligence and personality in human beings goes back for decades, and has been reaffirmed again and again. The recent, wholly justified and long overdue concern about the children of very poor and inadequately educated parents has led to a concentration of research into the ways in which learning can be fostered among such children. But the findings have been exploited publicly with little regard for the realistic differences in conditions affecting normal growth and development among the vast majority of children. Partial responsibility for this confusion lies in the fact that experimental research produces only small bits of information at a time, and the relation of these pieces to the total picture is difficult to see without a frame of reference that includes experience with children in the flesh and a good deal of background about total development. It is all too easy for an intelligent bystander to exaggerate the significance of any one small finding or even to substitute the small piece for the whole story as findings are reported. From such small beginnings it is again a small step toward stressing the possible implications of a piece of research as though its results were proven. And even intelligent journalists have done just that. The proliferation of printed materials possible under our advanced technology and the opportunity available to many to speak and write with certainty about education without being held accountable to children or parents for what they say creates misconceptions that are detrimental to parents and children alike. The meaning of learning and growth in early childhood has received excited and sensational treatment which has resulted in unjustifiably excessive pressure on all children at younger and younger ages.

Educational Research Cannot Find All The Answers

To clarify this further, it is necessary to understand the problems involved in educational research. In order to show that a given approach to learning is correct, or accomplishes what it sets out to do, results must be measured. Unfortunately, not everything learnable is measurable, even though what is learned may be very valuable. For example, how does one measure with accuracy the relative effect on a child of his father's teaching as against his mother's? Or how measure mathematically the quality of a home or the quality of a classroom? No matter how carefully anyone defines a human situation, the complexity of human life and experience produces an element of elusiveness and uncertainty which at present defies the researcher's instruments. As a consequence of these limitations, much of the research in educational psychology is inevitably limited to what *can* be measured, which too often means the obvious or the overtly observable. That, of course, sets limits on what is studied, since measurable behavior is not necessarily significant or far-reaching. Thus, it is possible to count the number of slaps given in a week by the father and compare that with the number of slaps given by the mother, but that comparison, while it can be treated statistically, tells us nothing of the relative effect on the child of either parent's teaching.

Carrying this into what is to be stressed or measured in learning, educators who have worked with young children are more concerned about how to foster and support curiosity in children rather than about how and when to teach letters. They reason that a curious child is a learning child, and it is simply a question of time before he is motivated about letters, too. Curiosity, however, is hard to stimulate if it has failed to develop spontaneously, but recognition of letters of the alphabet can be taught by rote and the results measured. For this reason, there is far more research on recognition of letters of the alphabet and on numbers than on curiosity or mathematical understanding.

Until the instruments of psychological measurement can handle the really complex problems of learning and growth, educational programs developed as a result of findings uncovered within the limited focus of measurability are in reality shortchanging children. In the case of the disadvantaged, there is, for some people, the defense that since we do not know how to kindle curiosity, we may as well give the children acquaintance with letters and shapes, although many educators would not settle for such limited goals for even supposedly limited children.

By implying that studies primarily designed to help children with difficulties ought to be applied to all children, popular writers have helped develop a state of anxiety among conscientious parents that has led to pressure of a kind which we cannot fail to relate to the increase in the number of ulcers and the use of tranquilizers among children of school age—and perhaps even to the use of drugs as an escape from pressure among high school and college youth. From previous experience with parental anxiety in other areas, there has accrued ample evidence to predict that such anxiety can cause far more extensive damage to children's power to learn than any such objective factor as the age at which formal learning is begun.[6]

Attempts to teach children earlier and earlier are not new, although the nature of the tasks to be taught keeps changing. A few generations ago, early efforts focused on physical skills like climbing or skating; today's efforts are in the realm of symbol-learning and abstract thinking. The early investigators succeeded in training youngsters to develop skills earlier than when left alone, only to find that those who came to the skills as they were themselves ready learned faster and in fewer

[6] M. Kellman Pringle, *Able Misfits: A Study of the Educational and Behavioral Difficulties of 103 Very Intelligent Children, I.Q.'s 120–200,* Studies in Child Development Series (New York, Humanities Press, 1970).

trials. It proved to be uneconomical to push skills early, and the lesson was learned by psychologists and educators alike. Whether in toilet training, skating, or reading, similar conditions within children make the pressure for too early achievement of dubious worth. This is partly because of the uncertainty of permanence and partly because of the question of side effects from excessive pressure.

The Meaning of Kindergarten Materials and Activities

It is with this in mind that the role of the non-academic materials and the play program can now be evaluated. Given the concept of subject-matter organization and book learning as a sole frame of reference, it is entirely logical to put block-building, painting, drawing, and dramatic play into the familiar sequence of vertically structured slots and assume that if these activities are suitable for three- and four-year-olds, they are surely babyish for more mature fives and sixes. But, as indicated earlier, the yardstick is not appropriate. The materials and media of value in the kindergarten are not subjects to be followed in a sequence from easy to hard. Nor do young children learn in the style of adults. The materials are no more than the means by which a *process* of learning takes place which is indispensable to later, formal learning. They are the tools by which a child can bring into focus, and then go on to clarify further, his personal understanding of a wide variety of content, both objective and subjective, *learned through his senses*. The ways in which a child uses these materials are very much related to his emerging powers to cope with abstract symbols, and therefore have genuine relevance to his future growth in reading, although not in an immediately obvious way.

Language is the major symbol system used by adults, but the full possibilities of language for the expression and development of thought are not fully utilized by children whose think-

ing is still strongly tied to action, and whose words are rooted
in the concrete and literal. Yet it is necessary to their learning
that they deal with their comprehension of reality in some
symbolic form.

Concrete Experience Must Be Used in Symbolic Form

Beginning at birth, every child is internally impelled to organize into his own understanding the many and varied impressions of the world that come to him through his senses and
through his parents' interpretations of that world. Such individual organization gives him the sense of knowingness that
makes him feel secure and serves as a base from which the further desire to know is stimulated. Each child's individual organization of his world becomes a chart of sorts, by which he
finds his way among things and people familiar to him, and out
of which he gains principles to apply to the as yet unknown.
Eventually, in order for him to clarify his understanding for
himself *and* to be able to communicate what he knows, every
child needs to express his experience in some symbolic form.
By transforming experience into symbolic form, every human
being is open to furthering his knowledge through exchange
with other people's symbolic rendition of their experience.
The ability to use symbols in a process of communication is
thus the basis for man's learning.

But, just as children still must see and touch to learn something, so they need symbolizing forms that are close to their
action style, and this is the role played by the blocks, the clay,
the paints, and dramatic play. Symbolizing processes have always existed in non-verbal as well as verbal forms. From the
time of the cave dwellers and sand painters, fluid, plastic, unstructured materials have been used to reproduce and imitate
facets of the world that seemed meaningful. In the process,
meaning itself grows clearer.

Materials used by children in play can be broadly classified
as structured and unstructured. Structured materials are defin-

ite in purpose and design and include toy cars, boats, planes, dolls, dishes, toy animals, musical instruments, and so on. These toys are clearly what they are supposed to be: miniature imitations of the adult world. Unstructured materials, on the other hand—such as blocks, paints, crayons, and clay—take on the form a child wishes to impose upon them; they have none of their own. The child is the determiner of sequence, form, and content as he uses them. They change as he changes.

In the past, parents bought their children the structured play materials, and the children found the unstructured ones in the natural world about them. Dirt, mud, sticks, stones, sand, clay, plant debris, and whatever else nature offers are all fair game for children's use. In industrialized, urban society such natural riches are harder for children to come by. Blocks, paint, manufactured clays, crayons, and various manipulative construction materials are the replacements both at home and at school for nature's gifts. The structured materials help the children to pin down the real world (a child notes details on the toy bus he pushes along the floor) and encourage imitation (a child wheels her doll carriage as mothers do). Unstructured materials allow for some imitation also. (For example, a child paints a man.) But more important is the part they play in assisting children to make the transition from dependency on concrete experience (touching, tasting, smelling as a way of getting to know reality) to the use of symbolic representation as a way of further clarifying it. It is this latter, most significant, aspect of the unstructured materials that is not generally understood.

Within such materials as blocks, paint, clay, paper, wood, and a host of others lie the possibilities for the simplest representations of reality to the most complex. Any study of children's uses of such materials across different age levels reveals an amazingly consistent sequence of development. Thus, at an earlier stage, a child may add block to block across the floor to build a road, later put two blocks crosswise over two others and repeat the pattern higher and higher to build a building, while, still later, five-, six- and seven-year-olds will struggle with engineering problems of staircases, floors, bridge supports, and clover-leaf constructions. The blocks do not change, but the children do. They continue to find the blocks valuable long after kindergarten, whenever grown-ups allow them to use them to assist learning.

The same pattern of developmental progression holds true for all the unstructured materials as it does for language development and other phases of growth. It is no accident that children's drawings, clay work, buildings, paintings, and constructions grow more elaborate and detailed as the children grow more mature. Children abstract what is to them the essence or essential character of an object, person or event when they initially reproduce it. They move on to reproduce objects, persons, and events in greater and greater detail, showing evidence of accumulated awareness, understanding, and clarity. When materials are not limited by boundary or form, they remain forever tools which a person uses differently as he grows to perceive the world differently. If children's perceptions are sharp and clear, their "products," although crude in technique, reflect that clarity of perception. If their perceptions are fuzzy and confused, their products will show that too. Since they learn through their senses, the degree and quality of a child's sensory experience will influence his recreation of reality in symbolic form. This, and not formal academic learning, is what gives quality to a kindergarten program, because it supports learning in a genuine way.

As far as we know, the power to symbolize progresses in stages. A child learns first that something can stand for something else. This rudimentary concept is obviously the underpinning for a later recognition that symbols in print stand for reality. The normal child, in his play, continues to be involved in "something stands for something else," activities which are really symbolizing processes, at increasing stages of intricacy and abstraction, working away at highly individualized perceptions of what the symbolic representation of reality should look like. Children who use blocks to build a skyscraper are actually putting their understanding of skyscraper into symbolic form. As they paste or staple together assorted cardboard tubes from rolls of toilet tissue and toweling to make a movie projector, they are putting their understanding of movie projector into symbolic form. The materials in programs suitable to early childhood must have an elastic potential that will allow symbolic processes to proceed in increasing complexity as children continue to grow in knowledge and emotional depth. Such increase in knowledge and depth is not accomplished by memorizing and recognizing specific symbols such as letters or numbers. There is a time and place for this, too, when the facility in the symbolizing process itself naturally supports the use of adult-determined symbols in a more abstract system of symbol usage. Stated differently, the child who has acted out, built, painted, sculpted, or danced innumerable experiences which he first encountered realistically in concrete, sensory form, is not only pinning down his understanding of what he has experienced; he is also building up a backlog of awareness of the relation between symbolization and reality, which is a necessity in grasping the subtle relationship between print and meaning. Without this insight, as indicated earlier, a child can easily become, and remain, a mechanical decoder of a symbol system in print without response to the message locked in the code. Insufficient experience in symbolizing through play and with materials, while not the sole cause of reading deficiency, is one of the phenomena repeatedly associated with poor reading in large numbers of children.

Symbolic Play with Concrete Materials Leads to Abstract Learning

Much that is intellectual can take place through play. Blocks are amazing resources for intellectual stimulation and encouragement, and several areas of understanding are developed simultaneously in good block play. In mathematics, there is the recognition of basic geometric shapes and their relations to each other through constant handling of the squares, triangles, rectangles, and curves which make up a block supply. Kindergarten children know in their fingers which two blocks can replace a single larger one, which two triangles fit to form a square or rectangle, which curves are part of a small or large circle. Problems of balance, height, and width must be endlessly resolved in buildings of differing shape and function; angles must be employed effectively in stairs, ramps, and bridges. The relationship of length to height is realized as children move blocks into linear placement as roads and into vertical placement as houses and towers. Spatial relationships in many dimensions emerge as children attempt variations in structure and design. Concepts such as "few" or "many" are refined into sharper understanding as they recognize their need for two more, three more, five more blocks. They gradually add to their physical sense of five blocks the feel of five crayons, five beads, five cups, and five children, which enables them to abstract the concept of numerical quantity as such, unrelated to the characteristics of the items one is measuring. The meaning of five (and other numbers) grows easily and naturally into a certainty out of such experiences.

Aside from the mathematical learning in block play is the whole matter of relationships, not between shapes and forms, or between children, but between social need and fulfillment. The garage built by two children serves the cars of three others; the store built by one child is open to all who want to clarify for themselves the nature of financial transaction; the boat, the plane, or the helicopter is used to get people where they want to go.

Not only in the blocks, but in dramatic play generally, children try on for size the roles of adults and the relationships they perceive among adults. With mere suggestions of costumes and props, the children recreate that world as they try to understand it. An observant teacher offers them the information that will help them expand their play in breadth and depth. She straightens out misconceptions and confusions. She takes the children to see for themselves the bridges, boats, barns, garages, airfields, dairies, houses in construction, irrigated rows of crops, or whatever else in their environment will give them a clearer perception of work processes and specific aspects of the natural and societal structures related to survival. Such first-hand opportunities to observe are supported with books and pictures, models of the real thing, and perhaps conversations with the adults involved.

Observation Is the Base for Science Learning

Much science-learning takes place in a good kindergarten. Science to the average adult is a course in memorized detail: the names of the solar systems, the names of rocks and minerals; the names of the elements, the placement of body organs. But memorizing labels is not the essence of science learning. Under good direction, the factual information spontaneously gathered by children in the natural process of observing, exploring, and experimenting is pointed toward the recognition of repeated occurrence of phenomena and a grasp of the principles involved. Correct and accurate terminology added to this basic experience makes possible discussion, questioning, and plans for further study, inevitably leading to the extension of knowledge. Children permitted to experiment safely learn the properties of materials as varied as sand, water, or magnets; the function of pulleys, inclined plane, pendulum; or changes in natural and man-made materials, such as oxidation on an apple core, or the effect of water or fire upon paper. All are genuine science concepts. Children watch the cycle of life in a small animal and gain an awareness of a life cycle as natural law. Comparing their own and animal bodies and behavior, they strengthen their knowledge of themselves, of animal life, and of the relationships between man and the animal world. Adults who speak indulgently of "sand-box learning" have much to learn themselves. A great deal can be learned before books!

Literature Is a Source of Deepening

But stories and poems of literary value also increase information when they are read to children, even though the major purpose of reading to them is not for information but for pleasure. For example, as children hear *The Story of Ferdinand*,[7] their emotional response is to a bull that is different from all others, yet survives; but, incidentally, they are learning exactly what a banderillero, picador, or matador does. As they identify with Ping and his troubles in *The Story About Ping*,[8] there is also incidental learning about life on a Chinese junk. From *Make Way for Ducklings*,[9] they learn not only about animal life, but something about islands; from *Down Down the Mountain*,[10] they gain knowledge about rural mountain life, while feeling at one with children who succeed in achieving an utterly childlike ambition.

The Kindergarten Must Be Evaluated By Its Own Yardstick

A critical approach to the kindergarten year need not concern itself with the repetition of materials and play. Five-year-old children enjoy, and are able to make excellent use of, unstructured materials like blocks, clay, paint, and crayons, and their dramatic play is meaningful to them. What they need from the kindergarten program is the continuing expansion of the experiential base on which they can sharpen their perceptions so

---

[7] Munro Leaf, *The Story of Ferdinand* (New York: The Viking Press, 1936).
[8] Marjorie Flack and Kurt Wiese, *The Story About Ping* (New York: The Viking Press, 1933).
[9] Robert McCloskey, *Make Way for Ducklings* (New York: The Viking Press, 1941).
[10] Ellis Credle, *Down Down the Mountain* (New York: Thomas Nelson & Sons, 1934).

as to have something to impose on the materials as they shape and form them. It is here that kindergartens need strengthening, and learning the mechanics of reading will not do that.

Just so long as an area of learning lends itself to concrete experience, or springs from it, it is suitable for young children's learning. Mathematics, science, literature, social studies, art, and music are the content of the kindergarten. All are rich sources of learning which the good kindergarten teacher taps for the children's growth in mind and spirit. If children are bored in kindergarten, it is because the content is dull and children have to play with little to play about. Arts and crafts of a gimmicky character, plus some marching and banging on percussion instruments, do little to challenge and stretch the inquiring mind of a five-year-old. But when children are actively involved in seeing, hearing, smelling, tasting, and touching what goes on in the world; when they are actively involved with peers in play which takes off from the literal to become imaginative and untrammeled; when children ask, and find answers to, questions; discuss, exchange, and argue; when they can turn to an adult for corroboration, information, contradiction, or help, then the kindergarten program is more likely than not to be a good one, and parents should be able to enjoy the children's rich painting, intricate block building, detailed drawings, joyous singing, and absorption in stories.

Kindergarten and the Parent

. . .

As children enter kindergarten, a first matter of importance to parents is the teacher. Parents expect, and have the right to expect, that she will be a warm and affectionate person, although she need not be overtly demonstrative for the children to feel her lovingness. She must accept and respect children, be aware of their stage of growth, and be sensitive to individual differences among them. She must be tolerant of their awkwardness, yet not brook behavior which is destructive to the individual himself or to others. She must be able to accept without prejudice their immaturity and even socially unacceptable behavior, while at the same time opening up the possibilities of more mature behavior for them. She observes each child's style of functioning, his problems in relating, approaches to handling materials, vying for leadership, and relating to her.

A good teacher slowly releases her children from dependency on her, so that a visit to an excellent kindergarten in the middle of the school year might find the teacher barely visible amidst the active, self-directed bustle of the children. The teacher who herself doles out each piece of material, who controls each activity of the children's day, and who gives directions for assembly-line productions to be pridefully carried home, is not doing the children a service, even if she genuinely loves them and is hard-working. Nor do children need to be entertained in the kindergarten, kept busy because "idle fingers get into mischief," or prepared for first grade. Living is itself learning for young children, and the interaction with their teacher, with children, and with materials has to be genuine, uncontrived, and steadily conducive to growth in several important areas at the same time.

Basic to a child's growth at school is the teacher's understanding of what the immediate and far-reaching objectives are for that stage in life. A teacher must be sensitive to the interests that have appeal to young children, be clear about the ways in which young children learn, and be prepared to help them in their learning without imposing herself upon them. This she does by her selection of materials for exploration, experimentation and use, and by her arrangement and organization of materials for group and individual activity. She reflects her knowledgeableness by her choice of literature and music, both of which can have taste and quality, as well as appropriate simplicity for the age. She reveals continuous concern by changes she makes in the abundance and variety of stimuli for sensory and intellectual pleasure. She recognizes children's right to fantasy in their play, yet insists on their responsible handling and care of materials as well as the materials' proper return. A good teacher listens to children and hears what they say. She savors every question, every comment, and seeks to extend their meaning for the child by her use of supportive information, questions, or concepts. At the same time that she takes children seriously, she discourages children from taking themselves too seriously when a lighter touch would do better.

The teacher has the responsibility of acquainting parents with her philosophy and goals, of sharing with parents the unfolding program and the children's experiences. All too often she struggles to do this against the shortsighted ambition of some parents. Hopefully, she has the ability to clarify the negative effects of precocity, but while it is likely that a good teacher in today's schools is a good practitioner, she will find it hard to articulate the reasons for her practice. She knows from experience that premature striving to achieve too often leads to feelings of inadequacy and inferiority that do not give way with the years, even in the face of objective success. From following her kindergarten pupils through many years of school, as teachers report back to each other, she is likely to know that the greatest danger to children between five and seven is to move on into academic learning and peer relationships without a sense of competency and self-worth. But articulateness is not necessarily her greatest strength, and parents must learn to evaluate the teacher by her performance more than by her verbal persuasiveness.

Social Relations Are Vital to Kindergarten Children

It is probably safe to say that, to the kindergarten child himself, the most important matter is not his teacher or learning his letters but his position vis-à-vis other children. It is true that there are children who are still quite dependent on adult appraisal of their behavior, and therefore need a longer period than others of relating to the teacher before they slowly find their way to other children and materials. And there is the occasional child who is frightened, excessively shy or timid, and who needs more teacher support at the beginning to find his way. But few five-year-olds cry at leaving their mothers, most are happy to accept the teacher uncritically, and most move into the serious business of making, keeping and changing friends, which to the children is the real meaning of kindergarten.

A piece of research concerned with the effect of the teacher on children's group cohesion examined kindergarten classrooms in which the teachers were clearly authoritarian or as clearly democratic, to see which kind of teacher encouraged greater group feeling among the children.[1] To the investigator's surprise, the children's feelings of closeness to each other were as strong under the authoritarian, controlling teacher as under the more democratic and permissive one. The reason was plain enough. At this age, friendship is so compelling a need that healthy children will ignore the adult and even be surreptitious in their peer relationships if necessary, rather than deny the impulse to move closer to others their age. In the study, incidentally, while race was not a factor in the children's choices, sex was. Boys chose boys as friends, and girls chose girls.

The road to successful friendship is not easy, and the effects of the struggles at school are often brought home. All parents prefer to eliminate suffering from their children's lives, but this particular kind is necessary for maturing. Children endure it, because ultimate success is far more important than the temporary discomfort associated with the learning involved. One cannot dispatch the children's feelings with a flippant, "It's not serious when they're that young." To the child involved, the ups and downs are serious. They are the stuff of his life, and he knows it.

Friendships develop in stages, something the teacher often knows rather better than parents do, but which parents need to understand, too. First, there are the beginning contacts, which children handle differently, some with caution, some with fear, some with open confidence and some with defenses reared. Then comes the development in depth, in which again there are individual differences and varied methods of coping. Some children persist in the face of frustrations and disappointments, others withdraw. Some persist with tact and good humor, others with badgering or bribery; some withdraw quietly and others withdraw in anger and protest. The change-over from

[1] Elizabeth Hirsch, "A Study of the Influence of the Teacher's Role Upon the Social Behavior of Pre-School Children: The Influence of Dominative and Socially Integrative Behavior of Teachers Upon Cohesiveness in Pre-School Class Groups," Doctoral Dissertation, New York University, 1967.

starting to maintaining relationships often causes dramatic changes in a child's feelings about himself and about school within a fairly short period of time. The reverberations are bound to be felt at home.

Within each child the egoist and the social creature are in genuine conflict. As every child in the class seeks his place within the group, the assertion of the many selves intent on ego-enhancement causes all kinds of feelings to be experienced and expressed. In addition, there are idiosyncratic factors that further complicate the dynamics of interchange. For some children, the position within a family may be such that finding a place of importance among peers takes on the intensity of a last-ditch battle for survival. For others, the experience of never having been denied anything by adults makes the resistance of peers an unexpected deterrent that they must learn to cope with before they can proceed. For still others, ideas are so important and the urgency of their organization and thought about what and how to play so impelling that there is neither time nor patience to hear anyone else out.

Individuals in a class gradually merge into a number of subgroups, as egocentricity adapts to the social urge to find mutually satisfying arrangements. The five-year-old who is the oldest of three may enjoy being the baby to the five-year-old mother whose bossy sister never gives her a chance. The timid and non-aggressive little boy might be very happy to take a subordinate role as long as he is invited to play at all, and he looks with admiration at the confidently assertive five-year-old who knows just what to do. The child who insists on being the doctor finds willing patients; the airline pilot readily locates an obedient crew and passengers. The choice of friends is thus more than a matter of proximity, common interest, or like-sex. It is very much a matter of children serving each other's deepest needs. The influence of the inner life, the fantasy life, is strong at this point in choice of both play partner and play theme.

Yet the continuing life experiences of the children with each other tend to alter the expectations of the fit. The timid child of the beginning of the year may swing into stronger self-assertion as he grows more secure in the school situation. Admiration can turn to envy and then desire to emulate, in which case he will no longer put up with being a passenger—he will want a bus or a plane of his own! And so a new round of interaction begins. This is the process that goes on for much of the kindergarten year, as children expand or curb their burgeoning social selves to meet the insistent needs of others in a play life that all require and want. The struggle for leadership can grow very intense, especially among certain kinds of children, all of whom have something to offer. One of the consequences at home is that kindergarten boys or girls may release this tension in nightly bedwetting during the period when they first compete for a position of dominance among peers.

Of course, there are children who prefer to play alone much of the time or with one other child, and who skirt the central battles for power. This does not necessarily mean unhealthy behavior. It could just as well be idiosyncratic. Not everyone is outgoing and extroverted, nor need everyone be. The important aspect is not the number of friends or drama of conflict so much as the ability of a child to feel affection and reach out for friendship, even if with one child and in smooth untroubled serenity. But the child of five who does not have any friends at all needs to be looked at carefully, especially if, at the same time, he gets along very well with adults. A conference with his teacher is probably the best way of shedding light on the causes for the lag.

Children Need Support as They Struggle to Grow

Trying to see one's child as a social being confronted with social realities calls for a shift in parental perspective that is not easy. But it is probably a basic prerequisite for giving the child the best support and guidance he needs in order to work things out for himself. The kindergarten year is, for many children, the beginning of what will continue to be personal responses to their very own experiences, a style of functioning in which parents play a decreasing, but nonetheless significant, role. It is good to remember that there are deep satisfactions as well as conflicts for children in their experiences and, in fact, that there is no greater satisfaction to a child than his own mastery of conflict. Children can return home after playing at school with a contentment and personal strength which are good. But, on the bad days, they will turn to parents for sympathy and reassurance, or even turn on parents as an alternative to facing and solving the real problem. The parent who tells his child "not to play with the other children if they bother you" has to be sure that that is genuinely helpful advice. The parent who is always sure that it is his child who is at fault in the quarrels is probably unrealistic, as is the parent who assumes that it is always the other child who is wrong (or has not been "well brought up").

For most people, at some place and at some time, there is the chance to assert oneself sufficiently to be a leader in a situation. The chance depends in part upon oneself and in part upon the particular group to which one is relating. In a school group of sufficient size, there are always children who fit each other's needs, except for those children who simply do not know how to find their way among people their age at all and need more help than most. It is here that a good teacher has so much to offer struggling children.

Minds Stretch in a Good Kindergarten

Life in the kindergarten is not only a matter of emotional and social relating. As indicated earlier, it can, and should, be intellectually stimulating as well. Children are quite aware of this aspect of their schooling and of the teacher's knowledgeableness, too. One youngster came home from kindergarten and described a walk to the park during which the children picked acorns and carried them back to school. His parents asked if he knew where acorns come from, and he answered, "Yes, from the grass." His father explained the relation of acorns to the oak tree and the reason why acorns were available at that time. The child listened with interest and then commented sagely, "If Mrs. Wilson (last year's teacher) was my teacher, she would have told us all about that, but I guess Miss Harrison doesn't know it."

Intellectual content is developed in the kindergarten through many teacher-led activities specifically geared to thinking processes and fact-gathering as well as through support of children's play. For example, discussions that push thinking take place regularly in a good kindergarten. Often, they are simple exchanges of information. Just as often, they are probes into new areas following an expression of curiosity by one or more children. In the following discussion the reasoning was related to practical decision-making, and subjective preference gave way to objective logic.

> The class had made pancakes, and they were going to have them at juice time. The teacher asked the children whether they preferred to have their juice or the pancakes first. (This teacher generally involved the children in the group organization whenever she could.) After several expressions of personal taste, one little girl carried the day with her reasoning. "I think we should have the juice first because the syrup is very sweet and the juice is not so sweet, and if we have the juice after the syrup it won't taste good, and no one will want to drink." The class voted unanimously to have the juice first.

In many kindergartens the children are encouraged to give their versions of group experiences or of ones that individuals have had outside of school. The opportunity to do this strengthens not only the ego but the sense of narrative sequence that is indispensable to following the details of a story through the maze of print one later reads oneself. The following stories dictated by the children to their teacher and then posted on a wall of the classroom came out of a class trip to Battery Park in New York City. The first one shows two boys, Sam and Hank, grappling with concepts of size and perspective as well as variety of detail.

> "We saw the Statue of Liberty," said Sam. "It was very small, because it was far away," said Hank. Sam was at the Statue of Liberty before he came to school, and he says, "It's big when you are next to it." Hank said, "We saw an old fort that they are changing into something different." "We went all around the fort and when we saw a nice little window we climbed into it," Sam said. "We saw men working inside the window."
>
> "On our way to the park we saw a statue of an eagle," said Hank. "It was huge, bigger than any live eagle. There were lots of big cement walls with the names on them."
>
> "As we were walking along we saw ferry boats, ships, and I don't know what else," said Hank. "And then we went to the park and climbed trees and had juice."

At a later date, the teacher used these observations to supply more information through books and pictures to all the children about river traffic, which she considered more suitable to the children's further study at this stage than information about forts and their purposes or the building of a monument. At the same time, she recognized that the strengthening of narrative sequence was taking place also for children whose content was not as information-laden as Sam's and Hank's, even though they were drawing inspiration from the same trip.

Katherine and Ellen—"What we did at Battery Park"
> "To go to the trip, we went on a bus. We went to the fire station and saw the Statue of Liberty. Ellen and me said, "Don't go up to the lamp any more or else the arm will get wobbly because of the person's weight, because it is already wobbly. Then her arm will be right behind her and if you look behind, you still can't see the arm because it fell into the sea. And nobody knows it's in the sea last of all."
>
> "There might be a guard in case someone comes anyway. You can still go in the Statue of Liberty, but not up to her lamp, but the bottom of her arm."

Feelings as well as thinking went into that one, but the last is pure feeling.

Martin and Paul

"We went to Battery Park and we made a trap for the girls and boys on the monkey bars. We put ropes on the different areas on the monkey bars. When someone gets in the monkey bars we tie them up. We tried to kill them but they escaped. We go and get some more prisoners in our trap."

And, of course, there is the pick-up from children's play and comments that gives a teacher clues to their need for support and help through experiments, trips, pictures, books, films, or whatever. Thus, a kindergarten teacher who heard some children talking about who had sneakers on and who had shoes quietly prepared a chart of two columns ruled into two-inch squares, one column headed by a picture she drew of a sneaker, the other by a picture of a shoe. From her closet she took some small, bright-red gummed paper circles. At snack time, she sat the children around her and suggested that each child with sneakers paste a little red circle in one of the squares in the sneaker column and each child with shoes paste a circle in a square in the shoe column. In time, the circles dotted out to become lines, and excitement began to run high as it became evident that the sneakers were "winning." But this had to be verified, so a count of sneaker circles was compared with a count of shoe circles. There were indeed more sneakers than shoes on kindergarten feet that day. Then the children counted all the red circles on the chart and compared that number with a count of themselves and found that these sums tallied. And then, because they were five, the shoe children made noisy resolutions to arrive in sneakers the next day!

Bringing Things Home from School

The kindergartens have a long tradition of arts and crafts, from which stems the custom of children bringing productions home to show "what we did in school today." This still happens to a greater or lesser extent, depending upon the school. But today, two different kinds of products are likely to be involved. One kind is a finished-looking, generally prefabricated item, which is done in conjunction with a holiday or other special occasion, such as the Thanksgiving Pilgrim and turkey, the Easter basket filled with eggs, the pinwheels to blow in March winds, and the Mother's Day presents. They are often charming construction paper models, usually conceived and organized by adults, sometimes even executed by adults for children who do not have sufficient coordination to be neat workers, and carried home in triumph by the obedient ones who followed the teacher's directions. Few kindergarten teachers today believe that children's use of materials ought to be confined to such controlled projects in which ability to follow directions and the child's stage of coordination are key elements leading to success. There are many who prefer to do this kind of thing sparingly, if at all, and allow children's originality and imagination free rein to be the spurs to their individual levels of coordination and skill. But teachers are afraid that parents will assume that nothing is happening in kindergarten unless the children bring things home to show "what we did in school today."

It should be obvious that much can, and does, happen in a kindergarten geared to principles of child development. Assessment of a program must be tied to more subtle and far-reaching influences than the pleasantly shallow productions that are reminders of one's own days of innocence in the kindergarten. There is no question that children enjoy learning techniques of pasting, stapling, cutting, and sewing, and that they love bringing things home to admiring relatives. But this is peripheral learning during their sixth year. Parents owe it to their children to expect greater depth in their children's schooling, even at this stage.

The second kind of production is the item conceived and executed by the child himself. Sometimes there is adult help, as when a teacher shows a child how to hold a saw for most effective cutting, or when a teacher offers a child an empty jar so he can mix colors to get just the shade he wants. But while this kind of help expedites the child's own effort, it does not control it, and often there are no tangible results to carry home. But when there are, and it is the child's own creation, parents are likely to feel that there is something special about it, and that there is something special about their child, too, who has done this wonderful thing. And indeed there is.

Yet children do not need or want effusive, undifferentiated praise for everything they make or bring home from school. Like adults, they have their good days and their bad, their better productions and their poorer ones. They know from experience that some things turn out more successfully than others, and unmitigated praise for every effort confuses them and hampers the development of their own emerging standards for themselves. Even though the adult's motive is to protect the child from feeling the hurt of criticism, complete uncriticalness does not leave a child feeling good about himself. It is *unjust* criticism that needs avoiding.

Whereas adults who fuss about a child's productions out of proportion to their meaning in the child's growth are at one extreme, at the other are adults who smile amusedly at the efforts of younger children and can see nothing of value in their accomplishments. They may respond indifferently to the child's work with a practical, "Yes, yes, now go and get washed," or they may stand by unconcerned while an older sibling teases and deprecates the younger child's productions. Obviously, this is not helpful to a striving young person and leads to its own set of distorted perceptions. A child may end up believing that not only his productions, which are extensions of himself, but he himself is worthless. Or if he does not yield to this idea, he may embark on a lifelong competition with others to prove his worth. Since he will never quite believe his worth from objective evidence, he remains forever cheated of the comfortable conviction of competency that comes with realistic acceptance of one's strengths and weaknesses.

Children are very sensitive to the genuineness and honesty

of appreciation and criticism. They accept both graciously, if they are well meant. But they also sense when they are being tolerated, and often will not bring things home from school when they feel that their efforts are a source of exaggerated praise, amusement or indifference. Without knowing normal levels of workmanship for this stage of growth (and there are developmental levels), it is hard for many adults to know what is admirable and what is not, what is good and what could be better. Obviously, young children's drawings, clay work, woodwork, stories, poems, or songs are going to have a simplicity and even a crudeness that compares unfavorably with the more sophisticated versions by adults or older children. But all children's original work has sincerity or superficiality. The sincerity shines through, and one can say with conviction, "I like that," or "I can see you worked hard at that," or "That's good." With the same child, there will also be days when one can comfortably say, "Well, I guess you didn't work too seriously at this," or "I think I like last week's better," or "I think you've done more interesting ones than that." This honesty is not the same as technical advice, such as, "You should have made that line equal to this one," or "Why didn't you use blue for the sky?", or "Don't you know all the legs on a table are supposed to be the same size?" In the kindergarten, children's projections onto materials represent the most telling impressions to *them*. They capture the important essence of something as they see it and pay little attention to the accuracy or completeness of detail, balance, appropriate size relations, or color—things that are important to adults.

If the height of a tree is what impresses them, then in their drawing or painting the color of the bark will be secondary. If the wingspread of a plane is what really counts, then the wooden model they build could be painted a potpourri of color for all they care. They are not striving for accuracy, only for meaning to themselves. Precision will come, but later.

But every child needs to grow in the power to evaluate himself and his efforts realistically. Facing both his assets and his inadequacies of the moment, his planning for himself will be likely to hold better possibilities of attainment and fewer possibilities of unnecessary failure. This is not to say that one wants a child to play it safe and not try anything unless he is sure of succeeding. (Some children do just that.) But there is such a thing as a calculated risk based on realistic appraisal of the positive and negative factors in a situation. One would want children to learn this, and while most children learn it the hard way, adults can help them by being fair to them in indicating standards. Standards must not be out of reach, nor so easy as to be a disappointment. It is not an easy balance to achieve. But children's self-evaluation is considerably influenced by the adults who play a continuous role in their lives. Reassurance and moral support liberally mixed with realism give children the most useful assistance in developing judgment about themselves and their achievements.

Bringing Things to School

Children will often reverse the carrying process and bring things from home to school. Sometimes they complain that the teacher did not let them play with their possession, or she did not use it for the whole class, or that other children took or spoiled it. Parents need to recognize the several possible meanings behind this kind of reaction. It is important first to examine why a child wants to bring things to school, something a child may not verbalize easily, although he is usually aware of his motives. His reason may be logical and completely valid. For example, he needs the rope, the hat, or the box as a prop in some play he is involved in with others, or he wants the class to hear his new record or see his new book. It may be reasonable from the child's point of view, yet not valid, as when children bring things to bribe or impress others so they will be allowed to play. It is the latter type of motivation that should give parents pause for thought. Since neither bribery nor making an impression is a permanent solution to the hurdle of making friends, a teacher may ask a child to keep his offering from home in his locker, so that she can help him tackle the challenges presented by children in more basic ways than bribery and boasting. Parents owe it to their children to be honest in admitting inclinations of this kind and to ask for a conference with the teacher to decide jointly upon the best approach to the problem. Parents need not be embarrassed to discuss a child's less than perfect behavior. Every teacher has only imperfect children in her class, marvelous as they might otherwise be.

The teacher may also prohibit play with things from home for reasons quite unrelated to individuals. It can happen that teachers believe that what a child brings from home is not a constructive contribution either to himself or to the life of the class. An extreme example can be made of the military toys and games which teachers feel exacerbate the existing violence children sense in the adult world, and which, in the teachers' view, hardly needs reinforcement. This view merits a moment's attention. There was a time in early childhood education when the adult world of violence, war, and crime did not enter every little child's living room daily via the mass media. At that time, it was considered suitable to allow children the props they wanted to carry out the normal fantasies of childhood that include aggression, hostility, desire for power, fears, rivalry, and so on. It was often helpful to a timid youngster to reach into his double gun holster and feel braver as he faced children no older, but more forceful, than himself. For children whose angry feelings overwhelmed them, so that constructive play came hard, a certain amount of release in make-believe violence seemed to do no harm. But with the advent of television in an age of unending crises in adult human affairs, children become aware of violence and sadism as a style of adult life too early and without enough basis of comparison with the constructive in human relationships. While, of course, they have their families as models, experience within the family necessarily includes punishment and anger as well as love and tenderness, and in the mind of the young child, the balance is not yet too clear. Childhood fantasies of getting even or achieving power are completely normal. But today's child sees the unbridled, primitive quality of his fantasy enacted as appropriate reality in the world of adults; his fantasies of anger or fear are discharged and glorified by grown-ups on the television screen and throughout the news reports, as though there were no alternatives. There is, therefore, a less than clear line between rationality and fantasy confronting any child growing up in an age of mass dissemination of the horrors concocted by man against his fellow man. It is necessary for somebody of authority to say firmly and convincingly to children, "Violence is not the only way."

Still another reason why a teacher may declare a home possession out of bounds may be the numbers of books, records, toys, and games brought from home which reflect poor judgment on the part of well-intentioned adults. Items sold for children are frequently designed to appeal to the adults who will buy them. Grandparents and bachelor uncles may buy what has nostalgic or sentimental appeal for them, what looks "adorable" or "cute," or what looks impressive from any one of several adult points of view. In the teacher's eye, they may be too old, too infantile, too limited in possibilities, or otherwise unsuitable for her particular class. In a sense, the play materials at school are sanctioned by the teacher, and she may be reluctant to give status to a story with a moral which talks down to children, a chauvinistic puppet, an insipid record, or anything else that violates her standards of suitability. While she may be willing to have an occasional "impurity" in her classroom to support the need of a particular child, she may be swamped as children compete for her favor and the praise of their classmates, and may ultimately have to say with complete reason, "Enough." A child is a member of a group, and there are occasions when the life of the group has to be protected, even though an individual may be disappointed in the denial.

Living in the Group

Group living holds many challenges for a young child, aside from the ones which have to do with child-to-child relationships. Mainly, these are demands made necessary by the exigencies of group existence, which cause every young child a degree of distress while growth in the capacity to share is still taking place.

If a child has been to nursery school, this phase of kindergarten may be easier for him. But even nursery school may not quite have resolved a child's desire to be the sole person in his teacher's heart, nor have helped him control his impulses to the point where group need tones down his own. This is not necessarily a shortcoming in the nursery school. Some children are harder to socialize than others, and at five there are many who still need help in becoming reasonably cooperative members of a group. There are routines and rituals that are necessary if many children are to share a classroom limited in equipment and supplies—a circumstance true of the best equipped school. The sharing inevitably calls for some curtailment of personal desires and liberties, and not all children react with equal cheerfulness to this fact of life.

Parents need to be aware that a child's happiness or unhappiness at school may have to do with his ability to give up some of his individual desires for the greater good of the group. Many activities which are completely reasonable when acted out by one child at home become impossible to permit in a setting geared to group life. For example, singing is a delightful and joyous experience, but one child's singing can ruin the story for those who want to listen. In a school where the outdoor space has to be allocated, individual children may find themselves having to stop the most interesting thing they are doing before they are ready, so that the class can go outdoors together at the allotted time. Or take the fact that boys have a tendency to monopolize the blocks in any classroom. A teacher conscious of this may deliberately squelch some of the boys' ambitions in order to get the girls out of the housekeeping corner and into a type of play which calls for a different style of symbolization. Since this immediately extends the numbers who must share even a good sized set of blocks, it may cause some resentment among some children. Or, despite the fact that during rhythms the teacher urges the children to run in the same direction, so that they won't bump into each other, a child might, without thinking, run any which-way, as he would in a room alone at home. When he does get knocked down, the resentment will be against the child who ran into him, and the tale a tale of injury.

None of this is extraordinary for children this young. But it needs to be understood for what it is, since this and the struggle for leadership are frequently disguised to parents as complaints of a very different character. For example, there are children who, in their eagerness to start building, pile their blocks on the floor directly in front of the cabinet, inadvertently keeping others from getting their share. Eventually, the teacher may say, "Unless you remember to take your blocks off to a space away from the shelves, you may have to give up playing with them until you do remember better." But the story of despair that comes home is likely to be, "Jackie and Harry played with the blocks, but the teacher wouldn't let *me.*"

Tales from School

Tales from school must always be listened to with one ear cocked for the fantasy and feeling that color the facts. Children cannot help being egocentric, nor can they help twisting things a bit, so that they themselves come out in a favorable light. Often they are right, and what they say is completely verifiable. But any tale from school that is a matter of concern ought to be checked with the teacher, because there are usually two sides to the story. Sometimes a busy teacher, like a busy mother, may not catch every detail of what goes on, and a child may come home with a scratch or bruise that the teacher has no explanation for. But, on the whole, teachers do know their children and can clarify much that parents need to know, provided the parent has not already discouraged the teacher by attacking her on the basis of a child's story that has not been checked.

Teachers have the same problem at their end. They hear many things about the children's home life which they learn to take with a grain of salt. They know that one episode that is incomprehensible can seem like a trend to a child. They understand how a child's fears will magnify the importance of so commonplace an event as a normal family squabble, or how a momentary expression of dismay will be taken as a sign of permanent disaster. They also know that a child may say, "My mommy doesn't want me to play outdoors today," when he means that he prefers to go on crayoning, or is worried about the competition on the slide. Without a note from home, teachers must use their sixth sense to help them use good judgment about a variety of tales and confidences.

Conferences

The practice of teacher-parent conferences has existed longer in the kindergarten than at other levels of schooling, and conferences are valuable aids to teacher and parent when used intelligently. Report cards have a restrictive and judgmental character and are therefore unfair to children who are very much in process and quite unfinished. Nothing really compares with a good heart-to-heart talk between the two people who see and deal with a child most. But the conference requires trust and goodwill. Both parents and teachers are human beings given to the usual range of human responses. Their investment in the child they share may be different in intensity, but not necessarily different in sincerity, and each must assume the other's good faith. They may not agree on what is best for a child, but both would want "the best" for him. Each is eager to be successful; indeed, each needs to be successful in order to justify the role of parent or teacher.

Teacher and parent have much to offer each other. The one

thing a parent cannot know about a child is how he looks to others—to another adult, to children his own age, to strangers like the school custodian, to the older children who help in the kindergarten, and so on. Nor can parents know for sure how their child reacts when confronted with unexpected challenge, resistance of others, competition for leadership, deprecation of ideas, opportunity for independent decision-making, or choices of desirable alternatives in new areas of experience. The group situation is an unknown for a young child, and he plays it by ear as he gets increasingly involved. All this the teacher sees and, if she is a good teacher, she does not pass judgment upon a child, but tries to help him accomplish what is most satisfying to him without allowing his interference in the rights of others. An expression often heard in the kindergarten is, "I cannot let you do that to him, but I will not let him do it to you either."

Yet teachers need, and are grateful for, the knowledge a parent and a parent alone has. Teachers are often reassured to find out that the shy little girl who has been watching for weeks is at home both competent and a leader, but always takes her time testing out new situations. Teachers are alerted when a parent confides a history of fears in a child, or a series of traumatic events that has upset him, or a special relationship with a sibling that accounts for behavior with younger children. They are glad to know which children are worried about new bathrooms, which do not like noise, which have been taught not to get messy, which are inclined to long periods of concentrated play at home, which have had no friends in the neighborhood, which have fathers who expect too much of them, which have expectations for themselves that are unreasonable. They are as interested in knowing the children who have persisted in their questions about letters and spelling until they have taught themselves to read as they are in the children who cannot write their names.

Shall They Go to Kindergarten?

There are parents who support their children's inquiries and exploration even to the point of having many kindergarten materials at home, and they question the value of sending children to school to do what they already do at home. Where this is so, there may well be a point to giving a child who has been to nursery school "a sabbatical year." [2] On the other hand, if one recalls the way in which materials are used, it can be seen that the same approach can serve very different content, so that home and school may both extend a child's interests and knowledge without too much overlap. But one must bear in mind that activities without other children are not as fully satisfying to a child as the opportunity to share with peers.

The special quality of intimate exchange that an adult and child can develop with each other must not become the sole means by which a child learns. Where the parents act as teacher, one would want to be sure that playmates are also available. One must also consider that the kind of focus on children which is ever present and alert to their multiple needs must at the same time be objective and free of anxiety about achievement—something harder for parents, perhaps, than for teachers. In any case, whether they stay at home or attend a public or private school, children at this level of maturity need a more informal than formal educational experience, a more concrete rather than abstract style of learning and a chance at independent functioning in a safe as well as stimulating environment. They must be allowed imaginative free rein as well as offered realistic challenges. Most important, their openness to what the world has to offer must be preserved, so that they will become, and remain, enthusiastic and self-generating learners.

[2] John Levy and Ruth Monroe, *The Happy Family* (New York: Alfred A. Knopf, 1938).

Developmental Aspects of
Sixes and Sevens

· · ·

In folk wisdom, in medicine, in moral and religious teaching, as well as in education, there has always been agreement that seven marks a turning point in the life of a child. Mothers become aware of it, because the children no longer cry as readily as they did and seem less vulnerable to the round of physical disorders that worry mothers of littler children. Schooling, where it has been part of the picture, has most frequently begun in the seventh year. Philosophers speak of seven as a time when the child is formed. "That which he is at seven, he will be at seventy," they say, and to a large extent this is true. Personalities are clearly defined in such areas of constancy as the pace at which a child does things and temperament, which might be sanguine, intense, overreacting, easily irritable, bland, or a model of endurance. Morally, children of seven are quite aware of right from wrong. But values and beliefs will undergo many changes, and multiple techniques of living have yet to be learned. What lies ahead in the way of development is different enough from what went before to require a reassessment of the parental role.

The Middle Years: Six to Twelve

The primary years are part of the more inclusive middle years of childhood, in which changes of an emotional, social, and intellectual nature occur in a steady trend toward the assimilation of adult ways of thinking and behaving. The progress is uneven, there are many regressions, and falls from grace occur regularly. Nevertheless, one can see three major thrusts taking place in the period as a whole, that is, during the years from six to twelve. One thrust is in the direction of increasing facility in physical and neurophysiological skills, although no dramatic bodily changes take place before the end of the period. A second is an unmistakable move away from the influence of home toward the greater influence of peers. And a third is the steady growth in power of logical thinking, conceptualization, and use of symbolism closer to the adult's than to young child's in style. At the same time, the middle years are years in which character is formed and personality traits solidified, years in which there is great interest in learning, high curiosity, and a strong drive toward independent adventure. But, as we shall see, sixes and sevens have ties of kinship with the five-year-olds they were, as well as with the eights they will become.

The Primary Years

The growth taking place in children at six and seven impels them toward a strong declaration of individuality and a separate psychological existence while they are still children in their parents' homes. This is revealed initially in two ways. One is the dramatic assertion on the part of a child of his right to personal privacy, which many children claim by posting a sign on their bedroom door which says quite unceremoniously, "KEEP OUT!" (Sometimes the sign is ornately decorated with flowers and designs, but the message is the same.) The other is a degree of self-absorption which blocks out adults quite effectively. Without being openly disobedient, in fact appearing even agreeable and compliant, they simply turn stone deaf when it suits them. When these things happen, it is clear that the children have entered the middle years of childhood—a time when their own interests and involvements are far more gripping to them than anything parents may feel or say.

The stretching of the silver cord, which has been going on for many years, now takes on specific attributes. The first of these is the changing response to parents as authorities. In his earlier years a child welcomed and found security in the authority of his parents. He quoted his parents as law and never questioned their omnipotence. When he was inclined to resist them, he did so in a direct gesture of defiance, like running away from them at two, or saying "No" at three, matters ultimately settled by a mutually acknowledged recognition of the authoritative status of the parent. At six and seven, feelings of needfulness give way to feelings of "I can do it." A child no longer rebels daringly in defiance of the acknowledged authority. He now begins to stake out his rights and argue. He is much preoccupied with the idea of fairness to himself, which is a natural consequence of the greater consciousness of himself as a person separate from parents, and he wants his rights. His perception of adults is shifting from that of unassailable authority to somewhat less impregnable authority, one with whom one tries a little jockeying, thus lifting oneself up a notch in selfhood. Since a new relationship is being tested with parents, children are often belligerent and on the verge of tears at the same time. But they fight, nevertheless, for what they think they are entitled to, asserting, between the wails, "You're not my boss!"

Yet the shift is no more than a preliminary stirring of the foundations of dependency and hardly a major move into independent living. It should help to know that children of six and seven are beginning to ask not so much for an equal, as a less unequal, partnership in their upbringing than was the custom before. They will increase the demands as the years go by.

Sixes and sevens seem to be toying with the idea that one can eventually act like a parent oneself, which is a step in the direction of ultimately assuming responsibility for one's own behavior. While this is valuable for a child's growth, it is disconcerting to a parent. To be adored and needed, to feel the trust and dependency of a small child are the rewards in ego expansion for the sleepless nights and restrictions upon personal freedom that are the price of parenthood. When the helpless, trusting dependency goes, a phase of parenthood has ended, and many people react with uncomprehending disappointment at having to step down from so gratifying a position.

In reality, the child of six and seven continues to identify with the parents he still loves and whom he still needs, both as models to imitate and as supports for his growing independence. It is logical, however, that if children are to take a stab at aiming for adulthood, adults must begin to seem at least a little less than perfect, or the goal of adulthood itself would appear unattainable. Children, after all, know from their subordinate relation to adults, just how imperfect they themselves are. For this reason, the adult faced with an excited, negotiating child can afford to let go of his position of superiority, although obviously not his good judgment. Adults who listen to the reasoning of a child, who honestly admit not knowing something, or confess to having made a mistake themselves, present a far more realistic, and therefore attainable, model to the children in their lives. Since adults do know more and do have the final authority, the lapses from omniscience and omnipotence should not be too damaging to their self-respect or to the child's basic affection and admiration as the new relationship is forged.

No parent would knowingly keep his children at a level of dependency that would make it impossible for the child to function autonomously in adulthood. Problems arise because the changeover, unfortunately, does not come at the parents' moment of readiness or convenience, but in response to a steadily maturing but secret inner plan of the child's. Parents are always caught by surprise when their children attempt to alter the status quo. However, despite the gradual but steady decrease of parental involvement in a child's life, the need of a child for his parents does persist for many years.

A significant form of child need emerges precisely at six and seven, as the new areas of independent functioning beckon and encourage self-testing and experimentation. The parent who wants his children to be independent and is willing to support the children's ambitions has some dilemmas to resolve. Children of six and seven generally do not have a clear, objective sense of their true abilities or deficits. Nor have they had enough experience to evaluate the skills and assets necessary for situations with which they are as yet unfamiliar. They decide to try the physical skills and games they have watched older children execute for years, even though they may not be quite up to them. They ask for privileges before they are ready for them and, as a matter of fact, do not see why they cannot try anything that appeals to them. A six-year-old who wants very much to see a department store Santa Claus does not hesitate to assure his busy mother, "I can take the subway myself!" Thus, they are as likely as not to overestimate what they can do, since the drive to do is strong, the urge to be independent of parental help is insistent, and they are totally inexperienced. If a parent relinquishes too easily the responsibility for curtailing overly ambitious aspirations, or abrogates the right to supervise activities of unpredictable outcomes, there is the danger that the child may end up having more latitude than he can deal with and more responsibility for himself and his actions than he is quite able to handle. Instead of becoming more competent as a by-product of successful coping, he may come to feel more inadequate as a consequence of repeated failure. Furthermore, with the paradoxicalness characteristic of children's relationship to their parents, parents who are uncritically permissive are often seen by the child as indifferent rather than kind. Children are not ready for complete independence. They run away from home with the full expectation that their parents will find them and bring them back. But they want to try out independence, to test and build their competency, and they expect their parents to know how much is too much and how much is just right. Since they go right on aspiring to activities and privileges they cannot handle, it is a matter of constant evaluation and judgment on a parent's part to decide whether the child stands a reasonable chance of mastering the challenge involved or whether it is really impossible. What complicates the matter is that a parent cannot always be sure of what a highly motivated child might, in fact, be able to accomplish. To top it all, if parents support their children's ambitions, they are magnificent and understanding parents in the children's eyes; if they forbid them, they are cruel, unjust adults treating a grown child like a baby. If a parent bears in mind that the ultimate goal for the child is independence based on true competency, then it is easier to bear the ambivalent position of liberator-releaser, tyrant-protector, as one tries to assess a child's real abilities and real limitations, all the while supporting his ambition to grow in independence.

Competency must accompany independence, and competency is the goal children strive for in their primary years and thereafter. Added to the "I can do it" is a stubbornness in persisting with what they want to learn that is quite remarkable. Think of the hundreds of efforts expended in learning to catch a ball, bounce a ball, jump rope, and hit targets with precision. Think of the drive to use the tools that adults use in the way adults use them. Of course, children at this stage (and for long after) show persistence primarily in dealing with things which interest them, and they can lose interest fairly quickly in things which once had appeal. It is typical of children of six or seven cheerfully to become competent at certain chores—perhaps dishwashing, stacking the dishwasher, or taking out the garbage—only to reject responsibility for the chore once they handle it well. Yet, in relation to what they consider important to themselves, they will continue to use and refine the skill, as in ball-playing, for example.

The literalness of the pre-school child seems somehow transformed at this stage into a rigidity and absoluteness which can be annoying unless understood. Routines which the parent takes flexibly enough are given a solemnity out of all proportion to their meaning, as children carry them out without humor. One seven-year-old boy sat down to dinner alone with his mother one evening when all other members of the family were legitimately involved elsewhere. There was a rule in this family that one waited to begin eating until all were seated and ready. The mother sat down after serving the two of them and lifted her fork. The child said accusingly, "You are supposed to wait." A little startled, the mother answered, "But we are the only ones tonight, and we are both at the table now." "Yes," said Mark, "but I haven't unfolded my napkin yet." This same child, who was afraid to go swimming at his day camp, used reliance on the sacredness of routine to avoid the swimming pool when he had the chance to. At the day camp, wet bathing suits and towels went home on Friday to be washed and dried for a Monday return. But Mark was out one Monday and Tuesday with a virus, and was sent back to camp on a Wednesday, which was a cloudy day. The child commented that there would be no swimming, because the sun was not out, to which his mother optimistically responded, "But the weather may change in the afternoon, so why not take your swim bag with you just in case?" He looked at her scornfully and answered, "But it's not Monday" and refused to take the swim bag.

Sixes and sevens seem to be building structure into their beginning independent life by deliberate design. This is no better exemplified than in the slavish adherence to rules in games, which makes a first appearance at this stage. Younger children are good-naturedly sloppy about the rules of a game—impulses carry them more. But sixes and sevens are trying to deal with life in rational terms, not on impulse alone. A rigid commitment to the rules they think important is the beginning of such rationality. In keeping with the character of much of middle-years behavior, when new patterns are often tried and tested *outside* the home, the same seven-year-olds who do not follow a home rule to hang up their clothes, undertake to play a group game with peers by arguing about the rules with such intensity that no time is left to play the game itself.

Perhaps because, up to now, adults have been able to "fix things," and life has probably had a certain ordered simplicity for them, children of the primary grades assume that life resolves itself into basic yes-no terms. Everything that requires a solution must have a solution, and every question must surely have an answer. They show a resistance to ambiguity and to what adults call flexibility. They are reluctant to adapt to unexpected ways and choices. If they know the route to Grandma's, they do not care to try a new one for a change.

It is probable that children hold on to the pattern of orderly predictability they needed for security in early childhood because now this gives them a feeling of control over their own world in the face of their newly-emerging sense of themselves as separate from their protective parents. The childish belief in the magic of one's own power to control (if you wish hard enough for something, you can make it happen) is, of course, due for painful disillusionment as reality is more clearly faced and recognized in the years of self-directed, and therefore less protected, living. The possibility of alternative solutions, or the reality of no solution in some instances, has to grow upon them, hopefully with adult guidance which avoids cynicism or fatalistic resignation.

While they are great ones for clarifying rules and are not easily shaken out of the rules they have accepted from older children or adults, sixes and sevens are not at all averse to cheating if that will make it possible to win. Once they are at play, winning is terribly important. They are poor sports and take losing badly. Two children, one seven, the other almost eight, whose mothers were visiting with each other, were heard to say, once they had gotten past the hurdle of the boy-girl distance, "Do you want to play checkers?" "O.K." "I cheat you know," said one. "That's O.K. I do, too," said the other. And they proceeded to play.

Yet sixes and sevens are at that point in life where what we call a conscience is beginning to operate. Prior to that time, children differentiated right from wrong as a matter of association with praise or punishment. They knew what was permitted and what was not, but they were concerned less with the moral issues than with adult reactions to their behavior. Somewhere about six, the admonitions of the parents begin to take hold, and children develop personal guilt over wrongdoing and righteousness about being right. While this is taking place, children know perfectly well when they are not on the side of the angels, as the two above confessed to each other.

At the same time, their wrongdoing has a poignant other side, which is perhaps best seen in a widespread and common practice among first- and second-graders—tattling. On the face of it, one child's telling on another for misbehavior hardly seems sportsmanlike or loyal. In reality, neither sportsmanship nor loyalty has anything to do with it. For all their bravado, these children are still very much concerned about adult opinion and approval. The internalization of parental standards has not yet proceeded sufficiently for adequate self-assurance. They still want, and need, important adults to know that they do know right from wrong all by themselves. Consequently, when a first- or second-grader sees a classmate break the rules, he feels impelled to inform the teacher, so she will clearly know that he, for one, can be trusted to know the difference. Teachers as well as parents are often horrified at this behavior because it violates the taboo against informers which is part of our moral code. But all that an egocentric primary child is asking for is adult recognition and approval of how good he is. "I am pleased that you know the right thing to do" is what he wants to hear. He will be helped to learn the social code, too, if an adult follows this with some such non-judgmental perspective as "I don't think it makes John happy when you tell me about his naughtiness. Why not let me watch John from now on, and I will count on you to know what you need to do"—a response that need not embody sarcasm. Children are in a real bind here. They need support for persistent needs as well as a sense of direction for future behavior from the same important adult at the same time.

Almost all children tattle at one time or another in the years between five and seven. It does not break up friendships (at least not among the children!). There seems to be a common understanding among them that tattling does not involve malice toward others. As in the cheating, they acknowledge the legitimacy of frankly selfish, self-protective behavior. Two years later, by fourth grade, the need for such approval from adults has diminished to the point where tattling on classmates receives the same scorn that adults give it. At that time, loyalty to one's peers overrides considerations of adult approval, and the fourth-grader who is still willing to betray his peers is likely to be an insecure child with difficulties in relating to other children. But in first and second grades, tattling is not the antisocial phenomenon it will become. If it is handled for what it is, the children do learn the requisite social codes.

The period of conscience-formation could be characterized as a time when "the spirit is willing, but the flesh is weak." Lying and stealing are carried off with great finesse, although with perfect awareness of their social meaning, and in ways very different from pre-school lying and stealing. Four-year-old lying has an element of confusion between fantasy and reality in it. A four-year-old who is caught in a misdeed not only wishes he had never gotten started to begin with, but moves easily from that wish to the illusion that he did not even do it, and he speaks convincingly of his wished-for innocence with the contrary evidence right in front of him.

Sixes and sevens are clearer about wishes and reality and have no illusions about their misdeeds. They are simply practical, and lying is the expedient to resort to if one is reluctant to face anger and punishment. Thus, if a child wants something which he knows is not his and which he knows he is not to take, he becomes temporarily deaf to the as yet very small voice of conscience within him, closes his eyes to the reality of law, takes what he likes, and enjoys it. Knowing that it is wrong, he knows he deserves censure. But he prefers pleasure to pain and so he defends his lapse with the best kind of lying of which he is capable. There is no relationship between the morality of this stage of development and the adult morality we expect him eventually to make his own. It is simply that the steps along the way are fraught with temptation, and the struggle to resist temptation is human. Children need, and want, help, as the following story illustrates.

The father of a family of three children generally emptied the contents of his pockets on his night table before retiring. A time came when he developed an uneasy feeling that his loose change did not quite add up to what he vaguely remembered from the day before. He dismissed the feeling and assumed that he was more forgetful than usual. But when bills as well as change seemed to be missing, he mentioned the matter to his wife, who tentatively suggested that it might be one of the children. Both were reluctant to accuse the children, but even if they did, which of their three children could it be? With gentleness and tact, they asked all three and received three negative replies. They were relieved, and the matter was dropped. But one day the mother of a second-grade classmate of the little girl in the family called to say that the two seven-year-olds had been seen by a neighbor stuffing themselves outside the school with candy from an apparently abundant supply. The neighbor was sure both mothers would be interested. Suddenly, it was clear to the parents in our story that money had indeed been missing for several weeks, and that they knew where it was going and by whom it was being taken.

The father and the mother conferred and then had a conference with their little daughter. True to the childhood instinct for self-protection, she lied valiantly as long as she could, but since she really could not account for the candy she finally "confessed." Her father was curious about how she had managed to elude him, but she made it clear that that was easy enough, given his habits. The parents talked to her about the difficulty of resisting temptation and how they understood this. They also talked about the deleterious effects of candy on teeth and how perhaps the little girl was now ready for a small allowance of her own, if she would agree not to spend it all on candy. And finally they told her that people who live together as a family under one roof must be able at all times to feel safe and secure about their possessions, that it wouldn't do for her older siblings to have to guard everything they owned, or for her to worry about who would take her things. The importance to each member of the family of the trustworthiness of the others was stressed to the child, and she was asked to try to keep that in mind when she was tempted.

The conference ended on a note of forgiveness and hope for the future and, for several weeks, the father's money (which he was now counting each night) remained intact. But several months later, money was missing again, and this time from the older siblings' dressers as well. The parents went to the child directly to confront her with their unhappy news. And this time the little girl did not lie. Instead she looked her parents squarely in the face, and said accusingly to her father, "Why do you leave your money around? You know I am a stoler, so why don't you put your things away where I can't find them?" Both parents gasped, but they did catch the message. Sevens say, "Give me a little help while I struggle and don't make it so easy for me to be tempted."

This is the reality of this stage of childhood. It is the reason why teachers of first- and second-graders must cope with problems of stealing in every kind of neighborhood in which they teach. The wise teachers do not leave their purses on their desks, nor anything else which could be irresistible to burgeoning, but still weak, consciences. And parents might do well to be aware of the same thing. True morality grows slowly. It is not based on fear of punishment, but on regard for others, a standard that for a long time must seem strangely unrelated to children and their egocentric feelings. Yet their normal drive toward maturity and their trust in their parents help them to assimilate such standards in time and to develop into socially responsible human beings.

There is another kind of behavior which, to some parents,

might seem to fall into the area of morality and conscience, but which, from a mental health point of view, does not. That is the area of sex interest and sex play, some of which exists at this age as it exists almost from toddlerhood on. For most children, both the interest and the play carry completely normal connotations. For the emotionally healthy child, interest in matters of sex is one small part of an expanding array of interests and skills. It would be most unrealistic to expect any child of average intelligence to be unaware of the existence of two sexes fairly early in his life, and from there to grasp the reality that a combination of the two in adulthood leads somehow to a new and third being. How could anyone coming upon this miracle for the first time fail to be impressed and to be curious about how it happens? Parents need to recognize the ongoing character of children's interest in this vital aspect of human functioning and to be ready for the many opportunities at different stages of growth to give their children information and deepen their concepts at the same time that their attitudes toward their bodies and toward people are being shaped.

The child about whom one needs to feel concern is the one for whom sex interest and sex play take on a persistence and repetitiveness which show exaggerated need for body pleasures at the same time that satisfactions from materials and other children are not being explored fully. We must remember that body experiences are the first to have meaning for all of us and that experiences beyond the body represent an extension of ourselves into intellectual and social powers. At the same time, these extensions are not a replacement of healthy body experience. A child's heavy reliance on body pleasures at a time in his life when he should be learning to enjoy an increasing variety of pleasures beyond his basic body feelings must be seen as having special meaning. The continued dependency on the body for comfort, or a return to such dependency at a stage well past infancy, when such dependency is realistic, is a sign that a child has been blocked from maturing into the larger scale of living more typical of older children. Forms of such regression could be thumb-sucking, excessive or exhibitionistic masturbation, bedwetting, repetitive sex play with others, and even excessive eating. The problems with which such a child is struggling are often created by adult mismanagement of their lives, problems which are likely to be incomprehensible and unsolvable by a child. The compulsive sex behavior is a symptom of the resulting distress and confusion, and a child so burdened needs help.

In a child of a relatively stable background, the quality and degree of pleasurable body involvement is markedly more casual and less frequent than in the troubled child. Nevertheless, the curiosity about the man-woman relationship is real in childhood and, since its meaning is just about impossible to grasp when one is a child, it continues to be a matter of curiosity and interest until finally resolved in personal knowledge, no matter how many facts are picked up along the way. The childhood play of pretending to be adults engaged in sexual encounter is therefore hardly cause for alarm. Children in all societies do it, and if western adults were not still trapped in a centuries-old tradition of regarding sex as evil, no one would be the least bit concerned when children try to learn in this area in the way they learn in others—by playing out what they are trying to understand.

Their early curiosity about where babies come from continues at this stage as an interest in the birth process itself. They ask the tantalizing question of how the baby got into the mother in the first place and its corollary—how does it get out? Not all children ask such questions openly, since even in intellectually aware homes there are still emotional residues of the repressive attitudes of earlier days. And not all parents are comfortable talking to their children about sexual matters. Children sense what is, and what is not, likely to cause discomfort in their parents or others and react accordingly. Two young brothers whose dog had given birth in their home were eager to share the details of the event with a neighbor's children. About to run and spread the news, the seven-year-old thoughtfully said, "In their family they might not talk about such things, because they pretend that babies are sent by God, so maybe we had better not go."

Whether or not children ask or speak openly, there is the likelihood that, at this stage, when imaginative thinking and fantasy still guide children's logic to an extent, the interest in sex matters takes two forms. One, as indicated, is sex play, alone or with another child, in which children try to figure out the man-woman relationship by taking roles. The other is a search for explanations that make sense, given what they already know. To sixes and sevens, it seems obvious that babies come out of one of the orifices in the body which they know about, and they fantasy that babies come out of the anus or the mouth, or else the stomach is cut open and the baby lifted out. It is hard for them to understand the existence of an intricate, hidden interior of a body. They can locate the spot (perceived from the outside) where the baby lies in the mother. But everything else is inconceivable, because the body's integrity and wholeness continue to be preserved in their minds. The information they are given must therefore take into account how much they can grasp. There is no harm in telling a child that some things are better understood at a later time. Parents often feel so guilty about postponing answers, or so afraid that the question won't be asked again if they seem to be evading an answer, that they will deluge a child with information he can neither understand nor do anything about. If one remembers that the best learning at this stage of growth is through concrete experience, and sexuality is hardly the area in which one gives children concrete experience to educate them, then it should be fairly clear that the words and pictures one does use to answer questions have to be imaginable to a child in his own concrete style of thinking. Obviously, much will be left unsaid.

If one can establish a comfortable sense of the reasonableness of inquiry about *anything,* then one can feel assured that the questions in the area of sex information will recur in changing context, even if at any one point a parent does not feel he has covered the ground adequately. The interest in the question of

how life is formed cannot ever be fully satisfied, and certainly
not in childhood. Parents who cannot verbalize can be reassured that the knowledge about male-female relationships that
matters most is learned in two non-verbal ways: first from the
parents' attitudes toward the human body and a child's right to
his own body, neither of which is simple when the background
has been shame and guilt; and second from watching a man
and a woman—his parents—relate to each other in the thou-
sands of details that make up a marriage. The two sets of attitudes, learned early and deep, have far more influence on the
adult sexuality of a child than any information passed on to
them verbally.

From Self to Group Identity

If family life gives to children a basic sense of who and what
they are, it also prepares them for a concept of groups and
group living, which allows them in time to become members of
a community, a country, a world. Six- and seven-year-olds
have known for some time that they belong to something
called a family, but they learned it in relation to flesh-and-
blood people: father, Bob Harris, mother, Susan Harris,
brother, Ken Harris, and self. Included also in the concept of
family are Grandma Harris, Grandma and Grandpa Miller,
Aunt Carol and Uncle Don, cousins Judy, Stan, and Barbara,
and some others less familiar. Immediate and distant family are
differentiated, but only the known relatives are real. But now
children also begin to perceive themselves as members of
groups beyond the family. They speak of themselves as black
or white, as Catholic, Jewish, or Protestant. They say knowingly that they are American, or perhaps Italian, meaning Ital-
ian-American, Irish-American, or Czechoslovakian-American,
before they have any real understanding of what these differences actually mean. It is a time when the normal identification with socially constituted groups can have built into it
an acceptance of difference and alternative ways, or the sense

of in-group can be frozen to exclude any other possible way of life but the one with which they are identified. Thus, normal developmental growth beyond the self can become the basis of prejudice if parents do not give their children a view of the many groupings of mankind at the same time that they give them a sense of pride in their own ethnic, racial, or religious group.

The children, in their daily lives among each other, are beginning to identify with groups of their own making and starting the process of learning how groups function. By seven, sex groups are pretty much the style, and boys and girls begin to identify with the socially accepted activities of their sex, even though no one sits down to actually tell them what these are. Girls will fuss about hair and clothes, confide in each other lovingly, and complain about each other loudly or prissily. Boys will wrestle like puppies, strut in exaggerated masculine fashion, and compete openly in the physical arena.

Group life begins to shape up at first out of self-interest, but gradually out of shared interests. In imaginative play, which does not depend on preestablished rules (as hide-n'-seek does, for example), the children are able to reach collective agreement as to next steps in their free-flowing fantasy, allotting roles and activities in a who-does-what-when sequence that all obey, unless all agree to change the order. The use of each other in mutual fantasy that satisfied individual needs at five now gives way to more persistent sharing of the ideas that shape the play. Children stay longer with the role they have undertaken than they did in the kindergarten, weaving greater detail into it. In time, the ability to stay with ideas in group play and to assume the role that is called for develops into the lovely and satisfying childhood experience of "giving a play."

Several factors affect the success or failure of a child's entry into group life. The first of these is the degree of dependency carried over from babyhood. If he is afraid to venture forth, to try things on his own, if he needs his parents' approval for whatever he does, then he cannot muster the necessary courage to give up their protection and to try to make it on his own among peers. If he does try, he may be so awkward that the children, with a cruelty common at this age, simply taunt and reject him. An indication of a child's degree of dependency can be the way in which he meets this age-level challenge of membership in a group of his peers.

A second factor influencing the success of group admission is the child's feelings about himself. If he thinks he is a pretty good fellow, he will probably exude confident expectation that people will like him, and sure enough they do. If he is not sure he is a competent, likeable person, the feelings of uncertainty that reach out to others can have the effect of turning them off. It is startling to see at how young an age the inner feelings about oneself influence the reactions of others of similar age. A child can feel inadequate even though his parents think he is wonderful, which is why parents may have trouble recognizing the particular cause of a child's difficulties.

A third factor is the readiness for skill-learning which binds children of this age together. The child who is able to climb, who learns to skip rope, who shows steadfastness in practicing ball-catching, who can turn a phrase, or otherwise offer something, is welcomed into the forming groups, which as often as not coalesce around commonly held skills.

While groups begin to take on a certain stability around games and play, they continue to be fluid in the primary years and even beyond to an extent, as children keep testing themselves and others in new relationships. Groups form for rather obvious reasons. Children living physically nearest to each other naturally get many chances to know each other and often become friends for just that reason. Beyond propinquity are the elements of interest and opportunity. Those who attend the same ballet class meet around their love of dancing. Those who watch the big boys in the park join each other to attempt to form a baseball club. Those whose homes are open to other children share eating, drinking, watching programs on T.V., and playing games. This is the stuff of childhood, and parents must make it possible for children to meet and play with each other.

Intellectually, children in the primary grades fall in the stage between five and seven that the Swiss psychologist Piaget studied so intensively. Those unfamiliar with Piaget's work will find that he uncovered things about this stage of development that are very different from the conventional views of children of six and seven associated with a child's attendance at school. Parents and the community generally seem to feel that once children have entered the elementary grades, they have somehow taken a major and magical step toward maturity. Psychologically, there is the feeling within the child, his family, and his community that going to first grade means being big and turning away from babyhood. The child is now firmly pointed toward the adult world. But he has not suddenly become an adult, and this is what is overlooked in the pride of seeing him grown-up enough for first grade.

The first-grader of September happens to be the kindergartener of last June—a matter of two to three months. Summer does a lot for a child, but it does not transform a little boy or girl who learns through play into the kind of scholar who will sit willingly for hours and learn from books. That will take quite a while, and ready though most six- and seven-year-olds may be to start the long haul, they can best meet the immediate challenges of formal learning in their own basic style of thinking and learning. That style remains true to their stage of growth and not to the adult world of symbol-learning upon which they are about to embark. It is an active style, heavily dependent on first-hand, concrete experience, and includes a way of seeing reality which is completely childlike. Parents actually know this, but school tradition, which began long before psychological studies of children existed, is strong enough to convince parents that their children must conform to the school's expectations in first grade, or something will go seriously wrong.

Piaget's studies are a great service to children because his findings make clear that the schools must change their curricula to suit the thinking processes characteristic of children. In some ways, children of six and seven think like adults, but in many ways they do not.

Thinking processes must not be confused with I.Q. scores. I.Q., or Intelligence Quotient, represents a ratio between the number of right answers on a specially devised test and the age at which the child has accumulated all the information for the answers. The assumption is that, from this ratio, one can predict a rate of learning that will continue in the future. Learning capacity is then labeled high, average, or slow. While this is in part realistic, it is hardly the whole story. For one thing, psychologists are discovering that intelligence functions in many different ways, and the I.Q. test by no means accounts for all of them. Second, the amount of information a child absorbs is, as far as we know, as dependent on opportunity, exposure, and the kind of adults who answer his questions as on innate capacity to absorb. Third, I.Q. scores have been known to fluctuate as much as forty points in either direction for some children, when certain conditions in their lives at home or at school changed.

I.Q. scores have been useful in predicting success in school learning because there is a certain relationship between the two. Binet used school curricula as a basis for devising an instrument to evaluate children's intelligence. The school curriculum has always been based on the memorization of facts and the repetitive drills of skills. I.Q. tests, in the main, measure information retained by the child. School curricula, as now constituted, therefore, correlate with I.Q. in a gross, general way. But, in practice, the placement of children in classes according to I.Q. has proven inadequate for the bright as well as for the not-so-bright children because children are far more complicated than one numerical score of one mental attribute—memory—could possibly indicate.

For example, school under-achievers frequently have very high I.Q.s, which is confusing to schools and parents alike. Could there be a connection between this fact and the finding that some of the best and most original adult thinkers in fields as separated as science and literature did not do well at school? Or is light thrown on this apparent contradiction by the study of creativity which found that more children who scored high on intelligence tests were conformist and unquestioning and that the children who showed originality in thinking did not answer the questions as they were supposed to, thus reducing their I.Q. scores?[1] I.Q. scores have their usefulness in evaluating a child, but unless they are used along with other criteria, they are not the best prognosticators of learning, once we expand the concept of learning to include more than memorization.

What we are concerned with here is not how much a child can learn in a given period of time, so that we can predict his future and judge his potential accordingly, but with the ways in which a child does his learning so that it means something to him. This is related to what a child can understand rather than what he can retain. An obedient child will memorize nonsense if necessary, which is no help to his intellectual development. The criterion of understanding is the more far-reaching one, because out of understanding comes further inquiry and further learning. The large amounts of information "learned" and forgotten by the time children are out of the elementary school should be convincing evidence that to learn without understanding is wasteful of a child's time.

Because children are children, there are limits to the kinds of things they can understand. According to Piaget, the young school child is still egocentric, meaning that he and his experiences continue to remain the points of departure for his learning. It is not really possible for them at this age to think objectively about matters which do not impinge on them. They do not know why the Pilgrims came to these shores, nor Columbus before that, nor do they particularly care. They will repeat it all if they are good children, but it doesn't mean anything. One evidence of this egocentricity is that time is still

[1] J. W. Getzels and P. W. Jackson, *Creativity and Intelligence* (New York: John Wiley & Sons, 1962).

very personal. A child perceives as a long time his wait for his mother at the cashier's counter in a store, and as a short time, his ride on a pony which, on the clock, lasted twice as long. Although they are fascinated by the information that their own parents were once children and may even start their questions by saying, "When you were a little boy . . . ," six- and seven-year-olds are fuzzy about their father's having been a little boy. The existence of this very moment in time is so strong in the consciousness of children that the existence of a time before the important now is really hard for them to conceive. Even in relation to their own growth, they feel that they are as they always were, although they take it on faith that they were indeed once babies. The future, too, seems remote, and when someone asks, "What are you going to be when you grow up?" they are a little embarrassed, shrug their shoulders, or perhaps give the latest passionate idealization—a ball player, an astronaut, a ballet dancer.

The same confusion holds true of space as of time. On the way to school the candy store seems much closer than the cleaners right next to it. Sixes and sevens can know by rote that Los Angeles is in California or Canada is up north, but not before they are closer to ten do they understand the spatial, part-whole relationship, that is, that Los Angeles is part of the larger spatial area known as California, and north is a direction related to an imaginary point, the North Pole. Adults take this kind of knowingness about time and space as something that has always existed and assume that it exists in children, too. But careful study reveals that it does not emerge before a certain amount of maturing has taken place. While such maturing can be helped to come about, it cannot be hastened. This maturing, according to Piaget, is partly a matter of physiological development, partly a matter of a child's own experiencing, and partly a matter of presentation by others. In the end, all sources are integrated by the child himself as he acts upon his understanding. In practice, this means that adults cannot expect as full comprehension from six- and seven-year-old children in history and geography as they can in math and science, in which direct relationships are easier to see. School curricula have not always taken this into account, but the time is at hand now when they will.

It is the way of the human mind to organize and classify experience the better to deal with it. The world is so big, and impressions are so many, that some kind of systematic ordering must be done by each individual to make it possible for him to function. Children start to classify the world of impressions and experience early, and there is a developmental progression in this as well as in other things. The power to systematize begins with the recognition that some things remain constant, or permanent, in one's environment. In babyhood, the game of peekaboo, and, in the middle years of childhood, the game of hide-n'-seek are still enjoyable, because the element of uncertainty about where people are and whether they will reappear is still tantalizing.

A sense of constancy is first associated with parents, who, sure enough, turn up whenever you need them, or at least often enough for most children so that they take on a quality of permanency for the children. The concept of permanency is then applied first to concrete objects. These take on life for the children and, when they are lost or broken, children cry. Ultimately, abstractions take on a life of their own, as concepts of quantity, size, weight, volume, space, morality become meaningful. But children do not mature in all areas of abstraction at once. For example, at five, there are still some children who confuse right and left. At seven, there are still children who distinguish right from left on their bodies, but cannot see that a person facing them does not perceive right and left as they do. Sensing directionality from *their* bodies, they are too egocentric to grasp that others sense it from theirs.

At six and seven, children classify things in terms of their concrete properties, e.g. the ball, the orange, the lollipop, and the plate are all round, but they can also classify according to less concrete aspects which are perceivable, such as color—the sky, the rug, the kitten's eyes, and the glass are all blue. And they classify by function: peaches, pears, and apples are for eating, balls, skates, and kites are for playing, pencils are for writing, and so on. What they find hard to do is to classify on several dimensions at once, and especially on abstract ones. It is hard, for example, for children to understand such concepts as a relation between distance and relative speed. Fifty miles an hour means very fast if your mother protests, or it is being stuck in a rut if your father complains about the slowpoke ahead of him. Ask sixes to get the big book with the dark green cover which is at the back of the shelf in the bookcase in the bedroom, and they are confused. Or tell a child of six that all apples and pears are fruit, and he may well assume that all fruits are apples and pears. Ask him a question involving seriation (what comes before and after what), and he is lost. Yet, in later years, when children are readier for this kind of mental operation, they play endless versions of the Piagetian problem: "If Edith is fairer than Susan, and Edith is darker than Lily, who is the darkest of the three?" and tell jokes about family relationships in which the father becomes his own brother, or the son is his uncle—just to test each other in logical skill.

There is only so much that sixes and sevens can remember at any one moment, if they do not see it all in front of them. Piaget discovered that the power to retain an abstract characteristic of an object (such as its weight, volume, quantity), while a child is confronted with other, more obvious, characteristics (such as size, color, shape), is one which develops in this period. But it is not necessarily or reliably there whenever we would like it to be. Thus, a child of this stage finds it hard to take into account both the height and the width of a container in making calculations; nor does he understand the principle of preservation of matter, the "invariability" of substance. Not until he does, will he be able to understand that one hundred pennies can be exchanged for one dollar and that the dollar purchases one hundred pennies worth. Counting to a hundred by rote is not the same thing.

Fact-finding is important to sixes and sevens, and they have a continuing interest in how things happen and why. But it is more likely to be things they can themselves see or imagine in sensory terms. They are still dependent on direct contact with people and things as a way of learning. They can learn from pictures, and television presents pictures from which they learn a good deal. But they can learn from pictures only as they have had, and continue to have, contact with people and real things. Children whose experiences with people and things have been seriously limited, as in the case of some children of seriously underdeveloped parents, do not learn from pictures.

In any case, children like to do their own exploring and experimenting, and boys and girls, but especially boys, find it hard to sit and listen for long periods while others explain verbally. At the same time, the length of time during which they can remain interested in a project or discussion has increased since five, and they are able to delve more deeply into areas that interest them as a result. This greater patience, or "stick-to-itiveness," is a readily observable growth in the primary years, although individuals vary in this as in other ways. The children at this stage are also coming to value accuracy and workmanship, especially as they work away at concrete materials like wood or clay or other construction materials. They take pleasure in completing their work and enjoy making things that seem "useful," or functional.

Sixes and sevens are ready to learn and to include academic skills in their battery of competencies. The big question is: Are the primary grades of the elementary school ready for the six- and seven-year-olds?

Intellectual Life in
the Primary Grades

· · ·

Long before the day of enrollment for first grade, children look forward to the time when they will enter the "big school" and be "big children." They anticipate learning to read and write and have high expectations for themselves. As with all new challenges, the excitement is tinged with a bit of apprehension. The most sophisticated pre-schoolers are subdued by the social significance of first grade. With the certainty of intuition, they *know* that first grade is a turning point in their lives.

It is a turning point in several ways.

In the adult perception, and therefore the children's, this is school "for real." What they learn and how they are expected to react to the learning will be more closely identified with adult ways than with little children's ways, carrying the full weight of adult concern and approval. Failure in the primary grades is understood by child and adult alike to be a matter of the utmost gravity. To fail at school is to forfeit the right to enter the adult world of status and significance.

The children's anticipation inevitably includes speculation

about the many things they hear from the child population just ahead of them at school. "In school you have to be quiet . . . There is HOMEWORK . . . You have to do your work . . . If you're bad, they send you to the principal . . . Some kids are bad . . . The teacher is nice, she helps you . . . The teacher yells . . ." Parents hear things, too. "At this school the standards are very high . . . They give too much homework . . . They never give homework . . . There's only one good first-grade teacher . . . There's a new teacher, and no one knows anything about her . . ."

The nature of the experience will probably turn out to be different in more ways than either parent or child can predict. The relationship with the teacher is likely to have in it a new, somewhat less intimate, quality of dependency than with parents or pre-school teachers, yet retain a measure of small-child need. The children recognize the first-grade teacher as an authoritative arm of society, the adult in the new world of grown-ups who takes care of big children and tells them what they need, and want, to know. If the teacher is at all kind and warm, they are prepared to fall madly in love with her. If she is not, they may feel bewildered and cowed. Their love for, and slight awe of, the teacher may provoke a twinge of jealousy in parents, except that parents sense intuitively that one of the reasons why children can learn at school is that they are able at long last to admire and emulate adults other than their parents. And a good thing that is, too, because, in the years ahead, as the children grow increasingly independent and slough off their parents' guidance, it is very reassuring to know that they continue to accept guidance from adults who feel responsible for them.

Life with other children at school is expected to settle down to constructive and cooperative activity. Yet, as they enter first grade, children have been known to feel confused by the numbers of new children with whom they have to cope. Unless the class has moved on from kindergarten together, it takes long weeks to know the name of everyone in the class, especially if the first-grade structure is somewhat formal. Timid and shy children are particularly sensitive to the more aggressive ones in the class. For those children who have cast their lot with adult demands and expectations, the antics of children who are resistant, frightened, hostile, or defiant is a matter of great concern. Personality differences are strong, and individuals can be as easily overwhelmed or intimidated as they can be happily stimulated and exhilarated by their contacts with each other. By the second year, of course, there is a sure-footedness for most children that is revealed in the greater tolerance with which they discuss the variety of behaviors among the children in their class. "Linda is bad," they say with a mixture of surprise and awe. "Mark is a cry-baby," they report with disdain.

As soon as they can, they turn to the important job of finding a place for themselves in the group and making special friends. Even though traditional primary grades have given little recognition to the children's readiness and need for group involvement, either by guidance and support, or by assimilating the group process into curriculum structure, the children's personal struggle with group life continues with undiminished intensity during this and later years of school attendance.

New teacher. New learning. New peers. All present unfamiliar faces at the primary school level, even if children have been to school before. But, heretofore, when primary children were facing something new, at least their parents were clear about what was involved. A child was sent to the primary grades to learn to read, write, and do arithmetic. Parents admonished their children to be good and pay attention; they never doubted the teacher's knowledgeableness; they assumed that their children would conform, as they had themselves conformed, to the traditional expectations of the first and second grade.

But what was is now seriously questioned. The educational scene is filled with doubt and tension. Parents are increasingly taking part in the struggle for better public schools, are deliberately choosing private schools, or organizing new schools on their children's behalf. One wonders what overtones children are picking up at this important juncture of their lives, at a time

when parents who might once have enjoyed the luxury of undiluted pride in having a child who was ready for the important first grade bring them into school with skepticism, uncertainty, confusion, and even anger mixed with the hopefulness.

Yet parents have good cause to be concerned. Despite all
that has been learned about children's capacities, our elementary schools continue to function as though everything meaningful to six-year-olds were expected to stop when they entered the primary grades. They are asked to set aside their
curiosity, interests, and penchant for active involvement in
their own learning for two or three years, while they are
taught to read, write, and learn simple math—in preparation
for later, "substantive" learning. At the proper signal—admission to an upper grade—they are asked to turn on again and
apply to the subject matter prescribed for them the skills they
have spent several years acquiring. In all but the smallest percentage of schools, including private schools, there seems to be
a widespread assumption that children need not, or do not, give
attention to anything intellectual before they are eight or nine.
This assumption is based on another, equally specious one, that
intellectual content must be *read* to be learned at all, so it is reasonable to demand that children learn to read before they
tackle thinking and real learning.

To suggest that the primary years can, and should, incorporate more than tools for later learning is not to deny the necessity of a beginning period for basic skills. And the primary
grades are suitable for such beginnings. But, given the children's intellectual, emotional, and social capacities, as well as
the possible maturing inherent in this stage of growth, the 3 Rs
are still too meager a fare.

There are a number of important educational objectives intrinsically related to needs in adulthood that require time for
full maturing. These must also be accounted for from the very
beginning of a child's education. For example, Piaget suggests
that:

The principal goal of education is to create men [and women] who are capable of doing new things, not simply of repeating what other generations have done—men who are creative, inventive, and discoverers. The second goal of education is to form minds which can be critical, which can verify, and not accept everything they are offered. The great danger today is of slogans, collective opinions, ready-made trends of thought. We have to be able to resist individually, to criticize, to distinguish between what is proven and what is not. So we need pupils who are active, who learn early to find out for themselves, partly by their own spontaneous activity and partly through materials we set up for them; who learn early to tell what is verifiable and what is simply the first idea to come to them.[1]

Sixes and sevens are not too young to start learning how to be critical on the basis of evidence, not too young to understand the difference between the proven and the unproven, not too young to be discoverers, not too young to grasp and formulate relationships. They may not be old enough to apply problem-solving approaches to matters which are adult in scope, and they are hardly ready to gather important information from the printed page alone. But they are completely capable of developing attitudes toward learning which will serve them well as adults, provided such attitudes are shaped around content that is intellectually valid yet relevant to children's level of experience and potential understanding. Children are eager and entitled to enjoy competencies that cut across intellectual, social, and physical aspirations. The 3 Rs alone hardly do this for them.

Piaget's view of educational purposes is consistent with his findings about children's capacities for thought. These suggest that the practice of keeping children at an intellectual standstill while they concentrate on the techniques of decoding is anachronistic. We must set aside the traditional, outmoded sequences in early education and begin with an assessment of children's capacities in order to think curriculum for them.

[1] The *New York Times*, May 26, 1968.

The first reality to consider is that children are born learners and, if given a chance, will become self-perpetuating learners who experience joy and satisfaction from finding out and being competent. At six and seven, they may overestimate their capacities, but they love challenge. They thrive on the struggle associated with learning anything, but are quickly deflated by too much inexplicable failure.

A second reality is that children in their early years learn in certain characteristic ways directly related to their stage of development. They are natural explorers, investigators, experimenters. They are ready to develop techniques of fact-finding and relationship-thinking while struggling with standards of workmanship. But they must be active participants, even in a bodily way, in their learning.

A third reality is that they learn best what they want to learn, yet they have few preconceived prejudices about what they do not want to learn. Their minds are open to a remarkable breadth of variety, but they need time and help to move toward increasing depth of understanding.

Children thrive on content of a solid intellectual character, and almost every area of human experience and expression can be suitably tapped to encourage genuine inquiry. There is that area of human knowledge which concerns itself with man's relation to nature, to his fellow man, and to the social organizations he develops. There is the specific knowledge man has uncovered of the natural and physical world. There is the field of literature, by which man scrutinizes and explains his motivations and feelings in order to deepen his understanding of life's meaning. There is mathematics, by which man tries to sort and order his knowledge of the material world. And there is the aesthetic experience of art, music, and dance—as important to human fulfillment as the consciously intellectual endeavors. All offer exciting learning to children. But in order for these content areas to become valuable sources of learning, two conditions must be met: first, that children be seriously respected for the honesty of their inquiry, no matter how naïve it seems to adults; and second, that the content to be studied shall be respected for its intrinsic worth and meaning and not romanticized, diluted, or emasculated.

On paper, and in all the syllabi, schools have acknowledged the existence of these areas of learning under the headings of social studies, science, literature, mathematics, aesthetics, art, and music. But their admission into the lives of children has all too often been as fact-laden packets mechanically attached to a meager, basic structure of skills. With the possible exception in recent years of mathematics and to some extent science, solid intellectual content has never taken hold in an intrinsic, and therefore sound, way in our elementary schools, and certainly not at the primary level. Far from being exciting to children, the knowledge available to man about himself and his world has been a bore. The traditional approach to subject matter is at fault.

Any content area gains its significance from its meaning to man, not from its extensiveness as a collection of facts. To gain understanding of human social organization and thought, children must be introduced to the basic concepts and relationships that underlie human, natural, or mechanical phenomena. Obviously, only carefully chosen aspects can be selected for, and by, children to study at different ages, because concepts exist at many levels of subtlety and abstraction in every area of human knowledge. These must be appraised in terms of children's capacity for understanding, adult bias notwithstanding. For example, American children in the primary grades learn about the voyage of the *Nina*, the *Pinta*, and the *Santa Maria*; or the first, long, hard winter of the Puritans. What possible meaning can these experiences have for them in terms of human suffering, aspiration, tragedy, or triumph, or in terms of their historical significance? How can historical events mean anything to children who do not yet understand time in its fullest sense, even if they can rattle off names and dates? Even the study of the farm, so often a first social studies unit, must be reassessed in an era when the distance between wheat and a packaged loaf of bread, between a cow and a container of milk, are not only different from what they once were but, in their totality, are so very remote from the experience of urban and suburban children. Studies of foreign cultures, distant geography, or large political entities cannot possibly be illuminating unless there are connections in a child's mind with his own culture and geographic relationships. Young children still personalize objective reality. To the typical American seven-year-old, the government of his own country is "a man who lives in Washington." [2]

Today's world is a very complex one, and it is not easy for adults, much less children, to understand. Yet a comfortable sense of knowing what is what, even in a small way, supports a child's feelings of security and competency. In the search for such security in knowing, two different sources of knowledge have particular meaning to the contemporary child. One is the reality of urban existence, which is increasingly a fact of life for the American child. The other is the effect of technological development in separating the human child from awareness of his relationship to the entire ecological chain of which he is a dependent and interrelated part. Study of the social environment leads to understanding of the man-made structure that envelops the child's immediate present. Study of the natural sciences develops understanding of an environment which is growing more and more remote in our children's daily lives, but which places them squarely into their past and future. In a technological age, the study of both urban life and the natural world carries special significance.

The key to understanding urban life at six or seven lies in the concrete and visible processes of interdependent relationships which make urban life possible. Understanding even a small part of the organization of urban existence encourages children to find their way with some feeling of competency in the complicated adult social structures surrounding them. At

[2] Robert D. Hess and Judith V. Torney, *The Development of Political Attitudes in Children* (Chicago: Aldine Publishing Co., 1967).

the same time, such groundwork in perceiving interrelatedness provides a base for understanding later the more subtle and abstract aspects of man's social functioning.

The key to the natural world lies in the persistence of evolutionary realities and interrelationships which affect man's very existence. These, too, exist in concrete and observable forms everywhere. Yet the important learnings available to young minds in the natural sciences provide the foundations for a philosophical approach to life that is humanist. The content of both the social studies and natural science is intellectual, but each supports qualitatively different experiences in children's lives. The study of urban life lends itself to a style of group learning among children which can capture and define, in physically dramatized form, the interdependence of city services and functions. The natural sciences lend themselves to possibilities for individual and/or group observations and experimentation that allow for sharing and exchange among the children, but the experience is likely to be deeper in personal, rather than social, meaning. Thus, a child will build a bridge out of blocks and seek others to use it. But while he will comment to others on the birth of the gerbils, the real relationship he feels is to his own birth and existence.

Illustrations of social studies and natural science curriculum will make their relevance for the primary grades clearer.

In certain independent schools in New York City, the basic curriculum for six- and seven-year-olds is a study of the city. This is also a topic at several grade levels of the public elementary schools. From the vantage point of content "covered," children in both kinds of schools learn about the firehouse, the police station, the hospital, the school, the harbor, bridges, roads, the traffic system, airports, banks, stores, the water supply, sanitation, and so on. But, in the independent schools to which we are referring, there is a vitality in the study that is markedly absent from any traditional classroom.

It is generally accepted in these programs that young children are more likely to learn from what they can experience in a concrete, physical way than from verbal descriptions of the same phenomenon. Words accompany and follow first-hand experience, but they are not the most direct routes to knowledge at ages six and seven. At the same time, the target of the study is not factual information as such, although facts are an important by-product. There is, rather, great stress on *relationships between observed facts* and the use of *childlike processes of involvement,* through which these relationships can be comprehended at a meaningful level. A first step in any learning in the social sciences, therefore, is exposure to basic information through the senses. After that, there must also be an opportunity for children to organize their new knowledge for themselves in ways that make sense to them. This they do by dramatization, discussion, and the use of art and construction materials rather than through recitation, which is convincing to adults, but not meaningful, except as a source of praise, to a child. The synthesizing processes encouraged by dramatization and raw materials are basic to children's intellectual growth. They have been consistently short-changed in traditional approaches to learning, because they require raw materials, and any materials other than books were, and still are, interpreted as "frills."

In the program under discussion, then, the children begin their study of the city by visiting and observing the subway change booth, the post office, the fireboat at the dock, the firehouse, the sanitation truck at work, a bank, a man at work in a manhole, the bridges, the airport, and so on. Direct experience of this kind is supported back at school by books read to the children, pictures, artifacts, films, records, discussions with adults and other children, or any other appropriate resource that can broaden and deepen the knowledge gained from first-hand observation. The children are neither tested nor judged at any time on what or how much they have "learned." Yet their efforts at clarification are constantly assessed in order to be supported and expanded.

Children can best understand the processes and structures of social and natural organization if they can act upon the information they are exposed to in their own way. Therefore, time, space, and materials are offered the children to work out their understanding of the relationships they see in their exploration of the city. Blocks and various other materials for construction, such as wood, clay, boxes, corrugated cardboard, and large rolls of heavy paper lend themselves particularly well to concretizing the processes and functions observed in the adult world, because they are flexible enough to allow individuals to use them in their own unique ways (no two houses are the same), yet to join each other in interrelatedness (they buy at each other's stores).

The process of working out their understanding of social and physical phenomena through symbolic reproduction is necessary and important, because the children are forced to come to grips with their confusions. Following are some of the problems perceived by a class studying the city in this way.[3] The questions and comments were raised initially in connection with the block buildings which were to be built as part of a permanent city on the floor.

Where will people enter the building?
How will they use it when they come in?
How will I use it (work with it) from above, from the side?
    (Therefore I have to leave one part of it open and accessible.)
A grocery store needs counters.
A post office needs a letter drop.
A library needs a place for books and a place to sit down.
A store needs a place for display and a place to pay for things.
How many doors do I need?
How tall should the doors be?
How high from floor to floor?
How big does the elevator need to be?
What would the roof have on it?
What is my building made of? (bricks, wood, concrete, steel, combination of materials?).
How can I make my building attractive?

[3] From a record by Pearl Zeitz of her first-grade class at the Bank Street Children's School, New York, New York.

Should I nail thin wood to thick wood, or thick wood to thin
    wood? Which is best for my purposes?
Will this work best if I glue it in place, nail it, or both?
What are the right nails for different sizes and thicknesses of
    wood?

Out on the floor, children shared physical help and suggestions
as each child mastered the problems involved in his own attempts to cope with the reproduction of one small aspect of the
world he lives in. Here are some of the competencies every
child in this class had to attain while doing this.

Using a ruler and pencil to measure doors, windows, distance
from floor to floor, both for fitting space to rubber people and
for sawing, drilling, etc., when working with wood.
Using a ruler and chalk, and understanding the special relationships needed to draw in bricks on a pointed building.
Mixing the colors appropriate to the building material the
child wanted to represent.
Choosing the appropriate wood for different needs. Measuring a paper pattern of the dimensions needed before cutting
wallpaper or floor covering to size.

As the city built of blocks grew, new kinds of problems had
to be resolved. They were discussed in class meetings held for
that purpose.

Where should my building be in the city?
Where would you put the airport?
Should the little grocery store be near the big supermarket?
Should a factory be near someone's house?
How can I let someone know what I sell?
What kind of furniture can I make?
Should some of the furniture be nailed or glued in place?
    (shelves, counters?).

Much later in the project, the teacher described a different
stage of development of the block city:

As the city begins to function again, small groups are taken
out to explore the concept of electricity and how it works, going

from the simplest materials—small battery, bulb and wire—to larger batteries, more than one bulb, and switches. Each child is given all the time he needs to solve the problem of how to light the bulb with one wire and one battery. Then generalizations are made, leading to the understanding of the complete circuit and the broken circuit. Many of the boys who have been mechanically attaching wires to the two posts of a large battery and then to the socket with bulb, have to do the most thinking and problem-solving when taken back to the simplest one bulb, one wire, one small battery first. When this is established for everyone, we take up the problem of how the city gets its electricity and make the analogy of the complete circuit from the source of power outside the city and its transformation (stepping down) to smaller amounts for the city's needs, and back to the powerhouse. At this point we can bring the transformer into our city, transforming the 110 volts used in the real city to the 6 volts used in our city and supplying each child with the power to light the bulb he has installed in his building.

The value of the whole group working in this manner is that it provides the opportunity for large group discussions on an endless variety of topics related to a city, provides a real opportunity for different groups of children to work together at different times on a variety of projects, provides for using the strengths of different children in different ways. Yet the individual child can pursue his interest through his choice of building and through his need to spend more or less time on how to make bricks, curtains, furniture, food, or other aspects on which he may choose to concentrate. Depending on the group, the teacher, the maturity of the children, their interests, and the kinds of concerns in the real world at the time, other aspects of city life such as water supply, traffic patterns, mapping, housing, etc., could easily be a focal point within an ongoing "Permanent City."

In another school that approached the study of the city in a similar way in the second grade, the class was taken to visit a local factory that manufactured children's garments. The children were much intrigued by the organization of the garment-making process. The pattern, the cutting, the sewing of parts and their assembly, the finishing, and the packaging were clearly observable and not too complicated to follow. Back at school, the teacher helped the children clarify the steps in the process they had seen and then examine the relationships by which many people's contributions brought a product to completion. The children decided to produce something themselves which would allow them to set up and practice such organization. They chose to manufacture a small cap called a beanie. Almost immediately, they ran into problems they had not foreseen, such as the question of the ownership of the factory, of the materials, and of the finished products. They settled for cooperative ownership as the only way in which all could share in the working processes and also in the hoped-for profits.

They did make the caps, and sold them, too, to other children in the school. They started their project by studying patterns as a mode of reproducing a design or form. They laid out cloth in different thicknesses and spatial arrangements, figured out the best placement of patterns on cloth, pinned the patterns down, cut, matched parts, and sewed. They packaged, figured costs and prices, and set up a school store. As in the first-grade class, these children, too, had many questions as they dealt with practical problems. Their discussions were lively and to the point. The teacher offered them the few books she could find on factory production for children this young—books like *The Lollipop Factory*,[4] *Let's Go to A Clothing Factory*,[5] and *About Ready to Wear Clothes*.[6] In addition, she herself explored and read on the adult level, preparing herself as best she could for whatever questions the children might raise. The project went on for several months, during which time the children were also involved regularly with their readers, their math, and their

[4] Mary Elting and Margaret Gossett, *The Lollipop Factory* (New York: Doubleday & Co., 1946).
[5] Harry Lazarus, *Let's Go to A Clothing Factory* (New York: G.P. Putnam's Sons, 1961).
[6] Terry Shannon, *About Ready to Wear Clothes* (Chicago: Melmont Publishers, 1961).

writing. But, although they valued their skill-learning because, happily for them, it went on in a non-pressuring climate, the real pitch of excitement was the "factory."

This kind of study is not patronizing baby-fare. Nor is it sterile, as is the case with routine memorization. For the children studying the city this way, the result is as deep an understanding of the world they were born into as their youth and limited experience will allow.

Compare this quality of learning with the following set of lessons taken from a notebook of a second-grade child whose class was also studying New York City. The lessons appear exactly as the child copied them, uncomprehending, from the blackboard. There was no reconstruction of the city in this class, just straight verbal presentation by the teacher.

Dec. 17   *New York City*
New York City has five parts called boroughs. We live in the Bronx. The other boroughs are Brooklyn, Queens, Manhattan and Richmond.

Feb. 5   *Map Study*
We have been studying a map of New York City. We saw ten bridges and four tunnels. These connect the five boroughs, and New Jersey too.

Feb. 17   *Manhattan*
Manhattan, the smallest borough, is called "the borough of business and finance." It has an Indian name that means "island of the hills." Mayor Lindsay lives and works there.

Feb. 27   *The Bronx*
The Bronx is called the "Borough of Universities."
You can find a Zoo in many parks there. Yankee Stadium is there too.
It has many houses. Some are private houses, others are apartments. We live in the Bronx.

Mar. 5   *Brooklyn*
Brooklyn is called "the borough of Churches." There are four large bridges connecting it to other boroughs. It is important be-

cause of its large harbor and waterfront. More people live there than any other borough.

Mar. 7   *Richmond*
This borough is called Staten Island. It is closer to New Jersey than to New York. It is part of New York because a boat sailed around it in 24 hours. We can get there by ferry boat or by going over the Verrazano-Narrows Bridge.

Mar. 9   *Queens*
Queens is our largest borough. It has many private houses that make it seem like the country. Our two airports are in Queens. It was named for the English Queen, Catherine.

Mar. 12   *Our City Government*
The most important in New York City are the Mayor, the President of the City Council, the Comptroller, the Councilmen, and the Borough President. They help to run the city. They are elected by the people. Their job is a hard one.

Mar. 14   *Our Early History*
The Dutch came from Holland to Manhattan. They called their town New Amsterdam. It was at the very end of Manhattan. The English tried to take this land away from the Dutch. They renamed the town New York in honor of the Duke of York.

Apr. 16   *Amsterdam—Old and New*
We have been studying about Amsterdam. We have seen the Canal, the windmills and the interesting buildings. We are still able to see Dutch-looking buildings here in New York. We will look for some of those buildings in our own neighborhood.

It is no accident that so many bright, eager learners of six, seven, and eight become unhappy, rebellious children at school. Their natural enthusiasm for pursuing ideas runs counter to the controlled and controlling teacher-child interaction around prescribed questions and answers. The narrow range within which their minds are permitted to function at school offers little opportunity for the brainstorming that sparks new thinking, or for the satisfaction of peer-group sharing. Perhaps learning so conceived is responsible for the finding that, in the first grade, 95 per cent of the questions are asked by children, but that, by fifth grade, the process is reversed.

Natural Science

Basic concepts in the natural sciences are especially available to children through the same concreteness of experience that is effective in the social studies.

Here is the report on the way a child learned that dyes can be made from natural sources. See how concerned she is with the very specific, practical steps she herself had to take.

Making Dyes Out of Bayberry

First I cut the bayberry into little pieces. And put it in water for a Day and $\frac{1}{2}$ Day. I boiled it and put it in the icebox for a Day. Then Mrs. M. and I put it in a pot and boiled the Dye some more. We poured a little Dye in a pot again and put some wool with alum in it and boiled it. Once I put copper in the dye. And I put SODA in too.

And here are the questions asked by a second-grade class that had a new garden snake in a tank. See how down-to-earth and practical these questions are.

How does he breathe?
How does he go to the bathroom?
How does he shed his skin?
Where does he find his food?
Where does he live?
Why is he called a garden snake?
How do snakes hear?
Do snakes have teeth?
How does he move?
How does he climb?
How does a snake have a baby?
Do snakes change color?
How do snakes get married?

How do they stretch?
How do snakes kiss?
How do snakes eat?
How do they protect themselves?

The important concept of a life cycle was studied by an urban first grade whose teacher was aware that sixes and sevens are capable of understanding what a life cycle is because they have already gone through preliminary questioning about birth and death at an earlier age. For the learning to be meaningful, however, a cycle must be seen in its entirety, within a time span children can encompass—something not possible for a child to see in the human cycle. The teacher provided the impetus for the study by bringing into the classroom in September some leafed branches that held eggs of the monarch butterfly. These she knew had a degree of reliability in indoor breeding. She encouraged the children to guess what the small white balls on the leaves were. With only a few days to wait before they would see one or more tiny caterpillars appear, the guessing was a challenge that did not grow too frustrating. The children did guess that the little white balls might be eggs. When the caterpillars appeared, they stimulated a storm of questions and comments that sent the children scurrying to the books and pictures the teacher had prepared beforehand. Before their interest had time to cool, the caterpillars molted, and the chrysalides began to form. While waiting for the butterflies to emerge, the children's questions flowed continuously: What do monarch butterflies eat? What is the chrysalis made of? What happens inside the chrysalis? Will the young monarch fly away as soon as it comes out? How long will it live?

The children kept a record of what they observed as the days passed, but the quest for information also carried them through books, discussion, writing, and mathematical computations. In time, they learned to identify and to understand the events they had observed as stages in the life cycle of a butterfly. Their own story, developed by the entire group and recorded by their teacher, is more dramatic than any outsider's description could be.

Once upon a time there were 13 caterpillar eggs. We had them two days. Finally they hatched. Rita saw them because we went home early noon because it was a short day. Stevie went home at 2, and Rita stayed till 3.

Rita said, 'May I look at the eggs for the last time before I go home?'

She saw a tiny little caterpillar head coming out with the feelers on the top of his head.

On Monday the rest of us saw them.

They changed color when they were 7 days old. They were white and black first, and then they became yellow.

They got bigger and bigger, and bigger and fatter. They ate a lot of milkweed.

Soon we are going to have 12 or 13 chrysalises.

When they get out of their chrysalis they will be a butterfly. That will take a week.

We gave the caterpillars milkweed for three weeks and four days.

We felt kind of worried after two weeks because they hadn't made their chrysalis.

We fed them and fed them. It was hard to find milkweed because of the weather. It was dry.

Finally, today, October 14, two caterpillars are making their chrysalis.

We felt happy because we finally had 2 chrysalises. Then we had a third.

The chrysalises look like green wax. They look like they would feel gushy if you could touch them. They were pretty. The golden spots made a pattern that shined and sparkled.

Jeanie says that when the caterpillar hung in a J she couldn't wait to see the chrysalis.

We only had to wait till the next day.

We watched the chrysalis every day.

From green it changed to blue green.

Suddenly one day we could see a butterfly wing through the chrysalis.

The very same day a butterfly emerged.

When we went to the roof at 10:15 there was a black chrysalis. When we came down from the roof at 11:15 we had a monarch butterfly.

We all crowded around it. We came right to the cage. We didn't even wash our hands. There was an orange and black butterfly. Halloween colors.

Now the empty chrysalis looked like a plastic bag.

It wasn't strong enough yet to do anything but dry its wings.

We could not band it till Miss Gray came.

She will tell us all about insects and she will show us slides about insects.

We saw the last butterfly emerge. First he put his back legs out of the chrysalis. Then the crack got bigger.

At first it looked like a bee. While the chrysalis was cracking the butterfly came out. Its wings were all folded up and crumpled. Then the butterfly started drying and flapping its wings.

It flew up to a branch and fluttered. It was black, orange and white. It was beautiful.

The very next day Miss Gray came and banded two of our butterflies. She showed us how to feed them after she banded them.

We had a male and two females.

On Friday afternoon one of the butterflies that was banded flew out the window. It was a lucky accident because that one was banded, and the other two died right after. It flew out when we were feeding it.

We were lucky that the eggs hatched.

We were lucky that the butterflies emerged from the chrysalises.

We were really lucky that the banded one flew out the window.

Group Interaction

Very important to the projects described was the way in which the children related to each other as they sought to understand relationships in the external world. Just about ready for group life—in fact already struggling with peer-group interaction—primary-grade children are capable of genuine camaraderie and group spirit despite their anxious beginnings.

Among themselves, children explore both the competitive and cooperative aspects of relating. Quite aside from the obvious social and emotional implications of such interaction is its potential contribution to the quality of intellectual life when it is properly harnessed around interesting content. The inclination toward group life and action characteristic of children in the middle years as a whole makes it possible for even primary-grade children to learn to think and plan collectively, although adult leadership is necessary for the development of this natural proclivity. Increasingly sensitive to the modes of the adult world and growing even more capable of seeing part-to-whole relationships, children can grasp meaningful concepts and accumulate much specific knowledge while satisfying social and emotional needs. But the curriculum must be truly suited in content and style to their stage of development.

The Meaning of the Skills:
I. Reading
· · ·

Despite the existence in modern life of film, radio, and television, the old-fashioned communication media of reading and writing continue to be the undisputed first steps to success in modern adulthood. Fortunately, all children, including retarded ones, can learn to read, unless organic damage exists. Some children may take less time than others, but that is not a virtue; others may take more time, and that is not a fault. But the spectre of learning disability haunts the contemporary parent, and that is a misfortune. Questions of how early to start a child reading, what is the most effective method of hastening the process (or at least to positively guarantee it), which materials are the best, how many hours a day shall be spent in practice—these are matters for worry and argument among parents as well as teachers, school administrators, and psychologists.

Since no contemporary adult remembers any such controversy raging around his head when he was himself learning to read, the current argumentation conveys an impression of progress over the ineffectual modes of the past. This does not happen to be quite the case. Although recent important clues about the influence of environmental limitation and neurological development are leading to deeper understanding of the causes of some failures, this information does not radically change the basic approaches to most children.

It is not generally realized that contradictory views about how reading should be taught have swung back and forth for decades with a reaction, counterreaction regularity that has presented the rejected mode of a past generation as the latest innovation of the next. Present disagreements fall neatly into that pattern except for the improved insights into the causes of failure mentioned above, with one added complication. In our time, the mass media have brought into the public arena an issue that formerly existed only in academic halls. Acquainting parents with the problems involved in education is a task that should long ago have been undertaken by educators, and was not. As a result, the fast and eye-catching appeal of the mass media has led to a mass hysteria about reading which is far more damaging to children's progress than any one reading method could possibly be. Not only parents, but schools, too, are caught in the web.

The general public has been led to believe that the current controversy turns around the efficiency of teaching phonics versus the sloppiness of not teaching phonics, with the edge at the moment going to the straight phonics approach (as it did before the 1920s). But the phonics-no-phonics argument is a misleading over-simplification of a complex teaching-learning situation. There are special difficulties involved in learning to read the English language that one does not find in certain phonetic languages, such as Russian, Hebrew, Spanish, or Norwegian.

The same historical development that accounts for the richness of the English language is responsible for the irregularities of spelling and pronunciation which make its printed form difficult to decode. English has been fed by many tongues and has adapted to a variety of cultural changes over centuries. Consequently, archaic spelling exists side by side with newer letter combinations for the same sounds, and identical pronunciations exist in a variety of appearances. Feud, few, and hue; knight and night; cite, psychology and site; to, too, two, and through; trough, off, philosophy, and fill; cat, kit, and chasm; bear, bare, and lair; bread and bred, are but a handful of the varieties of ways in which given sounds can be presented to a beginning reader of English of any age. Because English spelling is not phonetic, the twenty-six letters of our alphabet must stand for forty-four different sounds, making the decoding task far more confusing than if each letter had a consistent sound.

One might argue that complicated words need not be learned first, which is certainly true to some extent. Unfortunately, although 85 per cent of words, or parts of words, in English are spelled with phonetic consistency, the 15 per cent that are not appear about 85 per cent of the time in reading situations. When, for example, should we introduce contradictory-looking, commonplace words like city and sun, cat and kitten, garage, George, and jam?

The consonants prove to be reasonably regular, but the vowels are a forest of contradictions. For example, the "a" sounds in pan, park, and pall are not only heard differently, but there are spelling differences for like sounds, such as in pane and pain, pare and pear. There are also letters which appear, but are not sounded at all. Vowel combinations in words like cow and bowl, or guide and fried, represent still another level of instability of letter and sound combination. According to some experts, there are one hundred and forty-four representations for the thirteen sounds of the five vowels!

Concern with efficient ways of teaching reading has existed as long as schooling itself.

As early as 800 A.D. and especially in the days of Martin Luther, devices such as the ab-eb-ib columns were employed to assist children in acquiring fundamental letter and phonic knowledge. In 1532 an A B C book containing 'A is for Ape,' 'B is the Bee,' and similar sequences introduced the well-known couplet-picture device which in 1650 was advocated by Comineus as a significant and desirable reading aid. The widely used *New England Primer* . . . reflected in 1690 the universal assumption that the knowledge of letters was the basic element in successful reading.[1]

The assumption that prior knowledge of letters was basic to beginning reading remained an unquestioned view until the end of the eighteenth century. At that time, a breakthrough in a totally different area of thought laid the groundwork for fresh approaches to how children should be taught to read. That breakthrough was today's taken-for-granted insight that children are different from adults and that childhood is a stage in the total life of man. As a result of this conception, a sizable movement toward what is now called a child-centered approach to education had its beginnings early in the last century. Froebel established a special school just for little children; Dickens raised an outcry against the brutality accorded children and succeeded in influencing laws and practices; Mark Twain and Lewis Carroll wrote especially for children's pleasure. By the end of the century, the psychological study of the child was begun in earnest. Dewey's philosophy of education was a culmination of this interest in, and focus on, childhood as a unique stage.

In this climate of sensitivity to children, the whole-word approach to reading was advocated, in the belief that knowledge of a word's meaning rather than of meaningless individual letters made it easier for a child to remember the printed word. By 1912, psychology was offering support for the intuitive and philosophical approaches of those who had first questioned the historic tradition of teaching the letters first and then building words from letters. Research in perception led to the insight that the whole is greater than the sum of its parts, while the theory of Gestalt psychology underscored the importance of pattern, organization, and wholes in learning.

Since a relationship between the whole (the word) and its parts (the letters) is clearly basic to reading, the controversy that began in the nineteenth century and extends into our own

[1] Paul Witty and David Kopel, *Reading and the Educative Process* (New York: Ginn & Co., 1939), p. 294.

stems essentially from a difference of opinion as to the order in which the parts and the whole are best put together by the child. Obviously, the way words are constructed and the meaning words have are both vital, although they are very different aspects of the reading experience. The traditional, "logical" understanding is to start with the parts (the alphabet) and build to wholes (words). The mechanics of word construction are therefore used as entry points to the new skill. The historically more recent "psychological" understanding argues that learning proceeds from the general to the specific, that children perceive any new experience globally at first and gradually differentiate detail with further experience. It is also believed, in the psychological view, that children need to make connections between the familiar and the unfamiliar if they are to learn. It is therefore expected that, by associating the known meaning of a word with its new representation in printed form, a child's progress into the reading skill will be considerably aided. Therefore, the word itself is used as the entry into reading.

In contemporary reading methods, the alphabet approach does not discount the importance of meaning, but assumes that meaning will come in time. The whole-word approach does not discount the value of knowing the relationship between letters and sounds, but assumes that such knowledge is better applied to unfamiliar words after a child has understood that words in print are meaningful wholes. Both approaches happen to work under good teachers! Studies of various methods of teaching reading show that 70 per cent of all children learn to read by any method. The consensus among reading experts has long been that no one method of teaching reading works for all children. By the same token, 20 to 30 per cent have always had difficulty under any method, and it is for these children that contemporary research has been most useful in defining further the causes of failure and the possible solutions.

At the time that the present swing back toward a beginning phonics approach started, with the publication of Flesch's book,

Why Johnny Can't Read,[2] the approach to the teaching of reading was eclectic, and few manuals for teachers were omitting the phonics. The climate in the classroom, however, was more relaxed than it is today and, although there were children whose problems of non-learning were not understood, statistics showed that the majority learned, as the majority always has, and that they were at least at par with children of similar I.Q.s of previous decades. Had the concerns about reading been aired less frantically and more knowingly in the press in our time, it would have been easier to see that differences between the two basic approaches revolve around *timing,* that is, should phonics be a way to *begin* or a way to *continue* after a whole-word beginning?; and *stress,* that is, shall phonics be the main approach or shall other factors affecting growth in reading be seriously considered? In practice, there has not been a phonics versus non-phonics dichotomy except for a brief period in the 1930s, when the issue rocked the education world as part of the challenge to traditional education as a whole. What was, and still is, needed is greater understanding of individual differences that affect any learning.

Looking at the experience of learning to read from the standpoint of children's growth in understanding the task demanded of them, rather than of methods related to the mechanics of the process, one can identify three stages in learning to read which all children must master, whether or not these are recognized within the method. The first stage is awareness that print carries meaning. Many children learn this in rather commonplace ways from their parents. As pre-schoolers, they help their mother locate cans on grocery shelves and listen to her say "Wheaties," "corn," or "tomato juice," while they note letters on labels and see her stare at the small print. They stand with parents near a sign that says BUS STOP, or leave by a building door over which there is a sign, EXIT. They see UP-TOWN at a subway entrance, HOT and COLD on faucets, and

[2] Rudolf Flesch, *Why Johnny Can't Read and What You Can Do About It* (New York: Harper & Row, 1955).

LADIES, GENTLEMEN, or TOILETS in restaurants, theatres, and parks. And they see and hear commercials on television which present labels they may or may not understand, but which they come to associate with the pictured products. If they have also been fortunate enough to have heard stories since they were toddlers, then they are old-timers to the meaningfulness of print when they enter first grade. But even with a strong background of this kind, there are first-graders who still need help in bringing into awareness the recognition that symbols carry meaning. Teachers who recognize this make certain that the children have such understanding before urging them on to the next step. Too often, unknowing and anxious parents characterize this period in the primary grades as time wasted. It is not.

In classrooms where attention is given to this need, words and meaning come together in many ways long before a formal reader is put into a child's hands. There may be messages on a blackboard each day which the teacher interprets. "That says, 'Good morning,'" or "That says 'John has a new tooth,'" and the connection between symbol and message is strengthened in the children's minds. Children write their names and read their own and other children's names on various charts, such as attendance and job charts. They tell stories individually or as a group to the teacher, and she records them in manuscript. Individually or as a group, they "read" their stories back. At first, the reading is no more than remembered chanting. But after enough experience in connecting what they have to say with how their message looks in print, a remarkable thing happens which brings them into the second phase of the task.

Out of the welter of black marks, out of the confusion of unfamiliar symbols, one small group of letters emerges to take on stable form, and suddenly a child can read a word. Wherever he sees it, he recognizes it, and he is not likely to make a mistake. He remembers the word as a unit, a *Gestalt*. Although he may know the letters of the alphabet, he has now come to understand that words have a uniqueness and intactness over and above their separate, specific parts. The process continues until many more words take on stability, and a child develops a small reading vocabulary. Words in print now have reality. The *meaning* of reading is clear.

In order to become effective readers, children must proceed through still another stage, and that is the analysis of what it is that makes words look and sound as they do, so that children can independently unravel new words as they encounter them in print. Words must be taken apart, put together again, and read.

In early focusing on the structure of words, children are helped to see that *elephant* has a different look from *if*, and *pretty* has a different look from *tippy*. They learn that everyday words like *play* and *work* change by adding *s, ed,* or *ing*. They also learn that single objects become more than one when *s* is added, as when *boy* becomes *boys*, but that sometimes the whole word changes to show more than one, as when *mouse* turns into *mice*. Children learn to see that some words are made up of two familiar words, as in *grandmother* and *fireman*, and to see words within words, as in *animal* and *candy*. Ultimately, they will learn about syllables and the rules for their formation.

The sound-letter combinations, or phonetics, are taught in simple to complex order, although the phonics-first adherents often go faster into the confusing alternatives than do the whole-word-first adherents. Stable consonants and their sounds, like *l, m, n, p,* and *t,* are generally studied before *c* and *g,* each of which has two sounds. Blends of two consonants and their sounds, like *bl, pr,* and *st,* are learned before combinations of two vowels or a consonant and a vowel like *oi* or *ow*. The vowels in all their diversity, along with the role of silent letters, obviously take up a great deal of time, even into the third year of reading.

It should be obvious that skill-learning so filled with tedious detail is hardly enough to fill a growing child's mind with enthusiastic delight in intellectual discovery. Yet a child ready for it can experience real pleasure from mastering so important a skill as learning to read.

It has, however, always taken about three years for a child to catch on in reading, if by reading we mean abstracting meaning from print with ease and continuity. Even though television commercials may support development of the earliest stage by associating pictures with words, there is no evidence to allow us to suppose that growth of the kind described can happen any faster than it ever has in children of this age.

For example, the complexity of structural and phonetic analysis suggests that this third stage is best begun when children have developed the capacity to retain in their heads the memory of the wholeness of words in the face of their dissolution into separate letters and sounds as the word is being analyzed. Children vary in this readiness, but, according to Piaget, they achieve it at about seven. For most children, that comes near the end of first grade, which is where phonics was taught for decades. Transition into any of the stages of the reading process remains a wholly individual matter. The child who takes less time may have caught on somewhat earlier than others to the fact that symbols stand for something, or he may have greater capacity to generalize readily to new experience. Very early readers are usually less distractible children than others of the same age, or not as easily thwarted by frustration as some others. They are also children who tend to enjoy quiet, sedentary activities more than others at the same stage. The child making slower progress may be no less capable, but he may be focusing on new friendships, or on the satisfactions of developing new skills with his body. He may be a dreamer, or he may for other reasons see no need for struggling with deciphering skills. There are any number of reasons why a child may not catch on to the basic concepts of any of the three stages or to any specific aspect of the third at this early age. There is no pushing him until he does. Only continued variations of the particular type of experience he needs will encourage his growth.

The rigid timetable of the traditional school, by which a

child has to be at a specific level at a specific time, denies this reality. There is not a single legitimate reason for the deadlines for achievement during the primary grades which are turning large numbers of youngsters into failures in their own and their parents' eyes before they are seven years old. Even "non-graded" primaries belie their title by using status-loaded reading levels to evaluate, compare, and slot children. As a result of grade-level standards, unrealistic expectations are projected onto children which provoke irrational distress in parent and child to the detriment of further growth in reading.

Let us examine the actual meaning of "reading level" or "reading score," those much bandied-about terms. Reading level and reading scores are interchangeable terms for an entirely arbitrary numerical figure related to the sequence of difficulty of the reading books in a basal series. The terms began as a guide to teachers, but have been distorted beyond recognition into a strait jacket for children.

Early in this century, educators focused their attention on reading materials in an effort to simplify the reading task. On the logical assumption that children would learn to read most easily simple words they knew best, studies of children's speaking vocabulary became the source for the words in the graded readers known as the basal series. Words most familiar and used most frequently were introduced first, followed by cautiously selected additions from the graded vocabulary lists. New words were repeated in the texts a carefully researched number of times to aid memorization, and pictures were also used as a further aid in encouraging recognition and recall. Time revealed that the simplicity of a word's construction and its familiarity in daily use are not always the major factors that help children to remember. Teachers struggled for years to drill "easy" words like *the, what,* and *they,* while children were learning at a glance words like *lollipop, umbrella,* and *hippopotamus.* In addition, the series were criticized for glamorizing white suburbia. As a result, a number of contemporary basal series now include content closer to life as all children experience it, as well as words that have meaning for children even when they are not mechanically simple. For example, *neighbor* and *supermarket* appear in texts, along with *mother* and *play*.

However, the basal readers were developed at a time when it was considered desirable to group children by age, the period when the inter-age schoolhouse of the rural regions was giving way to the consolidated schools of the village and town. The basal reading series were fitted into this organizational structure. Ranked for difficulty, they quickly became associated with age and grade, that is, pre-primer, primer, Book One First Half, and Book One Second Half, were to be "covered" in first grade, Book Two First Half and Book Two Second Half were to be "covered" in second grade. The structure was tightened by the erroneous concept that the neat levels of the reading books would be matched by equally neat progress in the children. The reading achievement tests that followed used the same criteria of methodically unfolding growth. What a fervent wish there was that teachers could chart the children's progress more efficiently!

The sequential order of reading material from easy to hard has much to recommend it. But children do not learn smoothly in month-by-month advances that match statistically developed scores. This association of learning pace with rigid time schedules of achievement has been a disaster. Children not at grade level at the right month of the right year have been scorned, and children at grade level before the right month in the same year have twiddled their thumbs at school until the next grade, when the next book would be distributed.

What we know about children's learning makes it abundantly clear that the timetable within which every child is expected to achieve in the basal series is completely unrealistic. Children simply do not do their learning in that kind of orderly progression.

Although children of approximately the same age follow the same general sequence in the capacity to learn, the timing of specific skill-learning is highly individual. Thus, the comparison of children even of the same age on reading scores or levels tied to age and grade is a punitive ax held over children's heads for performance that is, to a large extent, beyond children's control. This short-sighted reliance on grade-associated reading level as a basis for praise or humiliation becomes even more destructive when it is recognized that, despite the known existence of a variety of different causes for reading difficulty, the scores as now used do not identify these causes. The same reading scores can be achieved by a child who sounds out words accurately, but does not understand too well what he is reading; by a child who is afraid of tests, but reads extremely well for the time he has been taught; by a child whose reading skills are offset by impatience and carelessness, so that he loses out because of temperament rather than skill; by a child who has a specific disability which affects his total score without pointing to the training he needs; by a child who is an undiscovered partially deaf child, as well as by a child whose eye difficulties are also as yet undiscovered; and, of course, by a child who was ill or upset on the day of the test. Children who are impulsive, who can't sit still, who are highly energetic, who are very social, who can't follow directions, who have little patience with themselves, who give up easily, who are afraid of failure, whose standards for themselves are too high, who don't know that books can be a source of pleasure—all these children do not follow with predictable regularity the orderly, test-determined rate of reading progress. In the present system, such children are branded failures at six and seven, without an adequate diagnosis of whether their difficulties are due to maturation rate, poor motivation, fear of failure, or neurological impairment. The injury is further compounded by the insult done to children of forcing them to learn to read in competition with each other, a practice that distorts the individual's proper assessment of himself and destroys the possibilities for reciprocal, helpful relations with other children engaged in the same learning tasks.

When parents and teachers judge children competitively in terms of arbitrarily designated achievement levels that do not reflect individual differences or causes of difficulty, they open the way for a pattern of condemnation of those who, for whatever reason, fail to meet the timetable—and of inordinate aggrandizement of those who, without trying, meet it ahead of others. This is particularly tragic because the use of tight deadlines in early schooling leaves a residue of feeling about being a learner that affects the school career of children who learn quickly as well as those whose pace is slower. The whole syndrome of test anxiety is related to this kind of irrelevant pressure, in which the timetable has become more important than the progress itself. What makes the situation especially ironic is that reading scores continue to be used, despite their superficiality and teacher protest, primarily because they are administratively and economically easier to handle than the more complex, individualized diagnoses that show specific strengths and weaknesses related to the child's total functioning. Yet every child's progress in learning to read must be analyzed and evaluated as a very personal experience that takes place within a realistically broad time allotment.

Individual versus Group Teaching

Early grouping for reading was strictly authoritarian and efficient. Everyone was on the same line of the same page of the same book at the same moment, and all a teacher had to do was keep everybody quiet while one child at a time read aloud. The teacher's manual informed the teacher at which points to introduce or stress specific technical aids to all. In that system, some children finished the reader under their desks and sat it out while the rest of the class plodded along, and some children were in a constant state of bewilderment and confusion, while the class seemed to know where it was going. For this reason the monolithic reading group was in time broken into two groups, one fast and one slow, but the dynamics of life defeated this organization, because inevitably there appeared fast, moderate, and slow learners. So the two groups were turned into three, competition was disguised under non-prejudicial group labels like Robins, Bluebirds, and Sparrows, but no group ever remained neatly and consistently a fast, a moderate, or a slow group. The individual differences continued to appear until it became clear to many educators that the differences would themselves have to be the starting point of instructional approaches.

Interpretation of individual differences in terms of mechanical levels alone leads to the preparation of materials even more narrowly sequenced in mechanical difficulty. The programed instruction series, replacing basal readers in some schools, do just this. But interpretation of individual differences in terms of sex preferences, interest, and general maturity along with a skill level, leads to a different solution: individualized preference and choice of books within the range of technical difficulty a child can handle. There is evidence that children interested in the content of a book will strive beyond their immediate capacity so as to enjoy the story.

Obviously, the more one restricts early reading materials to the dependable regularities of the English language, the more contrived and uninteresting the text will be. Regularity and repetition may end up with such dreary reading matter as "Pat the cat, Nat. Fan Nan." Just as obviously, children cannot get into meaty and interesting reading until they have some decoding skills. This dilemma has been resolved by one school of thought, which urges using the children's own stories and comments as beginning reading matter. Knowing what they have said and mean to say, children then find the skills of symbolization and decoding vital to their own purposes. From their own writing, which is first dictated to the teacher and then handled independently, they move easily into reading the writing of others. The principles of Madame Montessori and the British Infant Schools concur on the use of children's own writing as the initial base for learning to read.

The problems of organizing a class so that each child is on his own reading program are not easy for teachers accustomed to monolithic, one-lesson teaching. This is why the programed instruction series in reading have become so popular. In both programmed instruction and basal series, teachers feel that some control outside their own judgment is being exercised in relation to the sequence of development in the mechanics of reading.

In all the prepared series, every step of the process is laid out, and word analysis skills are sequentially organized in the teacher's manual. Every teacher is guided as to which aspects of the structural or phonetical analysis she should introduce, in what order, and when. While the manuals give the teacher security and a sense of safety, they fail to meet the needs of individual children who have figured out the principles by themselves, or of others who are not ready for what the manual suggests for the given day if the teacher follows the instructions literally. The teacher may also be unable to adapt the guidelines to her class in less literal fashion than the manual may suggest, because the basic assumption behind the manuals is such that teachers grow dependent on their instructions to the point where they are reluctant to use ingenuity, even when it is suggested.

However, what is missing is the individuality of choice relevant to taste and interest that affects motivation and comprehension. For this reason, some teachers use story books as additional, supplementary reading materials to the series, or move directly into allowing completely individual selection by the children from an array of books that match their technical facility. In the latter case, children are brought together by the teacher in small groups when they show similar need for help in assorted skills—for example, perceiving similarities and differences among words, or substituting consonants at the beginning of families of words, or in recognizing vowel combinations, or whatever. The groups are then regrouped for drill and exercise as the children's needs change.

The teacher who breaks out of the mechanics-only pattern can obviously become more cognizant of individual children. But she must, as obviously, be knowledgeable enough about the many complex facets of the reading progression to be able to offer appropriate help to any child at any point at which he needs it without relying on the general instructions for the class as a whole. In her enthusiasm for matching story material to the individual child, she runs the risk of overlooking the necessity for careful and orderly attention to those specific technical aspects that call for diagnosis, drill, and practice, even though she is strengthening those aspects that deepen the motivation to read.

It is possible, therefore, for reading materials to be more or less suited to children's tastes and for teachers to be more or less organized and creative with whatever method they follow. From the parents' point of view, if the teacher seems competent, and the children are learning with a comfortable sense of faith in themselves, there is no point in becoming involved in the specifics of the reading method. Every parent can support an individualized reading approach by helping his child find simple books he can read with pleasure by himself. If a child does begin to do this, there are a few brief rules parents can follow.

When a child who is just beginning to read meets a new word, it is wise to tell him the word immediately. It can be repeated as many times as necessary, if he does not recognize it instantly, whenever he meets it in the story.

For a child who is at a first, second, or third reader level, encouragement can be of another kind when he meets a new word. He can be asked to "read the picture" if there is one; it may give him a clue to the unfamiliar word. Or he may be allowed to skip the word and read to the end of the sentence to see if its meaning helps him to identify the new word. Then he can check to see whether the word he has supplied makes sense in the sentence. If these two steps do not help the child identify the word, he should be told what it is, and the rest of the job should be left for the teacher.

The experts say not to spell a word out orally or have the child spell it out. This method may seem to work with one-syllable words like *hot* or *cat*, but becomes absolutely useless as the words become longer or more difficult, for example, words like *elephant* or *thought*. The spelling method has no place in today's more complex approach to reading. Similarly, it is unwise to insist that a child "sound out" a word. Phonetic skills are taught by the teacher as they apply to the material used daily, and parents may be urging the child to use a method not yet introduced.

There are books galore on the sequence with which phonics should be introduced, and they are not all in agreement. Schools follow one or another authority's concept of that sequence. But, basically, it is the children who must themselves integrate the learning so that all the many different parts merge to become reading. To be most helpful, parents need only be good listeners when their child brings home his reader to show them how he reads. In his excitement, he may not remember every word, and this is normal. What is most important is that beginners not be shamed when they make mistakes.

Causes of Reading Difficulty

Learning any skill is a long, hard task requiring practice, patience, persistence, and confidence. It need not be overwhelming, if the hurdles along the way are realistic for children who are ready and motivated. When they want to learn to hit a ball or jump rope, they spend countless hours in the persistent practice required and happily enjoy the mastery that follows. But in skills imposed by the adult world, such as reading or even playing a musical instrument, the gap between their beginning steps and the end goal is not so easily perceived or closed. Children need constant assurance and faith in their ability to succeed in order to carry them through the spurts of discouragement that are inevitable even after they have made some exciting initial progress.

Unfortunately, today's children must learn the skill of reading—which offers so much satisfaction when finally mastered —in an atmosphere laden with considerations of social status and practical expediency. They are more likely to be watched over-zealously for their errors than encouraged. Parents are understandably ambitious about reading and understandably anxious about delays in progress, but children are very quick to sense the disappointment and dissatisfaction of their parents and teachers. Excessive concern over reading disability, whether real or imagined, has even been known to influence personality. In the experience of those who have been involved in problems of teaching reading all their professional lives, every child undergoes some difficulties in learning to read just by the nature of the task. Most children do not have sufficiently serious problems to warrant the extra time and expense now lavished on children as a result of a mass hysteria about reading which is quite out of proportion to the magnitude of the problem.

Anxiety about reading has grown in the last decade or so, first as a consequence of the sense of urgency engendered by Sputnik and then by the failures among the very poor. These have caused the learning situation for children who learn to read at a normal pace to become somewhat unreal. Whereas it used to be a case of the less usual child in the so-called middle-class school, whose family struggled quietly with its shame over his difficulty in reading, today's suburban and middle-class urban school, like the inner-city school, is likely to have remedial reading teachers, speech therapists, psychologists, and perceptual training specialists for children under seven, despite the fact that, in many countries as sophisticated as ours, children do not even begin to read until seven, and at that in a phonetic language. Too many children are sensing a frantic undercurrent of adult uncertainty about their potential success, as schools and parents, to an alarming degree, confuse inequalities in normal maturation with genuine disability.

Confusing the situation is the reality that a small percentage of children do have problems in learning to read which require attention beyond the ordinary. Such problems are highly individual and must be individually diagnosed and assessed. Although the search for additional information about reading problems goes on continually, and new insights in hitherto unresearched areas are still being discovered, a good deal of knowledge about the causes of reading difficulties is already available.

Reading problems stem from several different causes or combinations of causes. The first possible cause is the simplest: inadequate intelligence. Yet that is the rarest cause of all. A second is the background frame of reference built up at home, within which reading is seen and experienced as enjoyable or not, so that the desire to read grows or fails to grow spontaneously before a child even enters first grade. The absence of such a desire is more likely to be true of children of parents who are not themselves readers than of parents who are. Children of parents who read seldom lack motivation or interest in reading, unless the pressure to achieve causes the children to reject their parents' goals in self-defense.

A third cause of difficulty lies in neuro-physiological development, about which information is at present scant, but increasing. Children with atypical development come from all kinds of homes. There is every likelihood that they can learn to read, but their specific problem must be understood. Dyslexia, a catch-all term for reading disorders, "appears to reflect a basic disturbed pattern of neurological organization," according to Dr. Ralph Rabinovitch, who goes on to say, "For some 10 to 15 per cent of intelligent children, a neurological disfunction interferes with ability to handle symbols of sight and sound successfully." [3] In contrast to Dr. Rabinovitch's 10 to 15 per cent, the widely used tests of reading disability show 30 per cent of all children with possible lags, ranging from borderline to severe disability. Dr. Rabinovitch calls the discrepancy between his estimate of 10 to 15 per cent with actual impairment and the finding of 30 per cent who fail the tests "a wide spaced net in which the slowly maturing child is caught."

Lauretta Bender's work supports the view that there are slowly maturing children who will appear to have disabilities

[3] Ralph Rabinovitch, "Dyslexia: Psychiatric Consideration, Reading Disability Progress and Research Needs," in John Money, ed., *Dyslexia* (Baltimore: Johns Hopkins Press, 1962).

when tested early, because the available tests do not differentiate between these children and those who have some neurological impairment. She says:

> Maturational lag is based on a concept of functional areas of the brain and of personality which mature according to a recognized pattern longitudinal-wise. A maturational lag signifies a slow differentiation in this pattern. It does not indicate a structural deficit, deficiency or loss. There is not necessarily a limitation in the potentialities and, at variable levels, maturation may tend to accelerate but often unevenly. Areas of the brain cortex serving such specifically human functions related to unilateral dominance as hand preference in using tools and in writing, and in learning processes for speaking, reading, spelling, and written language *show wider range in time of maturation* [my italics, D.H.C.] than do other maturational or habit patterns.[4]

Certain characteristic difficulties have appeared regularly in a sizable number of beginning readers—for example, reversing letters and words or seeing letters sideways or upside down. There are always some children who confuse *d* and *b*, or *u* and *n*, or who read *was* for *saw*, or *tap* for *pat*. An unknown percentage of these children outgrow the problem, which is to say that their space perceptions mature in time. The tendency toward reversals and upside-down viewing has to be quite pronounced and last beyond second grade for anyone to suspect that it is a neurological problem and not one of maturation. Very possibly, of course, if all children were expected to begin reading at seven instead of at six (and now even at five), the large group of intelligent, but neurologically slow, maturers would simply merge with the achieving children and there would be fewer "failures." Those whose rate of progress remained exceptionally slow would emerge quickly as the children in need of special help.

It should be obvious that any suspicion of such a condition calls for very careful neurological assessment, yet too many

[4] Lauretta Bender, "Specific Reading Disability as a Maturational Lag," *Bulletin of the Orton Society*, Vol. 8, May 1957.

anxious teachers and parents hand children a commercially prepared workbook and are sure they are solving neurological problems. Thus, although research is proceeding at a good clip, the diagnostic instruments for differentiating slow maturation from disability are not yet available. Nevertheless, because anxiety leads to desperation and desperation to clutching at straws, there has been undue haste in assuming apparent relationships between behavior and cause before the findings are in. Diagnosis for neuro-physiological difficulties must be made by experts who are experienced as well as trained. Mass screening of five- and six-year-olds should be viewed with utmost skepticism.

A fourth cause of reading difficulty is emotional disturbance in a child, sometimes centered upon the reading challenge itself, sometimes imposed upon the reading task from a broader base of general anxiety. A child in a fine teacher's first-grade class gave the clue to his struggle with reading out of an experience remote from reading itself. "He's very bright," the teacher said. "He knows everything. Why is he having such trouble with reading?" One day this child gave a detailed account, with apparent comprehension, of what makes a volcano erupt. The teacher suggested that he might like to make a model of a volcano out of a flour, salt, and water combination which would harden and could be painted. The day the teacher had the material prepared, this highly verbal boy begged off. "I am not really interested in making a volcano," he explained. This was so unchildlike a response that the teacher suddenly recognized that, for this child, there existed a serious gap between talking and doing. Physically small and undeveloped, he apparently found any effort dependent on physical competency overwhelming. He had managed all his life to evade applying himself to tasks calling for such effort by being glib with his tongue. Almost seven, he had failed to learn the patience and confidence it takes to struggle for mastery. When reading did not come as easily as he and everyone else had assumed it would, because he was so bright, he found it hard to cope with a task that called for effort, and not mere glibness, in order to achieve. This boy's I.Q. was high, his vocabulary was superb, he had charm, fluency, and understanding. But underneath was a little boy afraid of challenge, and that fear was the stumbling block to his progress in reading.

Reading difficulties due to emotional problems are the most difficult of all to solve. Emotional disturbance has its roots most frequently in the parent-child relationship, and mechanical aids and exercises will not cure such a difficulty. Children whose parents have faith in them are unafraid and relaxed about learning. They can be motivated to read by hearing enjoyable stories, or they can overcome lags in hearing acuity, eye-ear relationships, spatial orientation, or specific language disability by special training. But if children are afraid, confused, or anxious about themselves, no training works. This is why the excessive pressure to achieve, the hysteria about reading, the skewed priority given to reading in the primary grades, and the accompanying competitiveness add up to potential disaster. Adult faith in a child's power to learn happens to be critical to his learning. Denying the differences in readiness among primary-grade children is a way to build feelings of inadequacy and predisposition to failure into the program. Children who do not fit neatly into the prescribed schedule, even though they are normal, intelligent children, learn to worry about something they should enjoy instead.

The important indicator to a parent is the continuity of a child's growth and learning rather than grade levels. To cut down on unreal failure, the entire time schedule by which expectations are so narrowly pegged to age and grade must be discarded. Until such reason surrounds children's learning, it will happen that an occasional parent will be confronted with the possibility of a child having to repeat a grade, because he is not doing well, and because his test scores are poor. The end of first grade as now instituted is a critical turning point for this, since it is precisely at this time that a child may be tracked, condemned, or saved by wise counsel.

A teacher can do little more than describe a child's performance. Her judgment as to causes may be valid, but must be considered tentative. In some circumstances, repeating a grade may give a child who needs just that another year to grow. But it may, with equal chance, give a child a year in which to do more of the same useless thing he was doing before. Unfortunately, there is no guarantee that either promotion or retention works as a matter of course when a child is having trouble. Either may involve a calculated risk, which is why expert, all-inclusive diagnosis must be the basis for the best judgment that can be mustered to help a given child to grow. Unless there is a very thorough professional assessment of the multitude of factors that go into a decision of this kind, a child may lose out, whether he is allowed to move on or is retained. Considerations of status and neighbor reaction are obviously immaterial when the step taken may be crucial to a child's total life.

The Meaning of the Skills:
II. Writing

. . .

Reading and writing are alternate ways of dealing with the same set of symbols, so that learning to write simultaneously with learning to read makes good sense. Writing skill, however, must proceed along two separate lines—the mechanical and the conceptual.

When children are in the earliest stages of realizing the significance and value of letters and words, the teacher must of necessity give them directions for forming letters and encourage them to spend periodic sessions in practicing. A few basic generalizations are introduced early, and practice is carefully supervised so that far-reaching habits can be started and reinforced correctly. Children must learn from adults that letters begin at the left and move to the right, begin at the top and move down, that spaces are left between words, but that the letters of words remain fairly close. These simple, beginning guidelines are not as easy for children to follow with consistency as adults suppose. Many children give letters shape by moving pencils from bottom to top and from right to left, because it seems more direct to them that way. Considering that languages have been written from right to left and from top to bottom, there is nothing inherently wrong in these spontaneous and ingenious efforts. But English is read from left to right and written in the same way. There must of necessity be training in left to right direction when a child learns to read and write the English language, or progress will be impeded later, when speed and smoothness become important. The struggle with the two basic guidelines in writing—left to right and top to bottom—is enough of the mechanics to keep a child concentrating for some time. The precision of each letter's appearance is not of such momentous importance at this stage as the satisfaction of mastering the writing system in general. Only when a child has the basic rudiments down pat ought he to be guided toward such finer details as straightness of lines, fullness of circles, and even size of finished letters—provided, of course, that such emphasis never becomes an end in itself.

The emphasis on neatness in writing has had such a carry-over for most adults from years of punishing practice that few stop to consider that the really important characteristic of early childhood writing is neither beauty nor neatness, but legibility. Despite the fact that ours is an age of typewritten communication, the glorification of the nineteenth-century "fine hand" still casts its shadow on contemporary children. Neatness and precision are, after all, a matter of coordination and practice, affected, at least in part, by whether a child himself values the appearance of his writing, or is indifferent to it. For a long time, in the beginning school years, children are too busy learning to write so they can say something (anything at all) to be able to focus on the appearance of their writing. Boys are worse off than girls in this regard. Girls in the primary years have better sitting capacity on the whole and more patience with fine detail. By the end of the primary period, in third grade, many little girls have a neat and proper handwriting, while many little boys are still scrawling and sprawling over the page. (In some schools there is little understanding of the difference in development of boys and girls at this stage and in this area, and boys are made to suffer quite unnecessary humiliation and shame for their efforts.)

Parents and teachers often worry when young children do not establish proper writing form in the primary years, but the anxiety is misplaced. It is a response to the standards imposed on them as children in traditional schooling where, for years, writing, form, and content remained quite separate. While all children must learn to write in such a way that their writing can be read (or else why bother?), the pressure for neatness and precision does not belong in the first two years, nor must uneven writing be punitively handled in the third. It is worth remembering that while children are struggling to form letters, they must also learn that a sentence begins with a capital letter, and that periods and question marks act as stoppers of a thought (and sentence), and that introductory writing forms, such as Mr., Mrs., Miss, Dear, names of days, months, and streets offer special problems of capitalization. If one encourages the use of writing for the sake of communication from the very beginning, the need for accuracy in handwriting, punctuation, placement on a paper, spelling, and other aspects of form become rational and necessary in the eyes of the child, because he wants very much to be understood.

The traditional premature emphasis on form before the reason for form makes sense to the child has led to tension and fear about writing that every college teacher meets whenever he gives an assignment that involves writing at any length. The student reaction at that upper level of learning is far too often "How many pages? In what form?", rather than concern with the topic and whether it is to be explored in depth. On the other hand, parents and teachers point to the "progressive" school methods, which failed to teach any form under the guise of stressing content. In general, neglected form was not nearly as widespread in the progressive schools as the cartoons condemning the freedom in these schools would have people believe. If, as in all new movements which begin as a reaction against something, there were individuals who "threw out the baby with the bath," there were as many who learned how to integrate content and form so as to produce good writing which said something and said it so it could be understood as well as deciphered. There is a charming book called *They All Want to Write,*[1] which was first published in 1939 (the heyday of the progressive education movement), and which tackles the problem of integrating content and form at four grade levels. Written by teachers of elementary school classes, the book spells out their concern for protecting the use of writing for saying something at the same time that a child is dealing with the mechanics of the writing process. Revised for a third edition in recent years, its message is as timely as ever. As in the argument over phonics in reading, so in the stress on detail and form in writing, there is no real argument. The conflict is one of timing and consideration for the most teachable moment. Obviously, form strengthens content, yet form without content is hollow and meaningless. In the education of children, form must always serve content. If it is introduced in the service of content, children will understand its relevance, and learn it willingly, although not necessarily without struggle.

The two strands of communication and technical skill proceed separately and intertwine as children learn to write, until writing becomes a source of power, pleasure, and release. Individual differences are as marked in this competency as in all others, but it is still deeply satisfying to any human being to be able to say what he wants to say and to see his message in writing.

A child practices straightforwardly the technical aspects of forming letters at the same time that he is encouraged to see and use writing for communication. Thus, while learning to write his name and other letters by himself, he is encouraged to dictate stories that are as involved and complex as he cares to make them—stories which the teacher puts into writing for

[1] A. Burrows, *et al., They All Want to Write,* 3rd ed. (New York: Holt, Rinehart and Winston, 1964).

him. The mechanics proceed from writing surnames to copying the many brief, functional messages that grow out of a first-grade's activities and needs, such as the notices, invitations, or letters to their parents about celebrations, requirements, or shared experiences. As a class, they make up and copy announcements, invitations, or reports to other classes, the principal, or to visitors; requests for services or materials to almost anybody from the custodian of the school to the owner of a lumber yard; lists of materials for parties, projects, or group responsibilities; records of facts about gerbils, a visiting caterpillar, the behavior of magnets, or a recipe for chocolate pudding; records of interests such as favorite television programs. The children's facility in reproducing letters and words increases with such continuous practice.

But, at other times, they dictate individual or group stories about anything that has meaning for themselves—stories about siblings, a lost tooth, or reactions to trips, sudden frost, power failure, a moon flight, or whatever looms large in the world outside of school. They are constantly increasing their power to say what they mean at the same time that they are struggling to acquire the symbol system by which meaning can be put into print.

The following stories were either dictated or painstakingly written by first- and second-grade children, later to be copied after corrections were made by the teachers so they could appear in their school newspapers.

When I went to the Zoo, I saw a lot of crocodiles. They were opening their mouths. And then, my mother looked inside the mouth. And I did too. We saw their big, fat tonsils. Then we went inside the Zoo and saw a lot of monkeys. They were doing funny tricks. We saw bad, bad, bad bulls. (1st grade)

Once there was a machine. Now this machine was not an ordinary machine. This machine was a mystery machine. It is a secret. It will not let a crook in the door. The owner was the only one allowed in. This machine was not a robot. It was sort of a computer, but it's a mind reading computer. One day the computer wouldn't work. The man thought it was because of Halloween. And the computer thought it was a copy of him. So he let out a final blast and punched him in the nose. The next day the computer got a spanking, and the owner said, "Why are you punching your owner in the nose?" (1st grade)

I want to be a bus driver. I like to stay up late. Besides I have to know how much change to give back. You have to be smart. (2nd grade)

In the summer I went to the moon on a space ship. I landed on the moon. I looked all around to see what I could find. I found something strange, shaped like an egg. I did not know what it was, so I went back to Earth to find out. I went to the professor, and he said it was an egg. I told him it was lighter than the other eggs that we have. I tried to open it but I couldn't. (2nd grade)

The flowers look like balls on strings.
The daisies look like diamond rings. (2nd grade)

Parents can support the basic guidelines to forming letters, but, more importantly, parents can record their children's stories for them before their technical skill has caught up with their thinking and feeling. This meaningful story was dictated to a mother by her almost eight-year-old son, who could never have managed the mechanics of writing, but needed to cope with his feelings when his kitten died.

Tigerty Come to Life!

I remember the time when my mother went to get a dress out of the closet. The night before we did not know where Blacknose, the mother cat, was. Then she almost stepped on four little pussies drinking milk from the mother's breast. The first funny time I had was when Tigerty and little Whiteneck pushed over their mother, Blacknose. Then, after they were able to open their eyes, me and my friend Richard put them on the floor and Tigerty seemed to be the longest running and the strongest and the oldest, but she was really the youngest. I remember the time when we gave them names, me and Richard. We called her Tiger-ty because every time she would stand up her tail would stretch out to look like the letter "T". I remember the time when me and Popsy would go down to feed her and we would be greeted by her walking quietly up to her dish and looking happily at it. I remember the time when she was in our mop wringer and pail. I tried to get her out because that wasn't the place where she belonged, and she patted me on the cheek gently with her warm, fuzzy paw. I remember the time when she and the kittens were climbing into the flower pots, and the time she and the kittens, when I had no flower pots box, would break all the little flower pots. I remember the day when I went to water the front garden. Instead, Tiger-ty was in the watering can trying to poke her paw up into the nozzle. I remember the times when Tigerty and I would scamper in the garden. I remember when she was left out all night and I heard her meows and my mother and father came home from the movies and let her in.

And now it is the end of Tiger-ty because she died of a sickness and nobody knows what it is. And then the time I came down to the back garden and instead of being greeted by Tigerty's warm pats up to the dish and looking in, I was greeted by her lying sick on the floor. Me and Richard and Mommy and Pop were down there. And that afternoon, I came down to see how she was. And instead of being greeted at least by a sick kitty, she lay dead on the floor with flies all about her. And then we buried her gently in the back garden.

Tigerty is dead.

Respect for children's individual and personal expressions, offered hand in hand with unpressured, but clear-cut, teaching of mechanical stages of writing skill, leads to the protection of meaning and the use of skill proficiency as a tool the children can use to serve their varied purposes.

The Meaning of the Skills:
III. Mathematics

. . .

The third R, arithmetic, is perhaps the skill where the most radical changes in primary school practice have actually occurred. The changes grew originally out of analysis of the true nature of mathematics, but Piaget's studies of how children learn support developmental concepts in mathematics suggested for the elementary schools. A fuller understanding of Piagetian insights is necessary, however, to avoid the speed-up and pressure some people still cannot quite divorce from the education of children, even when good principles of learning are embodied in the materials.

Piaget, a biologist before he turned to studies in psychology, uncovered the existence of a basically evolutionary process in children's growth in the capacity to think. He found that they learned to understand concepts of space and time, of reality, of cause and effect relationships, of morality, of probability, number, and measurement, in a series of stages. While good teachers of young children have long recognized the differences between adult and childhood modes of thinking, it was Piaget who systematically gathered the evidence that gave support to the teachers' insights. What he uncovered about the progression in children's thinking proved to be quite consistent with other findings about social and emotional growth, indicating that all childhood learning follows a sequential order from less to more mature behavior. Developmental stages exist in the intellectual realms just as surely as they do in physical growth. It has simply been harder to recognize the developmental nature of intellectual growth, because children start so early to imitate adult behavior and speech. Since they can sound like adults, it is all too easy to assume that they know what they are doing and understand what they are saying in adult terms.

The evidence indicates that a general framework for thinking is built up gradually, starting with the child's first attempts to systematize the world he encounters so as to cope with it better. As he grows, the framework he has established for himself to give meaning to what he sees, hears, touches, smells, and tastes is filled in continuously by further experience in various areas, leading to broader as well as tighter organization of what he knows. The process of understanding starts with direct physical and concrete experience, moving gradually and unevenly to the understanding of more remote and abstract concepts. This process of grasping meaning in sequential stages is clearly seen in the understanding of mathematics.

Every parent beams with pride when his toddler says, "One, two, three," or when his pre-schooler counts up to ten and even further with only an occasional mistake. As it happens, the ability to count has very little relation to mathematical understanding. Learning to repeat numbers in the pre-school years is very much a case of parroting adults. The ability to imitate shows intelligence at this early stage, but rote repetition of numbers in their proper order is not the same thing at all as the comprehension of relationships among and between numbers. It is the latter type of understanding that allows flexible use of numbers in mathematical operations. And while rote learning, once fixed, remains fixed, conceptual understanding grows deeper in an evolutionary, developmental process. How does this growth affect a child's ability to use numbers?

Adults take for granted the fact that a number exists as an abstraction, that is, whether a number—four, six, or eleven—is used to describe a *quantity* of objects, people, or coins; whether a number is used to refer to a *place* such as a street, house, or television channel; whether numbers are on clocks or ascribed to days or years to indicate a moment in *time* or the passage of time; whether they are used to measure *distance* into the air, as in the story of a building; whether they are on a ruler to indicate *length, width,* or *depth,* or on a scale to indicate *weight,* the number itself is neither the house, the TV station, the building, or anything else that is tangible and real. The number exists in our minds separate from any particular, temporary relationship to quantity, distance, time, or space. It becomes a concept of measurement which we can apply to various dimensions that are quite different from each other, as length is different from years. In and of itself, any number exists only in the mind, not in concrete form as does the house, the street, or the TV set. Number symbols become in time to seem as real as something concrete, but the symbols stand for an idea, not an object.

Adults know this without giving it any thought. As a matter of course, they assume that children know it, too. But children do not, in fact, understand the concept of measurement or measurability, much less the concept of number in relation to measurement and measurability. They do not understand it, that is, before a given stage in their development, and that stage comes long after they have learned to repeat words and numbers that make it sound as though they do understand.

Piaget suspected that there might be a difference between repeating words and understanding their meaning. Accordingly, he set tasks for children between four and seven of such a nature that they would have to deal with measurement and number in ways that would make clear whether they grasped the true meaning or were just repeating words. For example, in order to learn what children understand about *quantity,* he set up the following types of tasks. The child is shown a row of beans, beads, or cubes, and asked to pick the same number from a nearby pile of the same items; or he is asked to bring a drinking glass for each bottle of lemonade on the table; or sort cookies so there will be enough for two different occasions, but the same number for each occasion. In investigating their understanding of *length,* a straight stick and a wavy length of plasticine are put side by side, so that the ends of the stick and the ends of the wavy strip of plasticine are in alignment with each other. The child is asked, "Are they the same, or is one longer than the other?"

This type of task is given to children within a wide range of mathematical concepts involving number, length, space, time, volume, and weight, and Piaget always rephrased questions, so as to be sure children understood what was expected of them. Time after time, and in every area, the responses fell into three stages broadly related to age. In Stage One, the children were inevitably attracted to the physical characteristics of the objects they were asked to measure. That is, they were more aware of the color, shape, or size of the beads, glass, or plasticine than of the numerical likenesses. Their response to color, shape, or size inevitably interfered with their grasping of the abstract number shared by objects that looked different from each other. A typical reply in Stage One to the stick and plasticine relationship went as follows:

THER (4.6): "They're both the same length" (indicating the end points).
Experimenter: "What if an ant walked along these two things, would it have to go further along one than the other?"
THER: "It would have further to go on the stick."
Experimenter: "Why?"
THER: "Because the [straight] stick is even longer."
Experimenter: "Run your finger along them." (He does so.) "Which way did you go further?"
THER: "That way" (snake).
Experimenter: "Then which is longer?" (He hesitates and makes no reply.)
(Snake is untwisted.) "Which one is longer?"

THER: "The snake."
Experimenter: (Twists snake.) "And now?"
THER: "It's the same as the stick."

In Stage Two, the children see the numerical relationships, but not reliably, or with consistency. Although they have themselves just seen the inequality as the clay snake is unwound, a typical response at this stage showed uncertainty.

> KEL (5.8): "That one is bigger because you pulled it." (Stick and clay restored to their original alignment.)
> "They're the same size but they could be bigger" (if pulled).
> (Appearance overcomes reality.)

But in Stage Three, children were as likely as not to regard the questioner as a little daft, because the answer was so obvious.

> AG (7.0): "That one's longer because it's twisted."

In these experiments, the percentage of children who failed to grasp the meaning of the numerical concept decreased consistently with age. For this reason, since most children move along in this graduated fashion, it is safe to assume a developmental progression in the conceptualization of mathematical insights, even though there are individual children who do not fall into any categories at all.

The developmental sequence that Piaget uncovered is one that begins with a child's having no notion at all of what a number means (even though he can count), progresses to a concept of number that gets mixed up with the likenesses in shape, color, or size of matched items, and reaches a point about two or three years later when a child understands that a number used to measure quantity, length, space, volume, weight, or whatever, will remain the same no matter what else changes in front of his eyes. Four is four, six is six, and eleven remains eleven, whether one measures beads, quarts, minutes, or holes. Growth of this kind is unquestionably helped to fruition by appropriate experiences. But it cannot be forced by training, because it is not possible to train for understanding. One can train for rote repetition; one can help understanding to grow in its own time and style only by offering the experiences which convey the idea.

The understanding of number is at first functional and not verbal, which is the point where some sixes and more sevens find themselves. This means that a child can do things with numbers in a variety of first-hand situations, yet is not able to explain what he did too clearly in words. For example, he may readily perceive the difference in size of two pieces of a candy bar, but not be able to explain the meaning of equality. His grasp is at first limited to familiar experiences, such as the size of portions among siblings, the matching of numbers of presents at holiday time, the numbers of new versus old toys, and so on. He develops a general framework of concepts about distance (far, near), length (long, short), area (big, small), pace of moving bodies (fast, slow), notion of distance traveled (miles), speed of time (minutes), succession (first dinner, then ice cream), durability, and simultaneity. As he grasps the non-concrete reality and durability of so abstract a concept as a number, he grows increasingly able to manipulate numbers and to recognize the relationship between parts and wholes within a unit he recognizes as a unit. That is, as he understands that three is a concept of "three-ness," regardless of whether the number is applied to weight (pounds), height (feet), length (inches), volume (quart), quantity (objects), he not only recognizes that three is three, no matter how applied, but that it remains three even when reduced to one, one, and one; to one and two; or two and one.

Thus, a child learns to retain the meaning of number despite the seductiveness of shape, size, or spacing. He can maneuver within the unit, because he can perceive the parts as consonant with the unit, grasping a true part-to-whole relation. At this point, he is ready to see relationships among and between numbers. He can differentiate between cardinal (one, two, three), and ordinal (first, second, third), and understand serial arrangements well enough to know that two comes before three and after one. Each number preserves its own character as the child learns its varied relationships with other numbers. Children achieve this operational facility with number generally between the ages of six and a half and eight, starting with the lower numbers, which they can handle more easily in their minds. This timing is likely to hold good even if they have learned to count to much higher numbers long before six or seven.

Relationship is itself a concept which must be understood before it can be meaningful within such an abstraction as a number. Children learn about relationship, however, long before they enter the primary grades, because they have experienced the relationship of socks to feet, food to hunger, and money to toys. At school they may be asked to formulate pictorial representation of experienced relationships they can understand—for example, a picture and then a graph of the children who stay for lunch and the children who do not; a graph showing how many birthdays there are in each month; a drawing of all the toys in a boy's room and all the items in a mother's pocketbook; a drawing of children on bikes, and children on sleds. The concept of relationship leads to a sense of group, which has already begun with the primary group every child knows best—his own family. Sensing relationship and group makes possible the sorting of objects. There are many games and exercises through which sorting and the formation of groups of items having similar characteristics can take place. All of this is on a concrete level, that is, it is done with things (or people). Sorting grows more complex (and a little less concrete) as children are asked to group all the dolls which are girls and need their clothes washed in one pile, and all the dolls which are boys and need new clothes in another pile. Slowly, the mathematical notion of a set—a group which shares certain characteristics (concrete or abstract)—emerges, and children can conceive of a set as a unit in spite of the fact that a set may consist of several objects or people.

The correspondence of numerical relationships follows, such as one cup for each child, one dime for each candy bar, and so on. Correspondence is pursued further to include more than one-to-one correspondence. "We each have two eyes, two ears, two legs, two feet, two arms, and two hands," the chart says. "Each child may have six crayons," says the teacher, and eventually the understanding will grow that five pennies correspond to one nickel, ten pennies to one dime, and ten dimes to one dollar.

Children put things in order—all the long blocks go on the bottom shelf, all the crayons go into the shallow boxes. But ordering goes further, to establishing size place on a line, to reproducing a line of shapes in the same order and then backwards, to putting pictures into sequence so that they tell a story. The concept of groups and ordering leads to the concept of inclusion—there are seven animals, of which four are horses, and three are dogs; there are twenty children, but only nine boys. These mathematical concepts, which make it possible for us to deal with our environment, have to be discovered anew by each generation of children. Making the discoveries at the stage when they are ready to understand and assimilate their meaning makes it possible to deal with them operationally, that is, with flexibility.

For some reason, addition comes more easily to children than subtraction, perhaps because subtraction involves a third and intruding element in the mathematical operation. Thus, in adding one to three as one builds to four, three remains stable. But if, to arrive at four, one subtracts one from five, then the knowledge that five is greater than four and comes after four in serial order must be understood before one can understand the equation three plus one is equivalent to five minus one. It all looks so simple!

Mechanical facility in addition and subtraction is not sufficient for grasping the meaning of division, multiplication, and fractions, and mechanical mastery, such as, for example, of the multiplication tables, is valuable only insofar as the mechanical aids are truly tools for carrying out one's understanding of concepts in the first place. Accuracy in computation comes quickly enough once there is real understanding of number.

Yet human computational accuracy in the age of the computer is hardly as significant as the understanding of the mathematical laws and relationships that can put the computer to work making order out of a welter of computational detail.

The mathematics materials in a contemporary classroom for the primary years must take into account the nature of the children's stage of growth, their dependency on concrete operations, their movement toward symbolic expression of their understanding, and the importance of allowing them to discover for themselves the truth of mathematical conception. Paper and pencil are hardly sufficient for this kind of learning. Quite the opposite, premature use of symbols leads to confusion. Take as an example the symbol for equal, =, which many of us learned to use to represent both "the same as" and "adds up to," i.e., one and one are the same, one and one add up to two. When we say that one and one are equal, that might or might not be true: one yard is not equal to one foot, one boy is not the same as one girl, and one gerbil plus one hamster does not add up to two gerbils. Thus, the important first learning is not the symbols for numbers and operations, but the understanding of the concepts they represent. When these are clear, and children have shown themselves able to handle the concepts in a variety of practical ways with efficiency, then, and only then, does it make sense to translate these concepts into symbolic form and use the symbols for the operations. Then children need a good deal of practice to stabilize the understanding, because they can still get lost among the unfamiliar symbols for the relationships. Greater precision and variety have been introduced into the language and the signs used in early mathematics, and some of them may be quite unfamiliar to adults whose last math lesson was longer ago than they care to remember.

This and the longer period of concrete operations may delay the appearance of familiar-looking mathematical symbols and examples and cause a parent to wonder what's going on. But the long-range results of this approach have proven the worth of the apparent delay. The sense of helplessness about math is over for many young people now. Girls as well as boys find math exciting and challenging, when they are allowed to make discoveries at their own rate of developing abilities.

Children need materials that encourage them to manipulate, order serially, count, contrast, construct, and reorganize deliberately or accidentally. The fact that they make discoveries does not mean that the teacher does no preparation. On the contrary, in addition to materials and equipment with which children can experiment, there are the tasks and challenges the teacher places before them to tackle individually as they are ready, but in sufficient variation of level so that every child has interesting problems to solve at whatever level of thinking he finds himself. This means that the math program, like the reading, must be individualized, with children working away at their own speed and without the pressure of time or grades to force them prematurely into shallowness and haste compounded by competition and anxiety.

In one sense, a similar approach to learning during the primary years runs through all the three Rs—reading, writing, and arithmetic—and that is a dual approach that guards the recognition of concepts during the period when the mechanical aspects are being painstakingly learned. As children learn the skills of decoding, they should be hearing stories and poems to keep alive for them the reason why they are struggling with letters and sounds. As children laboriously form letters of the alphabet and put them together to make words, they should be telling stories to their teacher or onto tape, so that the reason for writing will be quite apparent. And as children take on the writing of numbers, they must be clear about the meaning of number, the meaning of relationships among numbers, and the meaning of order and sequence in mathematics in practical implementation in their daily lives. Only as they recognize the meaningfulness of the skill, will the chore aspects take on the relation of necessary parts to an understood whole.

Eight to Eleven:
The Intermediate Years
. . .

In the 1950s there appeared a charming book about the middle years of childhood called *Where Did You Go, Out. What Did You Do, Nothing.*[1] In that small volume the author captured the essence of the middle years of childhood as most people then remembered them—years in which a special aura of magic hung over living and especially over the self-directed, out-of-school learning called play. The magic embodied a never again to be achieved sense of irresponsibility without guilt that permitted the free-wheeling activities of childhood. Enthusiastic and loving preplanning went into games, plays, and productive use of materials, yet all the organization and planning could be abandoned with equal enthusiasm when imagination called for spur-of-the-moment exploration and experimentation. Long hours of patient effort went into projects, yet there always seemed time for musing and dreaming. Make-believe had a quality of reality, but children knew the dif-

[1] Robert Paul Smith, *Where Did You Go, Out. What Did You Do, Nothing* (New York: W. W. Norton & Co., 1957).

ference and honored it. When they returned home from play, they reverted to non-committal, but obviously relaxed, behavior. They turned to the chores of home and school with more or less compliance, but never with the same zest they gave to their self-directed activities. Adults acknowledged more or less philosophically that the anticipation of being free to play after school was the spur for many a reluctant scholar to carry on through dullness and drudgery to the three o'clock bell. Such was the way of childhood—assumed by all, including those who saw it as regrettable, to be natural and inevitable.

There were, in those days, some schools and some teachers who utilized children's capacities for imaginative play and productive effort in developing their curriculum for the intermediate grades. For years, such schools and such teachers worked with happy, eager children in a mutually satisfying learning milieu. For a long time, there have also been parents who believed that if only all schools would involve children in their own true style of living and learning, much unnecessary heartache and wasteful frustration could be avoided. But while there is still much to say for this view, in the last decade or so something has been happening to children which is making it very difficult to develop a curriculum in which children of the middle years can feel seriously invested, even in schools which try to do just that. Quite aside from the obvious fact that the volume of knowledge has increased and information grows out of date at an amazing rate, Smith's book about the children has a nostalgic ring of datedness in certain important ways of a very different kind. Recent changes in child behavior make Smith's description somewhat unreal when applied unilaterally to the contemporary American child.

Too many of today's children of the middle years do not play after school or enjoy the pleasures of making and shaping things out of raw materials. Far from being organizers of self-directed activities, they are more likely to be organized and directed in a series of lessons in art, music, dance, religious instruction, scouts, television schedules, and homework that leave very little time for interests of their own choice.

This, however, is not the heart of the change we are concerned about. Over-scheduling can be readily rectified, if parents see the importance of free time for their children. Far more serious is the appearance of something quite new for this stage of life, something appearing in schools and among children who would ordinarily be considered the most fortunate in terms of opportunity to develop. It is the growing number of children who demand quick and easy gratification in whatever they undertake, have little patience with themselves or with a task, and show poor persistence in the face of failure. The child of nine or ten who once openly preferred play to formal school and chores at home, who responded to tasks with indifference, resistance, or a "get-it-over-with-fast" attitude, is not the child we are talking about. For such children, reluctant responses to the demands of home and school were expected; more importantly, they had little carry-over to the energy and pleasure with which the same children undertook to make a snow fort, build a shack in the woods or on a city lot, put on a play, or make clothes for dolls. No, it is not this child we mean. The new phenomenon is one in which children resist the effort it takes to be productive on *child terms*. These are children who are seldom enthusiastic; they complain, instead, of boredom and indifference. Their attitude toward life is unenthusiastic; little they do gives them unabashed pleasure. Their teachers say they suffer from ennui. At the same time, among these and other children, the reluctance to accept adult authority, which was always characteristic of this stage (Tom Sawyer is the exemplar), seems to have taken on a new quality. The children argue for their rights with a stubborn persistence and cold logic which often ends up evading morality or resisting recognition of the feelings of others in the resolution of conflicts with both children and adults. For example, a child who hits another in the face with a snowball is urged by the teacher to avoid hitting people in the face. The child not only fails to acknowledge the restriction, but goes on to outline the reasons why he had to hit, although the adult is arguing for not hitting *in the face*. The talk goes on on both sides, but the two do not meet on common ground. It is as though concern for people's feelings and recognition of a mutually beneficial code of right and wrong are not relevant aspects to children who argue tenaciously for their own wants and desires. "Words become a tool to undo the adult," is how one weary teacher put it.

The appearance, even minimally, of boredom and excessive protest against socially necessary limits on individual behavior among children who are offered every opportunity to grow and develop as individuals carries a particular weight when one looks at a trend among seventeen-year-olds from white affluent families who were studied over two decades by Dr. Douglas Heath of Haverford College. Over the twenty-year period, Dr. Heath found a trend within this age group toward deepening passivity and boredom, pervasive feelings of loneliness, emphasis on "my thing" and "nowness," dethronement of traditional academic authorities, and increased use of drugs. Yet, during the same period, he could see little change in the quality of parent-child relationships or in the emotional tone within families.

Serious as the adolescent problem is, it becomes more serious, and perhaps even cause for alarm, when attitudes and behavior similar to those of these adolescents appear during the stage of childhood which the noted psychologist, Erik Erikson so aptly described as the "Age of Industry," [2] i.e., of keen interest and intense involvement with materials and activity. Speculation about the causes for such changes in ever younger children points to the influence of society itself, rather than of the individual home. It suggests that ennui and cynicism among young children may not remain an isolated, transitory phenomenon, if our dominant social values remain unchanged. Dr. Heath believes that American families are now so subject to outside influences that they cannot function as readily as they once did as stable value centers for their children. It is his view that the role of the mass media in a culture given to sensa-

[2] Erik Erikson, *Childhood and Society* (New York: W. W. Norton & Co., 1950).

tionalism combined with the excessive academic pressures that were inspired by Sputnik are the two major factors responsible for the trends he observed. Certainly, few children have ever been so passive in their recreation and so pressured in their learning during early childhood as ours are. But there are other facets of the society that may be equally responsible and bear examining.

Our children are growing up in a society quite consciously and deliberately geared to planned obsolescence and constant replacement of goods. They are directed early by advertising appeals to become consumers. They experience the titillating vision of an endless stream of new inventions for their pleasure, along with the inevitable frustration of toys that do not last. Implicit in a policy of planned obsolescence is a subtle warning not lost on children, a warning not to invest themselves too deeply in the things they play with, nor take too long while they're about it. Whatever planned obsolescence may have done for the economy, there is a good chance that it has involuntarily helped to rob children of the middle years, who have normally been impelled toward imaginative and productive effort, of societal support for their creative use of materials and spontaneously developed play. Since this happens to be one of the ways by which children gain the satisfying conviction that they are competent human beings, the loss is serious. It is made even more serious by the growing shortage of alternatives to adult supervision and control available to the children. Urbanization, tight scheduling, and the pressure to achieve at school have together limited the possibilities for children to test their ingenuity and capacities in their own way and on their own terms. In other times, children could turn to the physical challenges and resources available in country settings and city lots when they had free time. Joining others who were older and younger in the informal camaraderie of childhood, they learned from each other and taught each other the special heritage of childhood games and lore which have been passed on from child generation to child generation outside the orbit of adult direction. According to Iona and Peter Opie, who have made two separate, careful studies of children's play activities, street games are disappearing, although they represent a childhood tradition that goes back to at least the time of the Romans. The speed with which basic changes of this kind are taking place is startlingly apparent in a comparison of the introductory remarks to both works of the Opies—a time space of a mere ten years. In 1959, in the introduction to their first volume, *The Lore and Language of Childhood*, the Opies wrote:

> No matter how uncouth school children may outwardly appear, they are tradition's warmest friends. Like the savage, they are respecters, even venerators, of custom; and in their self-contained community their basic lore and language seem scarcely to alter from generation to generation. . . . The same continuity obtains in their games and play songs.[3]

In their volume on *Children's Games in Streets and Playground*,[4] published in 1969, the Opies were no longer able to deal assuredly with the comfortable sense of continuity and stability in children's style of life. They go so far as to place the blame for the prevalence of so much angry, antisocial childhood behavior on the failure of adults to understand or provide for children's life-strengthening need to rely on themselves and their own resources, even under the new social conditions of mechanization and built-up cities. A little thought will show that in the lives of American children who are old enough to play independently, away from the eyes of supervising adults, neither communities nor schools have in any major way recognized, much less compensated for, the losses suffered by this stage of childhood in the change-over from natural to urban environments. Although this change leaves increasing numbers

---

[3] Peter and Iona Opie, *The Lore and Language of Childhood* (London: Oxford University Press, 1959), p. 16.

[4] Peter and Iona Opie, *Children's Games in Streets and Playground* (London: Oxford University Press, 1969).

of potentially self-directed children bereft of the materials and settings they have used since time immemorial to carry out their life style of action and productivity, almost nowhere in organized society does one see awareness of the problem the children face. Such response as there is defeats the children's needs. Children's play activity is organized by adults according to adult ground rules; children's responses are controlled and codified according to adult values of competition and rewards. The effect is to further cut children off from the internally motivated and intrinsically satisfying work and play that is their lifeline to growth. The Opies, from their British vantage point, place focus on an interesting comment in this connection, quoting Carl Withers:

> It is to be wondered whether middle-class children in the United States will ever reach maturity, whose "play-time has become almost as completely organized and supervised as their study."

It is obvious that the pace of our lives and the pressure to achieve leave no room for such slow-to-complete, old-fashioned, out-of-school tasks as whittling, knitting, making a cross-stitch sampler, or building a wagon out of broken boxes, carriage wheels, and pieces of wood. In and of themselves, these may not seem serious losses in an age of mass manufacture. But we do have to ask, with serious concern, what is replacing, for children who desperately need it, the kind of slowly developing experience through which challenge is met and conquered, and through which failure is overcome by self-effort. This quality of experience affects the power to cope, basic character structure, and intrinsic sense of self-worth. With so much in their lives prepackaged and done for them (as it is for their parents, too), where are the experiences through which children growing to maturity learn that doing is fraught with uncertainty, but wonderfully rewarding when brought to completion by one's own efforts?

A further aspect of the problem of non-investment and non-involvement in what is meaningful, is the real, if as yet unacknowledged, truth that there is no place for children or youth in the functioning of a highly mechanized society, where even adults find it hard to sense themselves as individuals who count. Child labor laws designed to be protective in one era have become a means of cutting children off completely from participation in the economy of another, although the conditions of life and work are quite different from what they were before. Nor is responsibility at home the answer. Longer years of schooling, large-scale social organization of tasks formerly done at home, and the extensive use of mechanical aids have made children's contribution to the economy of the home completely non-vital in most cases. Making one's own bed is not comparable to work in less mechanized eras. Children who chopped wood, darned socks, cleaned the fireplace, milked cows, hung wash, or watched the younger children, undoubtedly resented and complained about their chores. But what they were doing was essential and made them genuine contributors to the necessities of survival. This dimension of reality is experienced by fewer and fewer of today's children, except for the poorest. For them, the responsibility for survival needs, in combination with other factors of poverty, is as often an overwhelming burden of oppression as it is a positive factor for growth. Realistically speaking, the chores that the child in most homes once did are not necessary in a modern home. The created chores are, by contrast, quite thin.

Everyone is aware that a qualitative change has taken place in our style of life. But the pervasiveness of the impact on childhood has yet to be fully assessed. A recent study compared the professed ideals of elementary school children at the turn of the century with those of the same age now.[5] The children were asked to describe the person they would most want to be like when they grew up. The ideal person could be some-

[5] Thomas H. Hawkes, "An Empirical-Historical Study of Changing Ideals of Upper Elementary School Children." Unpublished paper presented at the annual meeting of the American Educational Research Association, Minneapolis, Minnesota, March, 1970.

one real, imaginary, or fictional, and they were also to tell why they chose the person. The contrasts between 1902 and 1969 were revealing.

In 1902, the children's models were historical figures of virtue (for example, George Washington, Abraham Lincoln). In the 1930s and 1940s, the models were contemporary political figures of virtue, such as Lindbergh and Franklin Delano Roosevelt. In 1969, the heroic models were figures from the entertainment and sports worlds. At the turn of the century, children were more likely to give intrinsic qualities of character as something to aspire to, but in the later study children of the same age chose as first and second choice for emulation those who had attained possessions and position.

Since the child population studied in 1969 included black as well as white children and ones from slums as well as from the suburbs, it can be assumed that the ideals chosen by the contemporary children indicate a social-cultural influence that cuts across all segments of society and is not a reflection of class or family bias alone. The shift from figures in history to figures known in one's own time can be explained easily enough by the prevalence of modern mass media in children's lives. But the switch to possessions and position rather than qualities of character as ideals worth striving for seems to be a reflection of the values of our mobile society, in which material wealth and possessions are the mark of individual achievement, and power in the world is the status role of the nation.

A comparison of a different kind also suggests some possible effects of the changes in society. This was a study that compared the hero in nineteenth-century folk and tall tales still read by contemporary eight-year-olds with the twentieth-century hero in comic books, also read by present day eight-year-olds.[6] The hero of the folk and tall tales (for example, Paul

[6] Judith Rosenthal, "Similarities and Differences Between Heroes of Folk Stories and Tales and Heroes of Comic Books." Unpublished Master's Thesis, Bank Street College of Education, 1970.

Bunyan, Joe Magarac, or John Henry) achieved power by the use of his own brain and brawn. He was ingenious and inventive and, although his physical capacities proved bigger than life, his talents were rooted in human abilities. He could run faster, climb higher, dig more iron ore, or fell more trees than the average man, but his characteristics were the characteristics of flesh-and-blood men. This suits the life style of the middle years child as we have known it. But the comic books, which first appeared around the turn of the century, deal with a hero with a very different set of competencies. The comic book hero can be male or female—surely a reflection of social change—but his power is not attained through personal strength or ingenuity. It is attained primarily through magic and with the help of the supernatural. At the same time, the comic book hero is a dual personality. In real life, he is likely to be meek, conventional, and dependent; when he puts on a disguise he attains superhuman powers. With these powers, he can go through walls, dispense with enemies against overwhelming odds, and perhaps alter the very direction of the earth's revolution on its axis by his use of magic.

For children at a stage when personal competencies of the adult type are strongly desired, and the power to function on their own is only painfully achieved, there is normal impatience with the tortuously slow bit-by-bit learning that ultimately adds up to competency. The world of fantasy is still compelling, and the superhuman hero, like the folk tale or the fairy tale hero, undoubtedly provides the needed escape from internal and external pressures that all people, including children, need. There is surely nothing new about magic wands and magic potions and magic swords to ease the frustration of having only limited human abilities for coping with daily problems. But fantasy serves a healthy purpose in childhood only when it exists in a total experience of reality-testing. When children grow up in a society of push-button magic, where the concern for their deep need to develop as human beings is ignored by the social structure, then faith in magic solutions to problems may be the only answer to helplessness. An inability to invest oneself in effort may be a logical result.

In a society as large, non-intimate, and technologically advanced as ours has become, where the mind and muscle of the individual seem increasingly less potent in the face of machines because of the impersonal organization of society, the message of the supernatural hero may be differently interpreted from the way it would be in another setting. Instead of offering a harmless release from tension and responsibility, such a hero may reinforce a sense of powerlessness in children who are deprived by society's indifference of sufficient opportunities to test and strengthen themselves in challenges related to their own internal motivation and physical needs as growing children. It is tempting to speculate whether the normal drive for competency and skill in living is petering out in the dead end of the Superman myth of magic as children are beginning more and more to find the answer to challenge in fantasy instead of in the experience of finding solutions through physical effort, hard thought, and persistence in tasks they choose for themselves. In a society where the elders bemoan dehumanization and alienation, we must ask whether children of the middle years who leave the protected boundaries of the family to function more on their own are being seduced into dreams of unrealistic and unattainable power because there is no way for them to achieve genuine competency in life-size, childhood ways. Is this the meaning of the drug culture which is creeping down to destroy younger and younger children? Is it a factor behind the excessive resistance to limits placed on their desires?

We can neither bemoan the past nor return to its more difficult survival modes for the sake of accommodating the children. But we must begin to face the fact that there is not enough in modern urban society that replaces for the child of the middle years what has been lost—a world in which a child can grow as a child. Add to this the special effect of exposure to grown-ups and youth who are questioning every formerly stable area of life, and we can begin to see possible causes for the change in the very nature of childhood. When behavior that is distressingly unfulfilling and destructive of the human spirit moves down to younger and younger ages in society, as seems to be happening, then there is much for parents to think about in dealing with their still formative children.

There is a tendency among some people to blame the unhappy state of so many of our children and youth on the "permissiveness" of parents. They even find a scapegoat in the benign and utterly reasonable Dr. Spock, who asked only that children be accorded the respect and dignity every human being ought to have. But the evidence is strong that blaming parents is an oversimplification. Parents as well as children are caught in the same web of skewed priorities that runs through the nation, in which people are simply not valued as highly as material goods and profit. We must recognize before it is too late that under such a hierarchy children are being seduced into a consumer instead of a producer outlook on life far too early for their healthy development, almost as though they must be made to pay their way in the system as a price for being. They are becoming cogs in the wheel of social efficiency and big business operation. A cursory look at the intrusion into their school lives of materials and curriculas devised and sold in quantity by powerful advertising rather than by thoughtful appraisal at the local level of what children need reveals how much they are being manipulated to satisfy these skewed priorities.

Fortunately, the home experience still seems to be the most salient and persistent one for most children, especially in areas related to self-feeling and inter-personal relationships. To a large extent children of the middle years are at a point where they repeat their parents' concepts as though they were their own, as children have always done. But the environmental influences are powerful, and parents must begin to recognize and understand the dynamics of the children's growth needs if they are to withstand prevailing values.

Because there are no dramatic physical changes through most of the middle years, and the emotional outbursts of early childhood have on the whole toned down, the period from eight to eleven gives an outward appearance of steadiness. By contrast with the turbulence of the pre-school years and the turbulence of the adolescence to come, this is true enough. But it is, in fact, a period during which the children must face and try to master alone or with other children many tasks which are full of conflict for them and have far-reaching implications for their adulthood. Although there is both struggle and suffering in such learning, the children can, and do, take great pleasure in meeting the challenges and overcoming them when the conditions of support are right.

The Major Developmental Tasks

Three important areas of value-laden growth deepen and take form during the middle years: the moral and ethical growth associated with carrying out one's responsibilities to oneself and to others in the course of social interaction; the attitudes and behaviors associated with assimilation of the sex role assigned to males and females in society; and the style and quality of learning by which one grows increasingly objective and realistic about the external world. Growth in all these areas is somewhat more complicated for today's children than in some other historical periods, because stability must be achieved while the adult society is being shaken by attacks in each of these areas. Although every aspect of growth is intertwined with every other and all undergo clarification and refinement during the middle years, they can be examined separately for better understanding of what is happening to the children.

Selfhood

The major thrust in the middle years of childhood is toward increasing freedom from adult authority and direction. This task must be accomplished, however, while remaining safe and secure in a nub of adult protection and acceptance—a difficult task for child and adult. To grow into mature adulthood, it is obvious that a child must develop some preferences, interests, values, likes, and dislikes that he does *not* share with adults, something which most adults would concede to be quite reasonable. In order to accomplish this, children's feelings of dependency on adults, and their attitudes toward adults as godlike creatures, must continue to change, or they will not ultimately be free of subordinate child status.   In the adult-child relationship, differing styles of protesting any interference with their pleasure shift now to doubting adult authority, without, however, rejecting it out of hand. As they learn to handle by themselves an increasing number of formerly adult-protected activities, such as crossing streets or facing on their own the consequences of their actions at school and among friends, they slowly develop the confidence and the courage to begin the process of undermining adult domination of their behavior. At eight, they no longer hang on the approval of adults with such passion as they once did, and they grow reserved in their responses. By ten, they may be subtly insulting. The following instances are to the point:

In a classroom of nine and ten year olds, the children, angry at their teacher because of her choice of social studies, greeted her one morning with a poster that reflected age and stage feelings, even though these were in a contemporary mode:

> KID POWER
> White is beautiful
> Black is beautiful
> Kids is beautiful.

In a fifth-grade class, where the children were a year older, a visitor observing the dissection of a fish suddenly had a fish eye thrust under her nose, simultaneous with a mocking, "Here, have a fish eye." "Thank you," the startled visitor replied. "I really don't want a fish eye." "Tough," was the laconic reply, as the boy shrugged his shoulders and ambled off without the slightest show of feeling. Later that same morning, however, the first group of children settled down without any resistance to their assigned tasks and, in the second class, the same child came with perfectly good manners and pleasantness to invite the visitor to stay for lunch. Contradictions of this kind are common; they grow out of a basic source of conflict during the middle years which children feel, but adults have difficulty recognizing. To satisfy the need for independent thought and action, the children must acquire the skills and techniques of the adult world. Under normal circumstances, they look forward to these with eagerness. Paradoxically, however, the people who can best help them attain the necessary skills and techniques they need are the very ones from whom the children are struggling to free themselves emotionally. Thus, their growth need to be self-directed comes into conflict with their childhood need for sufficient adult control and authority to allow them to feel safe and taken care of.

Despite the basic urge to separate themselves from adults, they turn happily to those they can trust when they need to. Eleven-year-old Sarah wrote her teacher in confidence:

> Kevin is a brat! Each day he starts tripping over my books or myself, he always has his arm on my desk when I'm trying to work and so I ask, "Kevin, please get off!" and he doesn't. I ask again and again, so nothing happens. Finally, I either 1) pull my desk away, 2) yell, 3) tell you. I know the last two aren't such good ideas, but he's always bugging me!
>
>   I don't know what you can do, but could you please try and do *something?* Thanks, Diane.

They push into the family conversation at the same time that their requirement for privacy takes on new forms. They turn a poker face to adults who seek to sense their feelings, or reply with a noncommittal "Fine," to questions about their achievements. Yet they enjoy chatting with adults when they are in the mood. They ask, "Do I have to sit here?" "Do I have to take a bath?" "Do I have to wear those clothes when we go to Grandma's?" And then they comply with sudden unexpectedness.

Group Alignment

In coping with the need to sustain and strengthen their sense of themselves as individuals, children now turn to other children as natural allies in a common cause. They band together to establish themselves as the coming generation, separate from that of their parents. Conformity to their generation in dress, language, taste, codes, and activities becomes axiomatic, and child allies support each other in a whole range of ideas, values, and standards that are often contradictory to those of the parents. The first serious challenge of parental authority thus begins with children hurling their newly-discovered gang outlook against their parents' standards and expectations.

The task of becoming a member of the peer group is not without its trials. The child who does not have a pleasant way with others, skills to offer, or the right techniques of relating, can suffer cruel treatment, rejection, and even scorn at the hands of otherwise very nice children. The fortunate ones are shaky enough as they start group life to fall back on scapegoating as one way of strengthening their own sense of being "in." It takes confidence and inner certainty to be open and welcoming to outsiders. At eight and nine, responses are as likely to be primitive as civilized.

Once a child is "in," there are problems intrinsic to survival which must be tackled and resolved. The peer world is one of rules, not only the obvious rules for games, but the special non-adult rules that govern life in general. These rules must be believed in and acted upon for true participation and acceptance. Rules imply consideration and feelings for others ("Always get chocolate ice cream for Nancy, she loves it"), along with obligations toward others ("You promised to bring the mitt. Where is it?"). There is open discussion of faults, and those who disobey rules are punished. In child-sponsored groups, there is a no-nonsense quality to learning the art of relating to others.

Children test and stretch themselves in constructive competition and cooperation. Unless they are seriously ill-equipped to begin with, or the chance of negative factors stacking against them is unusually harsh, they learn and grow. Within the group, individuals play different parts, sometimes jockeying for leadership in initiating activities, and at other times learning how to anticipate other people's reactions. There is learning of the fine art of compromise and a growing sensitivity to the unique qualities of individuals. The competition can be exhilarating and the cooperation rewarding. But both can be painful, too, as the burgeoning sense of individuality which causes children to question adult authority must be protected as well from the encroachment of other children and the tyranny of the group, even when the demand for group conformity is strongest.

Some of the rules are learned through the formation of clubs. Just as, every spring, someone thinks it is a great idea to sell something, and makeshift stalls of comic books or drinks appear on city streets, so among eight-year-olds someone inevitably dreams up a club. That dreamer usually designates himself as the President and convinces at least one other child to join. Even a two-member private club then sets down rules in writing, thereby giving them authority and status:

RULES

Never tell anyone about our club.
Always have meetings in rooms where there are no other people.
Meet Saturday—2 o'clock.
Ronnie can't belong.

The initial club is shortlived. Like the paramecium, it divides, and new clubs are started, with the original members each a president. The question of dues is argued and debated. By the time a decision is reached as to a proper amount, the club has served its purpose, and disintegrates over the insoluble question of what to do with the dues once they are collected.

The continuous formation of clubs and gangs leads many children to a level of social development they did not have when they started. Sensitivity grows to the existence of hierarchy and structure within and among groups, and children begin to sense the way in which they are perceived by others in that hierarchy. New forms of groupness are called for as they discover that the rights of individuals must mesh with the needs of the group. Democracy and social need are vaguely grasped as the children decide in time that the President ought to be *elected* and that the Treasurer ought to be someone who can add and subtract with some accuracy.

Turning outward from the family to enjoy greater equality than the parent-child relationship at that stage can possibly offer, the children commit themselves to helping each other find the way through the morass of considerations that accompany increasing intimacy and sharing among equals. "What shall I do to get what I want?" takes on the new tone of, "How can I please my friend, and how can I make him feel good about himself?" This is nowhere clearer than in elections of class leaders at school. All the children know, even if the teacher doesn't, that voting is by blocs of friends rather than by completely objective criteria. The adult may speak of aptitude for the role, but the children tally up their strength in terms of who can be counted on in the voting.

The friendships fluctuate, fickleness persists, but increasing stability appears in the friendships children value so highly. A few become the basis of lifelong relationships. Secrets are shared with dramatic seriousness and violated readily in the early stages of group commitment. Loyalty is a hard-won concept that makes its appearance closer to the end than the beginning of this stage and is then taken very seriously.

Small friendship groups develop norms of their own, a common lingo, common jokes, rituals, secret handshakes, secret languages, and their own unique flavor. While a major aspect of all the secrecy is the establishment of a child world separate from adults, it is also a mechanism by which a self-selected group establishes its identity even in the child world.

The conflictual nature, as well as depth, of the kinds of personal problems children must work out with each other is poignantly expressed by an eight-year-old who was rooting for his friend, Danny, during a ball game, even though Danny was from another third grade class and on the opposing team. "You have to be loyal to your team, Adam," his classmates argued. "But I *like* Danny," protested Adam. "You can like him out of the game," they told him, "but you must cheer for your classmates." Utterly confused, Adam could only say uncomprehendingly, "But I like him all the time."

At another level, a conflict of similar depth in the inter-personal realm was revealed in two letters from a fifth-grader to her teacher:

Dear Mrs. Simpson,

   Lisa has been treating me like dirt. Maybe it is my imagination, but it seems like everything she says to me is meant to hurt me. I do not know what to do. If I tell her how I feel she will probably dislike me even more and maybe get the others to make me feel uncomfortable. Do you think she does it on purpose? I feel better now that I've told somebody about it. What do you think I should do?

Kate

Dear Mrs. Simpson,

   I have solved Lisa without even talking to her. I now know I could talk to her. Even if she did run to the other girls they would ignore her. I like the other girls a great deal and Lisa will probably get over it. If she doesn't I will have to remember she is not the only one in the world.

K.

Morality and Ethics

The conflict of belonging and the dilemmas of relating occur in an expanding web of moral and ethical considerations, as developmental readiness and family and societal values now meet.

Adult rules learned by rote must be transformed into an internal sense of morality. According to Kohlberg,[7] who studied the development of moral thought across cultures, there is a sequence of stages in the grasp of moral concept through which all people pass, regardless of their cultural background or religious training. Gaps between moral understanding and moral action are characteristic of the maturing process.

As children grow, they change from the pre-moral level of the very young child, who responds to expectations of his parents for good or bad behavior completely out of fear of punishment or fear of losing their love, to taking on the pious morality of the conformer, with a certain pleasure in being good and acceptable to the admired adults. Prior to puberty, there is still a literal practicality which does not quite reveal the principled motivation adults hope for in children who do not yet sense the special importance of humans. Kohlberg, for example, asked a ten-year-old, "Is it better to save the life of one important person or a lot of unimportant people." The child answered, "All the people that aren't important, because one man just has one house, maybe a lot of furniture, but a whole bunch of people have an awful lot of furniture, and some of those poor people might have a lot of money, and it doesn't look it." If this sounds like undiluted American materialism, here is a similar response from some children in a village in Taiwan. Boys between ten and thirteen were told a story involving a theft of food and asked for their view of the matter. "A man's wife is starving to death, but the store owner won't give the man any food unless he can pay, which he can't. Should he break in and steal some food? Why?" Many of the boys said, "He should steal the food for his wife, because if she dies he'll have to pay for her funeral, and that costs a lot."

The capacity to conceptualize in terms of what is right and what is wrong is a process that develops separate from the spe-

[7] L. Kohlberg, "The Development of Moral Character and Ideology," in Martin and Louis Hoffman (eds.), *Review of Child Psychology*, V. I. Russell Sage Foundation, 1964. Also, "The Child as a Moral Philosopher," *Psychology Today*, September, 1968, pp. 25–30.

cific values to which right and wrong become attached. Growth in moral behavior in general follows a zigzagging path from self-interest to social responsibility. The tattling of the seven-year-old turns to unswerving loyalty and contempt for the informer by nine and ten; the wily cheating of the younger child gives way to demands for fairness from everybody, children and adults alike. Up to about ten or eleven, children everywhere seem to interpret right and wrong in terms of physical consequences or in terms of the physical power of the authorities who define good and bad for them. But at some point during that period, a developmental shift in the capacity to think in objective, rather than subjective, terms about matters that impinge upon them makes it possible for children to perceive the expectations and rules of the family, group, or nation as making sense in their own right. The process of internalizing such expectations as a code by which to live then begins. The former concern with conforming in order to avoid punishment or gain praise becomes concern with maintaining, supporting, and justifying the established order. The equating of things with people is open to new evaluation of priorities. On a personal level, they grow ready to replace a primitive "You scratch my back and I'll scratch yours" attitude with concepts of loyalty and justice. The team comes into its own during that period, because children can begin to deal with the laws of social necessity and justice as *principles*. Principles justify the subordination of individual desires to the well-being of the group as a whole, whereas, on a personal level, one could not allow such subordination to individuals and keep one's self-respect.

As they make principles their own, children grow very severe with offenders. A touch of the zealot conceals the uncertain faith they have in their power to live by principle. Adults who believe in children's independent decision-making often have to protect them from their own extremism toward each other when they become crusaders for the right. "An eye for an eye" is still an appealing philosophy at this stage and merges easily with newly formed concepts of fairness. The deeper compassion and social responsibility for others that is the highest morality must wait for further maturing. It stands a better chance of emerging if the conflict between moral judgment and moral behavior gets adult help and support in the direction of principles rather than expediency.

In the meantime, such matters as law and individual rights, attitudes toward ethnic and religious differences, toward national pride and in-group, out-group prejudice also enter the orbit of children's concern and beginning opinion. The world beyond the family comes to include not only the peer world, but the customs and attitudes of the nation, and, even beyond that, ideals embodied in literary and historic figures of the past. Children struggle to grasp relationships, meanings, and values in increasingly more subtle realms of thinking and judgment. They look with sharp eyes at the motivation as well as the behavior and attitudes of the adults who surround them; they idealize heroes of the past and present. Specific social attitudes become internalized, and moral issues can be resolved in terms of social fabric, not inner psyche alone.

Moral Development in Our Time

Thus, the process of moral development reaches a critical period during the middle years of childhood as children begin to come to terms with the meaning of moral and ethical thought and conduct. These are the years during which society's expectations take shape in children's thinking and feeling, and social attitudes coalesce in a rising crescendo of commitment to the values of the culture. As today's children of the middle years reach out to a style of life to make their own, they cannot help but be affected and shaped by the profound changes we have undergone as a nation since World War II.

The children of America today are taking on citizenship of the most powerful nation in the world. It must mean something very different to a child to grow up in a country that is never in the news as a world shaper instead of one that always is; in a country that is poor instead of one seen as rich. In the spread of our military, children must at least be confused by the contradiction between an apparent might-makes-right national policy and the ethical values preached to them. What does the nation's use of its might do to their personal struggle with concepts of authority and justice? When they are exposed so young to cynicism toward principled behavior in public and political life, what meaning can a moral code have for them? As today's children seek to identify with the society and yet learn to be critical of individual adults, the pressure of the times and the accessibility of adult news causes many of them to become aware of the overt and covert value systems much earlier than any previous generation of children of their age, leading also to cynicism and despair earlier than ever before. Witness this poem by an eleven-year-old about the frustration he feels in society's contradictions:

To Live and Kill

The world was brought about by neither you nor me,
At first it consisted of a fruit on a tree.
As there was made darkness and light,
There were rules made up of wrong and right.
Special things mixed, and together they ran,
So this magic potion had made a man.
The man was only made to keep a certain will,
That was to live, and NO, not to kill.

Man was built to be strong like a tower,
And love and thought was all in his power.
Then a sudden change took place,
For there was lots of trouble in the difference of the race,
Now we are having trouble, don't be of good cheer,
Cause at the rate we're going we'll be gone next year.

There is one thing I am writing this for,
Why don't we have peace, no, not war.

Nor are children immune to the moral contradiction of racism. The unfinished business of our having been a slave country while espousing democracy means that few children of the middle years who go to school and watch TV are not in some way emotionally involved in the residue of bitterness and hate from that heritage. They think, for the most part, like their parents; but many are questioning their parents, as they strive to equate history and morality. The age-need to be socially acceptable and to conform, the desire to be "in" and have friends, gets tangled in the skeins of prejudice and fear of prejudice. A white child wrote in despair to her white teacher:

> I really don't like Mary Ann and she *knows* it! Whenever something happens where my feelings about that come out, she makes it like, "You're white and I'm black so you hate me for that." (That's how I feel she thinks, anyhow.) Also, Joan said outside that Mary Ann was blaming us for what the white race years ago did to Negroes. (That's how I feel and think and I think Amy does too.) I hate to speak up like that because Mary Ann's been mad at me for a long time, and she can be a good kid when she wants, and when she is I like her.
>
> Betsy.

Another white child wrote on his reactions to a new, ethnically mixed junior high school:

> Like . . . you were afraid to be seen in the halls if you were white without a Puerto Rican and black friend, you know, just to prove that you're not prejudiced . . .

And what of the black child? How does he feel? In the normal give and take of childhood, how often does he have to defend self-value in the face of attacks tinged with racism? "Chocolate baby!" he hears, and he argues back, "People pay for chocolate candy. Chocolate is good to eat. I don't see people eating much white chocolate." "Hi, colored girl," a white boy calls. "Hi, colored boy," answers the black child. "I'm not colored," says the boy defensively. "Well, white is a color," laughs the girl in triumph.

But it does not happen only on the streets. In a school committed to the highest standards of morality, an eight-year-old black child returned to her classroom from the crafts shop in tears. As the teacher and, later, her mother pieced the story together, it came out as follows. During the fall months, one of the boys, Henry, had singled out the two black girls in the class, Carol and Eleanor, for an occasional, surreptitious taunting. The girls said nothing to any adult, but consoled and comforted each other.

On Martin Luther King's birthday, the teacher read an appropriate story to the third-grade class and led them in a discussion. Carol informed her mother that night, "The teacher told the children, 'A long time ago people didn't let people on buses if they were black.'"

Some weeks after King's birthday, the third-grade class was involved in a crafts project, when Carol asked the teacher for some striped paper. The teacher replied that that paper was for writing, and to use something else for the project. Minutes later, Henry helped himself to some of the striped paper and Carol said to him, perhaps righteously in the way of little girls, "You can't use that paper. It's for writing." Henry turned on her and called her a "dope," to which Carol retorted with vigor that *he* was a dope, and then Henry said with scorn, "Now I agree with why they wouldn't let you on buses and stuff like that!"

It was this last remark, so cruelly out of keeping with the situation, that reduced Carol to tears. In the context of the racial struggle familiar to her generation, she understood full well the level of insult in the boy's attempt to demean her.

In an ironic reversal of injustice, the fair-skinned eight-year-old daughter of an interracial couple was persistently called "Whitey" by a dark-skinned black child in her third-grade class. Under other circumstances, the aggressor would have been considered a hostile and malicious little girl and perhaps punished. The victimized child would have had to learn to defend herself against such attacks with the forces of right and wrong clearly delineated. But now, at eight, the two were participants in a political struggle, and the adults, white teacher and black mothers, were not too clear themselves as to how to separate the elements. In still another situation, a black child in the sixth grade of a suburban school came home to inform his prestigious father that his white teacher had slapped him and called him an epithet derogatory to blacks in front of witnesses. The frantic father called the school superintendent at midnight. At seven the next morning, the teacher was brought in, and she denied the entire story. By nine o'clock, the three supposed witnesses insisted that they had neither heard nor seen any such episode. By ten o'clock, the child who had told the story broke down and cried and admitted that it was all made up. But can we wonder that he used that particular avenue to his father's ear?

Children's struggles with the problems of group membership and morality during the middle years is in our time caught up with the unfinished business of the adults' in-group, out-group exclusions and hatreds. It is confused by the gap between adults' professed morality and their actual behavior. For example, the black child is invited to the white child's home, but the white child is not as readily allowed into his. The black father drives a white visitor home, but the white father is reluctant to drive into black neighborhoods. Do the children sense this?

Principles of right and wrong, fairness and unfairness take on living significance for children of the middle years through interaction with, and among, each other. The black child is told by his parents he is a good and worthwhile person, but as he competes on the ball field with a white adversary, does he remember *that*, or does he remember the bitter anger of his parents and their friends when they talked about the subjugation of their gifts and talents by whites? As the white child tackles his black classmate to block his passage to the goal, is he thinking of the blockade as part of the game, or is he remembering the pleas of his parents that blacks must have their chance, or perhaps the anger of his parents that Blacks are asking for more than they are entitled to?

In seeking guidelines for a moral code, children of the middle years read their adult guides as they actually live and not as they preach. To an alarming extent, children feel that grownups are letting them down. There are nine-year-olds who accept as fact that the world may end, that drugs are part of a way of life, that violence is unending, that people hate each other. They are skeptical about good outcomes to any of the crises in society. Among children of the middle years, a new generation's formulation of values and mores is beginning to coalesce. How representative is this eleven-year-old mistrust in the adult world?

> I have faith in the people who are *not in charge.* I do not have faith in the system . . . because at this point, look where it has gotten us, and they're saying, "give it a chance, give the establishment a chance."

Stability and Change in Sex Roles

The child group which supports the children in working through inter-personal relationships and principles of ethical and moral behavior serves in still another important way to help their growth, and that is in the affirmation of a style of masculinity and femininity. Yet that area, too, is no longer clear, and children must deal with transitional models.

Despite speculation within the intellectual adult community as to whether biology or culture determines masculinity and femininity, children at this stage are far more likely to continue patterns in existence than strike out for newly conceived roles. The adult search for meaningful definitions of male and female remains an academic question to most children, who assume at the simplest, most basic level that girls will become mothers and boys fathers; that women have their work and men have theirs. Although there is evidence that children of working mothers are extending the possibilities of adult female work roles,[8] children of the middle years still tend to separate into boy and girl groups, each of which takes on the mannerisms, recreational patterns, attitudes, and values they read as appropriate for their sex in the adult culture that surrounds them, most of which is still rooted in tradition. Boys and girls of eight make strong public displays of their contempt for each other, even though individuals of the opposite sex may enjoy each other's company in private, and in some cases even indulge in a little body exploration. Distances in public are maintained almost as a defense, it would seem, against confusion in sorting out the cues to appropriate sex-linked styles of behavior. For a few short years, certain aspects of getting along with others are worked out in companionships uncluttered by the intrusion of other-sex demands. By the time they reach eleven or so, they begin to look to the opposite sex with the curiosity and interest of a new discovery, raising fresh problems for themselves and their parents.

During the middle years, most of the boys surge into physically demanding activities which engage them fully; most girls settle for talk and imagination. More boys than girls are actively aggressive; more girls than boys are "catty." There are boys who do not like to fight and who happily enjoy the imaginative, aesthetic, artistic, and peaceful. But even when their families are happy with this, the peer culture and the larger social milieu make it clear that they must be good in sports and ready to take on a physical encounter, no matter what it costs them, if they want to be identified as a boy. Similarly, the girls who prefer an active style, the "tomboys," eventually succumb to the social pressure, although they are given more latitude than the boys when they break the stereotypes.

The problem is that stereotypes are not easy to break. Even when parents believe in complete equality between the sexes,

[8] Ruth E. Hartley, "Current Patterns in Sex Roles: Children's Perspectives," *Journal of the National Association of Women's Deans and Counselors,* Vol. 25, No. 1, October, 1961.

the residues of centuries creep into the child-rearing in subtle ways. Baby girls get ribbons in their hair when there is barely enough hair to hold a bow; baby boys are not put into a frilled bonnet no matter how liberated parents are. Parents who are quite willing to allow their three-year-old boys to push a doll carriage (because "men as well as women take care of the babies now") worry if their six-year-old sons are still playing with dolls when society at large says it is not normal. The mass media treat the problem with confusing contradictions as advertising, feature articles, editorials, and selective reporting reveal different values and biases on the subject.

But in certain important manifestations of child behavior, the adult struggle to change the relationships between the sexes seems to have made some difference, although this is more clearly to be seen among girls than boys. One apparent effect of the greater freedom enjoyed by women in this century is the appearance in recent years of unabashed, open sexual curiosity and scatological language among girls, now making such expressions a female as well as a male norm during the middle years. The kind of graffiti that once adorned only the walls of boys' lavatories now appear on the walls of girls' toilets at school and camp, too, and girls seem as devoted as boys ever were to the accumulation of smutty jokes. And some eleven- and twelve-year-old girls have begun to make Women's Liberation banners with self-conscious assertiveness.

More carefully documented effects of the changes in women's status are the findings by Minuchin[9] that, while conventionally reared girls continue to identify with the stereotype of the helpless, dependent female, the daughters of enlightened, educated mothers do not see their roles that way at all. In the same study, Minuchin found that boys from traditional homes continue to have fantasies in which aggression plays a big part,

[9] Patricia Minuchin, "Sex-Role Concepts and Sex Typing in Childhood as a Function of School and Home Environments," *Child Development,* Volume 36, Number 14, December 1965.

indicating that they, like their parents, accept the stereotype of the aggressive male more readily than do children from homes that do not see aggression as a necessary male characteristic. In the study by Hartley[10] during the late 1950s, boys and girls of the middle years showed up as consistently conservative about mothers staying home and fathers working. But they saw both mothers and fathers settling fights, helping with homework, and signing report cards. In Minuchin's study in the 1960s, the children reared in more modern modes were even less committed to specific, socially set sex-role imagery. Boys and girls were readier to share tastes and activities, but they gave no indication of what would replace the stereotypes of the past.

Images of outer appearance and form are shaped by the behavior of the adult men and women children see at home and on the TV screen. But interest in their own bodies and in the basic sexual relationship between male and female develops in any case regardless of adult emphasis. Although this area is an ever-present childhood concern, the interest tends to become more focused in the later part of the middle years, as the children sense themselves coming closer to the physical development that will prepare them for a sexual life.

It would be most illogical if it did not. However, an interesting mixture of verbal sophistication and openness among many of today's children conceals the developmental inability to grasp certain concepts that are completely outside their experience as children. Ten years ago, sex education meetings for children had to rely on anonymous questions submitted after a careful warming-up period. Today, mental health workers in sex education report greater freedom on the part of the children, with most of the questions still the same. There are some new variations, however, on the information sought that relate to current news releases. Ten years ago, fourth- , fifth- , and sixth-grade girls asked:

[10] Ruth E. Hartley, "Current Patterns in Sex Roles: Children's Perspectives," *Journal of the National Association of Women's Deans and Counselors,* Vol. 25, No. 1, October, 1961.

Can you tell when you are going to menstruate? How old do you have to be? What is the usual time of day you get it? Should you tell your friends? What kind of period do boys get? Does the same thing happen to men? What do you say when you want your husband to have sexual intercourse? How do you get a baby? What is a miscarriage? What is prostitution? What happens if you have to go to the bathroom and you have your pad on? What should you do if you begin to menstruate away from home like at the movies or at school, and what if you have a man teacher? How do mothers give their babies milk by breast feeding?

Today, among many boys and girls, there is a lack of inhibition about the questions on menstruation that marks a real cultural change, a result undoubtedly of the efforts of liberated mothers, assisted by the public relations departments of firms manufacturing feminine products. But whether submitted in writing or verbally, the children still want to know the same things and more.

What makes it a boy or a girl? Does smoking have anything to do with babies being formed wrong? Why can't you have a baby when you're not married?

One subject that still carries the same anxiety it always did is that of masturbation. More boys than girls ask about this, and, even in our enlightened age, they are still wondering if it is harmful in any way and if it is morally permissible—both a reflection of unresolved adult confusion. The questions on prostitution have given way to greater curiosity about homosexuality, clearly a sign that middle-years children listen to the news media. Along with this is a question that appears time and time again about the transformation of Christine Jorgensen, a case which is not of the children's time at all, but seems to have caught on as childhood lore. Since a basic focus of most of their questions has to do with an underlying, "What will happen to me?", the attraction to phenomena that deal with doubts about the inevitability of gender probably reflects the search for reassurance at this stage of childhood that looks ahead to, and fears at the same time, emergence into sexuality.

Because development into a sexual being takes until adulthood, the interest in that development is continuous. Both boys and girls wonder about their own bodies and, once past nine or ten, become absorbed in talk about the secondary sex characteristics—pimples, pubic hair, voice change, breast growth, and so on. And both boys and girls are interested in what happens to the opposite sex. Boys are especially intrigued by information about how females are made, fascinated by menstruation and pregnancy. Although both sexes are, of course, still seeking to grasp the meaning of conception, pregnancy is actually the more exciting area of interest for both. The children ask about miscarriage, abortion, and such anomalies as three-headed monsters and babies born with six toes. They are deeply concerned about illegitimate babies.

The psychological and physical remoteness of conception and sexual intercourse cause the children to work and rework their understanding at many stages of growth. An element of confusion is bound to remain until personal experience in time gives meaning to the abstraction.

Here is a chapter in a story about rabbits written by a very bright eight-year-old, who had obviously been given information and who accepted without question certain socially defined roles for fathers and mothers. He attended a school in which equality of the sexes and availability of answers were taken for granted.

Chapter Two

Once when Carolyn was knitting she wished she could have a baby. She told Jerome she wanted a baby. Jerome said, "Well if I give a sperm to the egg then we can have one." Well said Carolyn, "I am very fat maybe we could!" One day they decided to make a baby. They got in bed and then there was a new start of a baby. Now inside a little beginning of a rabbit was in the egg. When the egg was nearly 7 months Jerome made a few useful things for the baby, like a bottle, a crib, a playpen, a bib, and a rag to wip the baby's mouth with. Then

one day 2 months later peter rabbit was born, he was 17 inches
long and he weighed 7 pounds 6 ounces and he was very strong.

In a sixth-grade class that had been through an informal series of sessions with their teacher and the school nurse on
human reproduction, the effectiveness of the teaching was
evaluated by a questionnaire given to the children by their
teacher. The first question was, "What new information did
you get from this unit?"

While one child said jauntily,

I just wanted to make sure I got the intercourse idea right,

another confessed,

I didn't understand how the sperm got to the ovaries.

And two others showed their bewilderment. One wrote,

You told me a lot of things I didn't know. I didn't know that
was the way you have a baby. It seems like it would be a crazy
way. The way my friends told me seems easier,

and the other said,

I sometimes hope I'll never get married or get sexual desires because I just don't want to be that close to a man.

But if confusion about sexual intercourse is inevitable in
childhood, much information about the body does make sense
and carries children into speculation and thought about and
beyond themselves. In the same questionnaire, children wrote
about what they had learned and what else they wanted to
know in unexpected ways:

I learned a lot of new words that really help, and I learned how
animals like cats and dogs have intercourse. One more question,
How do elephants have intercourse?

I learned a lot about the fish when they die off when they reach
the sporing area.

I didn't learn much information *technically*, but as to how the others can accept it without nonsense it was amazing. It also made me think a lot (!). The thing that interested me most was what the fetus felt and its growth.

Children are not really interested in the feelings adults bring to the sexual relationship. They are as likely as not to say, "I hate that gushy stuff." They want more to know how they themselves fit into the picture and what are the scientific explanations that tie things together. As in all learning, they relate the known to the unknown. In the case of information about reproduction, they are more likely to make connections on the simplest childhood level of familiar bodily experience than on the higher level of spirituality and romance. Their body talk is rooted in body sensation as *they* have known it, and that is more likely to be excretory than genital in nature.

They are not sure of what their reactions are, or should be. In one sixth-grade class, where some of the children were already changing physically and beginning to enjoy tentative, sexually-tinged encounters, one girl wrote in confidence to her teacher:

> I didn't want to say it aloud, but deep down I think Roddy's group with Anne, Laura, Kay and Toni were mostly deep down interested in a new kind of flirting and this was it, don't you think so? Please tell me.
>
> Connie.

For most children, the interest in the body, in sexual relationships, and in their own masculine or feminine style of behavior are constants in a total battery of interests and concerns, but not out of proportion to the many challenges they are engaged in during these years of important growth. Where the interest is excessive, there is generally some skewing in their family experience that gives to this area of living a stronger impact than it need have. Children in the middle years are not driven by sexual feeling, although they do look ahead to their own development.

The whole person interests them, and sexual functioning

and attitudes are a part of this total interest. According to Gertrude Lewis, who collated the questions 5,000 elementary children wanted answered, the yearning was for self-understanding, of their body, their feelings, and of relationships with family and peers; it was for a philosophical code of beliefs by which to behave and which pertain to social problems affecting all society. They did ask, "Why do only girls have babies?", "How is a baby formed?", "How do we stay alive in our mother's stomach?" But they also wanted to know how the body grows and develops, what is inside, how the mind works, why some people are smarter than others, how the heart beats, how the cells work, why we have hair, and a host of other things about body mechanisms.

With the utmost seriousness, they wrote:

I want know about other people.
Why are Negroes treated differently from white people?
Why do my friends like me sometimes and sometimes not?
What is a real friend? What can I do to make friends?
How are habits started? Stopped?
Why do I sometimes hate everybody?
Why does my mother get mad at me when I try to do something right?
Why do people fight between each other within the same family?
Why did God make me if life is so terrible?
Who am I? What is Life? What makes me tick? [11]

Big questions never have simple answers, and it is the big questions that children are beginning to tackle between the ages of eight and eleven.

[11] Gertrude Lewis, *Teach Us What We Want to Know*. Published for the Connecticut State Board of Education by the Mental Health Materials Center, New York, 1969.

How Much Can They Learn?
. . .

By the middle years of childhood, children of both sexes are ready to examine many of the questions that man has struggled with for as long as history has been recorded. Like adults, they will not always find complete answers. Yet the content of their school learning can, and should, be significant both as to depth and breadth. In struggling to understand the why and how of human resolution, of social and economic need, of inter-personal relations, of man's place in the evolutionary chain and on this earth, they will gain the competence and skills of the adult world. But it is important that they gain these in such a way that they enter the stream of human knowledge with full support for their growth as thinking, feeling, acting human beings.

From Impulse to Control

Between eight and eleven, children are in an intermediate period that shifts and swings from primitive impulse to the ability to grasp the meaning of social organization and adaptation.

Both levels of response get rooted in learning, and both need to be accounted for in curricula at one time or another. As an example, the study of prehistoric animals satisfies the first level, whereas studying the development of the hoof is better handled at the second.

The children change their commitment to the purely personal to commitment to the universalized and non-personal. This means that the attractiveness of new knowledge becomes less and less determined solely because of its relatedness to personal experience as the connecting link with the outer world. Although at this stage children are on the road to dealing with abstractions of experience and are slowly losing their dependency on the concrete as a basis for understanding, the transposition of abstract understanding into words is even slower. The child who reasons: "A chicken is an egg's way of making another chicken," is groping to understand fundamental relationships beyond the obvious, but his terminology is hardly academic.

Opinions, tastes, values, and attitudes are formed and argued during these years; the differences between fact and opinion grow clearer in the process. Children are able to develop competency and enjoy achievement at many different levels of learning, from the most creative and imaginary to the most mechanical. They long to be involved in work and responsibility that are associated with functionally meaningful tasks. Normally, they should be developing increasing tolerance for postponement, although there are individual variations and some confusion in this as a result of the societal teaching of instant gratification. But they can project into the future and are capable of some planning.

Toward Differentiation and Flexibility

This is a period during which children are making the move away from their earlier rigidity and search for absolutes toward a growing capacity to see a situation from various perspectives, à la Rashomon. Such perspective allows them in time to recognize that circumstances condition judgment—a valuable asset in the study of history and in the response to literature. As they grow in capacity to see shades of meaning, the possibilities offered by alternatives begin to replace the either/or polarity of their younger years. Even such appraisals as "bright" and "stupid" take on degrees, and in their own self-evaluation they become capable of recognizing that they are neither all good nor all bad, but more likely to be "some good, some bad." On occasion, they can enjoy a joke on themselves, but generally they prefer the jokes played on others. The growth in capacity for differentiation that marks the way to more adult-like intellectual endeavor is clear to see in these elven-year-old descriptions of themselves:

Eric

I think my strong points are being honest. I have good judgment and good taste to pick out the right place or background for a thing. I try hard to be a good sportsman, but sometimes people cheat in the game and I can't stand cheaters so I argue about it until it is settled the right way. I think I would be responsible to take care of money and make sure it didn't get lost, and I would do the same thing for anything else.

Tina

To describe myself I will start with my "assets." I feel my main asset is art. I like to draw rather than toot on my clarinet. But I still like to play my instrument anyway. My hobbies beside drawing are that I like to collect post cards, and I pick up travel folders from different places. I have a private collection of magazines and books. My shyness is keeping me from telling you more about it. I admit I'm not good at sports, and I can do better in my work. (Social Studies is my favorite subject.) I am pretty good at ice skating and swimming. I like my friends to have a lively disposition or I tend to get depressed. It's pretty silly, but I guess I can't help it, I've been that way all my life. I want my life to be normal, but I do not want to be like my mother. I do want to have children, but I want to play a lot of sports. For awhile in Fourth grade, I went through a period of feeling sorry for myself, but I realized later, what a dope I was. Now whenever I get mad at myself, I remember what I did.

There do not seem to be any sex differences in intellectual functioning, although the social styles of boys and girls may differ. The results in I.Q. tests in which boys are matched against girls are inconsistent and probably vary with the test items, which have been devised principally by men. Certainly, as both sexes strive to be accepted in the world of real work and responsible functioning, the earlier exaggerated aspirations of their six- and seven-year-old style give way to greater realism in choice-making. But it is possible that the societal expectations for boys and girls influence what each sex sees as appropriate learning for itself and therefore to an extent probably color their "realistic" choices of action and preference. Both sexes are equally able, however, to gain differentiated knowledge about themselves as workers, learners, and members of a group. When the "self" can question and choose, and accept help without sacrificing independence, sex differences in learning capacity are minimized.

The developmental capacity for increasing objectivity in thinking, so clearly evident in the years from eight on, has barely been tapped in traditional elementary schooling. On the contrary, the exaggerated stress on rote learning and refinement of skills has violated the potential for genuine intellectual growth during these years. This has clearly been revealed in a number of studies of children's powers of inquiry. In one of these, the investigator showed ten-year-old children a short film depicting a simple scientific phenomenon and encouraged them to find the causes of the phenomenon by asking productive leading questions instead of waiting to be told what the reasons were. He hoped they would direct their questions toward categories within which to search for the solution. Although he worked with extremely bright fifth-graders, their reluctance to ask independent questions forced him to conclude that they had already learned by age ten to rely on being "spoon-fed"; they did not trust themselves to pursue a search on their own.[1] Yet games like "Twenty Questions" and "Coffee Pot," card games and games of chance, which children play independently out of school, are essentially games in which the areas within which to seek clues are systematically classified and eliminated in a process of searching, which is what the investigator hoped the children would do in the science problem.

A major reason for the discrepancy between children's capacities to think and their non-think school performance lies in the failure of education at this level to regard with respect the characteristic growth of the stage of development.

Elementary age children are avid for information and enjoy gaining skills. But they learn best when the appeal of the content is real for their age and stage, when the skill has some observable value, and when the style of learning is the childhood style of action. For adults responsible for children's learning, this means coming to grips with several significant factors in planning curriculum for the middle years: the stage-associated level of intellectual grasp (not I.Q.); the age-and-stage needs to be independent and competent; and the feelings that accompany learning at any age.

Obviously, this is not a simple matter of collecting data in the old style, although facts continue to be at the heart of sound reasoning. Nor is it an equally simple matter of letting children do what they want to on their own as an alternative to authoritarianism. Adults have a role to play in helping children's learning. It is not authoritarian and it is important in the eyes of the children themselves. They can play that role more, rather than less, wisely by becoming cognizant of children's growth needs and capacities before they attempt decisions concerning what should and should not be included in elementary education. Adults have their biases about what should be taught; children have their desires about what to learn. Adults

[1] J. R. Suchman, "Inquiry Training: Building Skills for Autonomous Discovery," *Merrill-Palmer Quarterly*, July 1961.

have their own perspectives, understandings, and style of learning; children are trying to attain perspectives and understanding through a learning style that is different from that of adults in important ways.

It is necessary for adults to ask new questions and to learn to think about children in new ways. They must ask, "What are the strengths of the middle years that lend themselves to intellectual growth and scholarship? And what are the limitations?" For, without a doubt, school is a place to learn. But, equally without a doubt, learning should make sense to learners.

We must affirm again, as with the primary children, that skills involve training rather than intellectual probing, and the purpose of children's schooling must be the expansion of their minds and the enhancement of their total selves. The learning of skills must be seen as necessary tools to children's continued learning, but hardly the end goal of their education during the elementary years. Children's intellects have to be nurtured on meaningful content; but meaningful, at this stage, refers to that portion of adult knowledge which can be conceptualized and responded to emotionally by children, so that it is meaningful to them as well as held significant by adults.

How Much Can They Understand?

Let us begin by looking at intellectual development at this stage in terms other than those of I.Q. scores, which came into use in the schools about fifty years ago and have kept us from seeing children ever since.

The capacity to deal with many variables simultaneously, for example, with time and space, as in geography and history, or with speed and distance, as in mathematics, is an intellectual capacity that emerges during the middle years—if opportunity and encouragement support the maturation possibilities. What must be kept in mind, however, is that the capacity to deal with several variables at once is only emerging and does not develop evenly in all content areas. Nor is it fully developed in most children by the end of the period we are looking at. Therefore, although we can speak of the period between eight and eleven as one in which there is growing objectivity, rather important differences actually exist between the younger and older children of the stage, differences that affect abstract thinking, judgment, and perspective. These are real enough to be given consideration in curriculum practices.

The capacity of eight- and nine-year-olds to understand ideas and concepts is clearly beyond that of children younger. Yet eights and nines have trouble with abstractions that are either completely outside their experience or that they cannot grasp by analogy. For example, the concept of necessity is clearer to them when it refers to food or the teacher's demand that they bring a pencil than when it refers to freedom of nations, or is described as the "mother of invention." Concepts of time, space, and number have deepened, but children at this level can extend their learning in only one of them at a time. That is, the challenge of numbers of hours in a day in relation to numbers of minutes in an hour is more appropriate to their capacity than the problem of how many miles could be covered in a given number of hours when the car is going at a certain number of miles per hour.

At the same time, they are still struggling with the fantasy-reality relationship that influenced their earlier years, although they are readier to grasp more subtle differences when helped. For example, the rabbit belonging to a third grade was not in the classroom after a weekend, and the children were perplexed as well as upset. Andrea announced that she had seen the rabbit on the street when she was coming to school just as he was entering an alleyway. The entire class got excited and suggested they all go out for him immediately. The teacher calmed them down by suggesting that they had to prepare for going out and perhaps a small scout party would be best. She then asked Andrea whether she was sure she had seen the rabbit, and Andrea was vigorous in her affirmation. At that point, another teacher brought in the missing rabbit, which had apparently wandered into his room. The children were delighted, of course. But the teacher went back to the earlier discussion and asked the eight-year-olds, "How come Andrea was so sure she had seen the rabbit on the street?" After a pause, one child volunteered, "I guess she wanted to see him so badly, she *thought* she really did." At which all the children shook their heads in agreement.

In style of learning, the children are more like than unlike their younger selves. They still need to act upon their understanding in a physical, doing way.

According to Susan Isaacs,[2] the development of thinking in the child thus largely rests upon: "a) the growth of his ability to hold together in one act of understanding a large number of facts and relations; and (bound up with this) b) the ability to pass from the simpler relations between things to the more subtle and complex." Therefore, a teacher making a decision to study another culture with her early elementary class as a social studies unit would choose such groups as Eskimos, Aztecs, Bedouins, or Indians in preference to Greeks, Florentines, or Romans. Although all are remote and foreign cultures to the children, the life styles of the first groups have reasonably uncomplicated physical reality that is readily observable to this age group, whereas the social and aesthetic implications of the latter cultures are too subtle for them. The work processes of Eskimos, American Indians, Aztecs, or Bedouins are fully integrated into every aspect of their lives. Their art is in the spoon, not separated from the needs of sheer existence. The directly physical response to the everyday needs of survival are dependent in part upon individual initiative and self-sufficiency, in part upon group endeavor. The total style is sufficiently close to the children's own penchant for activity to make it easy to identify with at eight or nine. The life of Florentines, Romans, or Greeks, on the other hand, was more complexly structured to begin with, and significant to posterity for the philosophical

---

[2] Susan Isaacs, *Children We Teach*, 2nd ed. (London: University of London Press, Ltd., 1965), p. 131.

conceptualizations inherent in the social interaction and aesthetic organization. These levels of functioning are only just becoming fuzzily apparent to eight-, nine-, and ten-year-olds, although they are profitably studied later.

The language of eight- and nine-year-olds is well developed for daily use, but such language of abstraction and conceptualization as they have has, for the most part, emerged from understanding gained from activity and experience. (They are perfectly capable of using words they do not understand and of sounding very knowing.) They cannot easily do involved thinking with abstract words alone, separate from some action. For effective learning in childhood, content must therefore mesh with the level of abstract thinking available during the developmental stage. When the content has reality for the children, it serves to stimulate further growth in the power to deal with abstractions.

Abstract thinking comes earlier and faster in the physical sciences than in the social sciences. That is to say, the principal of the pendulum can be grasped more quickly than the principle of brotherly love. It comes earlier in bright children than in slower ones, but it develops in a predictably *sequential* order, although it is not wholly predictable for *age*. In her study of children's concepts in the social sciences, Dr. Lois Wolf obtained responses to pictures of such social phenomena as poverty, war, old age, and the destruction of land and people. She found that perceptions of social problems deepened in a clear sequence of growth toward greater abstraction. Younger children are likely to give a straight, uninterpreted description of what they see:

> There's a boy here and there's a mother and baby's crying. And there's a cat and there's a dog over there. There's the stove. This here is for food, and there are some dishes and here's a towel. (Child 8 yrs., 5 mos.)

Somewhat later in age, the description of the same picture includes some explanation and elements of relationships, although irrelevant details tend to be given equal weight with important and central factors:

It's a lady having a baby and a child. It looks like he's eating
something and there's a boy or a man there. He's holding a
plate, and there's a cat down there and it's an old home. (Child
10 yrs.)

Still later, underlying concepts and broad relational structures appear in the place of immediately observable events;
possible alternatives and multi-causality can be considered, as
in this response:

It looks like these people are up in the Appalachians where
they're very poor and they don't have much food. Very poor.
And they're, say, like cut off from society altogether. (Child 12
yrs., 11 mos.)[3]

The important shift in depth of thinking between ten and
eleven which Wolf found when she investigated children's understanding of social concepts is consistent with Piaget's
findings that a similar shift occurs in a variety of abstract concepts from mathematics to morality at about eleven; and with
Gertrude Lewis's [4] finding of marked differences in the type of
personal questions asked by ten-year-olds when compared
with those asked by children from eleven to thirteen. The degree to which children must rely on concrete illustration in
order to understand concepts is, therefore, a basic consideration in curriculum planning.

As children mature, they can consider hypothetical conditions and solutions, provided these still have some connection
with concrete experience. The growing facility to deal with
several variables at once then lends itself to more imaginative
alternatives in solving problems.

Many ten- to thirteen-year-olds begin to abstract central
ideas and utilize them in the style of adults. Ten-year-olds can
study the social organization of animals, for example, without

[3] Lois Wolf, "An Investigation of the Levels of Abstraction Inferred from
Children's Explanations of Social Problems." Unpublished Ph.D. Thesis,
New York University, 1969.
[4] Gertrude Lewis, *op. cit.*

having to be animals. They can examine the variety of family groupings and leadership patterns they find in the animal world and make connections with the human experience without constructing a physical model. Their maturing enables them to better handle causes and their consequences and to relate the particular to the universal. At twelve, says Wolf, "children can study an underdeveloped nation in the context of the meaning of small nationhood in a large world; they can relate the distribution of resources to the distribution of wealth and prospects."

Events and cultures remote in time and space become accessible to their expanding awareness, making history-mindedness a new dimension by which to establish order in complexity. They grow interested in the political events of their time, and this, combined with their developing historical sense and capacity for perceiving alternatives, can open the way to using history as a guide to understanding the present. Yet, in a time of crisis, as ours is, adults need to resist the temptation to believe that abstract concepts of political conviction develop any faster than other social concepts. The relevance of developmental stages, even to the contemporaneous character of political crisis, is indicated in a number of studies of children's political thinking. These show that, before nine, there is only a vague realization of government as "something hovering over the country and caring for it." One study showed that children younger than nine said we have a flag because "God made it so they'd know who was the good people"; "If the Statue of Liberty was gone there would be no liberty"; a good citizen is "a person whose house is clean and who is polite." [5]

Another study, of the responses of children of eight to eleven to the teachers' strike in New York City in 1968, showed confusion as to the meaning of a strike and the role of the leaders. Not until about eleven could the children disassociate themselves from feelings about the changed routines in

[5] Muriel Beadle, "Learning the Political Facts of Life," *The New York Times,* September 20, 1970.

their own lives caused by the strike and deal with the objective issues involved.[6]

4th grade child

Q. What did you feel about the parents that broke into P.S. X? What did you think of that?

A. Well, I thought it was a pretty good thing to do because for one thing, I didn't like the emergency school. I was bored.

4th grade child

Q. How did you feel about the school strike?

A. I didn't like it that much. 'Cause we hardly ever got recess.

4th grade child

Q. Who was Shanker?

A. The President of the Board, President of the Union of the Board of Education.

6th grade child

Q. What do you think about people who want to get their rights by striking?

A. Well, I think it's very wrong, but like if someone has a right and a lot of people are with them, and at the Board of Education, the whole Board, Shanker and Donovan are against it, and you think it's a good idea, you know, you think it's a must, then I would, you know, I would . . . if it got to a point where I thought it was a must, a real must, like I'd go to City Hall and I'd picket.

6th grade child

Q. What do you think it was all about?

A. The strike?

Q. Yes. What do you think they were trying to accomplish?

A. They were trying to accomplish that it doesn't matter if, you know, it doesn't matter what school the teacher teaches at, the children are a different color or something, but just so long as every child gets an education.

[6] Lila Mukamal, "Responses of 8- to 12-Year-Old Public School Children to the New York City School Strike." Unpublished Master's Thesis, Bank Street College of Education, 1970.

The Role of Feeling in Children's Learning

Intellectual readiness and learning style are basic. But they are
not all that must be considered in planning curricula. Children
of the middle years do not do their learning unaffected by attendant feelings of interest, boredom, success, failure, chagrin,
joy, humiliation, pleasure, distress, and delight. They are
whole children responding in a total way, and what they feel is
a constant factor that can be constructive or destructive in any
learning situation.

On one level, emotional response can be to the nature of the
school work, as this child wrote so graphically:

> Something is wrong. I can't understand it. All this school work,
> I can't stand it. Every word I look up I *hate*. Every problem I do
> I hate. The picture dictionary I *loved*. The report I *hated*.
> What's more what I hate I don't do as well as I could.

At another level, feelings rise in response to the social interaction taking place during school learning:

> Dear Mrs. Dorsey,
> Roger and I had our hand up, then you called on Sarah so we
> waited. Then I called to get your attention by saying—'Mrs.
> Dorsey.' You said to stop interrupting, so I kept my hand up.
> Then Sarah wanted to say something so she did the same thing I
> did by calling out your name. I didn't think you would call on
> her because she had just been called on and I had my hand up
> longer. But of course, you did. I like Sarah very much but I
> don't have friends who are teacher's pets. I know Sarah is
> smarter and more talented and a very polite little lamb but even
> if you think she is much better you can still give other people
> chances and I'm not just mad, and I'm not saying it because of
> what happened about the talking, it's just that it isn't fair. So
> what if she's smarter than me. I'm not mad but it isn't fair.

And where feelings are dealt with least of all in traditional schooling is in the response of children to the meaning of the content to themselves.

The morning after the Kent State killings, the children of a fifth-grade class came into school filled with excitement tinged with awe, fear, and bewilderment. The teacher responded to their comments and questions immediately. She deliberately directed them toward looking at the problem of obtaining accurate information so soon after a calamity in which many were involved, and separate pieces had not yet been coordinated. The children accepted the reasonableness of the approach, but could not let it go at that. They quickly went into personal anecdotes of violence they had perceived. One told how a tall high-school student had attacked a short sixth-grader on the school grounds and had pummeled him mercilessly, while a crowd of children screamed at him to stop. The children had turned in desperation to the ice cream vender. "Do something, do something!" But he shrugged his shoulders and remained remote. Another told of a fight among teenagers on a public playground observed at night from the windows of houses. "People called the police, but they never came," she said. The accounts went on, and all carried the same theme: the children's helplessness in the face of brutality and violence. The teacher let them talk freely and shared with them her recognition of the validity of their feeling. The objective lesson about getting the facts before making a judgment had not been lost, but the children's response to adult betrayal of their childhood need to feel safe was at least as important, if not more so, and in this classroom, that feeling was not denied.

Curriculum Must Relate to Developmental Stages

To develop an elementary school curriculum that takes into account intellectual capacity, learning style, and children's feelings, there must be a complete and dramatic break with the

conventional way of looking at children in school—that is, as
scores, as high or low achievers, as badly- or well-behaved, and
as compliant with, or resistant to, rules. This is not to say that
achievement as such is undesirable, that socially constructive
behavior is unnecessary, or that rules are an anachronism. It is
to say that at present all three are exaggerated into caricatures
of their true meaning in genuine learning experiences for children. All are unhappily associated mainly with negative aspects
of living and learning, with the destructive aspects of competitiveness, conformity, and obedience, and with excessive test
anxiety. These interfere with honest intellectual inquiry,
which needs a supportive climate in which mistakes can be
made without fear of recrimination. All need to be reassessed
before we can come around again to realistic concepts of
achievement, behavior, rules of living, and evaluation of what
the elementary school child is learning.

The existence of an unnecessarily large number of "under-
achievers" among bright children in the elementary schools
must be seen in this frame of reference as the desperate, wasteful recourse of children whose feelings, imaginativeness, originality of thought and action style force them to protect themselves from conformity for the sheer sake of conforming to the
sterility demanded of them. No one who listens to children's
artificial responses to the contrived questions of the traditional
elementary classroom can doubt that docility, not thinking, is
what is being asked for. Nor are those who "make it," and
even make it well, necessarily better off than the under-achievers. Both success and failure in the traditional school exact a
price in this time of frantic competition and anxiety about the
future, because the goals themselves—grades—are so meaningless.

Skewed priorities lead to distorted expectations, and these in
turn can lead to unjust and even dishonest teacher-child relationships. Take this example as a case in point: Parents who
were visiting their children's school during an open school
week commented to each other on the exceptionally fine writing of the children in a bright fifth-grade class. Gradually, they

came to realize that, although the grading hierarchy was E, G, F, P, and U (Excellent, Good, Fair, Pass, and Unsatisfactory), the grades on the fine papers were mostly G−, with a rare G. One parent asked the teacher why. "Oh," said the young teacher, herself a Phi Beta Kappa member, "we no longer give E's." Perplexed, the parent asked, "But why not?" "The principal decided not to, because when we did give E's, we always had parents complaining when their child was not being sent to the junior high school classes for gifted children, and they could point to all the E's on the record. So we stopped giving E's." The children in that class were being taught to work as hard as they could to achieve excellence, although they would never, under any circumstances, achieve a grade evaluation of excellence in that school's own rating system. No one ever followed them up to find out how many developed negative or even neurotic attitudes toward schooling and the attainment of grades. But the consequences are not too difficult to surmise.

At the heart of the problem is the traditionally limited approach to a curriculum as simple accretion. Out of this approach comes testing to evaluate the amount and rate of accretion, and out of the constant testing come the pressure and competition for points of difference. What must be asked is whether all this is really as significant to the ultimate outcome in adulthood as the more vital attitudes toward self and learning, which neither traditional curricula nor standardized tests even recognize, much less measure.

The stress on the acquisition of knowledge at the expense of social and emotional growth has been criticized by child development experts and psychiatrists alike. It is no accident that ulcers are appearing in young children, with a peak period between seven and nine. Is that not when the serious pressure for grades gets under way at home and at school? Yet, aside from the mental health assessment, which is important in its own right, there is the sad fact that the curriculum for the middle years, out of simple respect for children at this stage of growth, deserves a strong focus on intellectuality. Ironically, intellectual growth is actually more fulfilling and stimulating when the children's feelings and interests, their stage of thinking, and social relating are utilized in the service of supporting their wanting to know. But this has yet to be recognized in school practice. When everything vital to children is ignored in favor of pressured exhortation to please parents and teachers by repeating senselessly what's in the books, the distortions that occur actually destroy intellectuality. What kind of learning, for example, is implied in this conversation between a ten-year-old child and her student teacher?

S.T.: Do you ever get mad?
Child: Yes.
S.T.: What kinds of things make you mad?
Child: I get mad when I know the answer and I raise my hand, and the teacher calls on somebody else.
S.T.: Why does that make you mad?
Child: Because then I figured out the answer for nothing.

This kind of non-investment in one's own learning is all too common in educational situations where rewards are unrelated to the satisfaction of knowing, and children cannot feel competent when they learn, only well-behaved and approved of.

Children of the middle years are ready to grow in many directions simultaneously. Their schooling can support such multiple growth only if the rigid, impersonal bases of skill- and fact-learning from which elementary education has proceeded at last yields to our greater understanding of children. At the same time, we must recognize the complex social requirements of our day that must affect their education. If we fail to do this at this stage of history, we will not only be betraying the demands of our time and therefore betraying our children's future, but we will be denying them, during their childhood, the feelings of self-worth and self-realization that come with competence gained from challenge perceived and mastered through their own efforts.

What Shall They Learn
in the Intermediate Grades?

. . .

How shall we select the content of schooling during the middle years? We can begin with children's interest in man and the world as the global starting-off point. From there, we must recognize children's profound need to order their world so they can feel competent and knowing within it. And, after that, we must act on the assumption that the ordering of the world's knowledge is a lifelong process of classifying and reclassifying categories of information, as increased maturity and increased knowledge interact in the individual mind.

Let us rid ourselves first of the old notion that it is possible to "complete" an education during the elementary years, or to "cover the ground." There is no such thing as covering all the ground in a time when the rate of accumulation of information leaves everyone breathless. What is far more important in childhood is that any informational search go hand in hand with attitudes and skills for inquiry that will support unending learning through many stages of schooling and all through life.

In the words of an old proverb: "If you meet a hungry man,

and give him a fish, you feed him for a day. But if you teach him to fish, you feed him for life."

We must teach our children to "fish."

In some measure, the selection of content must be determined by adults, because to depend only on what children want to know would leave too much they never heard of outside the scope of their choice. A good curriculum includes the search for answers to what the children want to know as a matter of course. But a knowledgeable adult also makes some decisions as to what might be useful, interesting, or of great value to inexperienced young children.

Organization of Content

Present classifications of knowledge into natural and physical sciences, social sciences, mathematics, literature, art, and music are as good as any to adopt for the purpose of determining educational content. But the classifications as they stand are not meant to be neat bases for scheduling subjects in class periods. Children have a way of crossing lines of subject demarcation without any difficulty. They integrate the information they assimilate into related wholes that often do not fall into separate school subjects at all. The problem adults must solve is how to determine entry points for children into the vast amount of knowledge available in such a way that children's own needs and desires to feel knowing about the world are satisfied, while, at the same time, they are stimulated toward further inquiry about it. The most valid criterion for selection in any content area then proves not to be the logical progression within the subject at all, but that piece of it which could be, or actually is, psychologically intriguing and conceptually comprehensible to children at a given stage of growth. Curricula in the elementary school can, and should, be man-centered in content, child-centered in motivation.

Two examples will clarify the difference between the logical and psychological approach to content. In traditional education, children are brought to the study of history in chronological fashion—this happened, then that, then that, in the order of the year of occurrence. The American Revolution comes first, then the War of 1812, then the Civil War. In reality, children might feel deeply moved to turn to history out of a need to find the roots of present conflicts in society. For example, as they perceive the clear challenges of the Blacks for redress of grievances, which no child of the middle years can avoid, they might well turn to the Civil War and the Reconstruction as more immediately significant antecedent experiences before they go back in time to the American Revolution. Or, in the same context, the Bill of Rights might be more germane than the break of the colonies from the mother country. Relationships between events thus become more pertinent than strict chronological order, although chronology is sure to emerge as meaning is sought.

In another, non-intellectual branch of learning, the same style of entry would hold true. A folk dance taught to eleven- and twelve-year-old boys meets with resistance when it is taught in "proper" order, that is, fourteen little running steps, a vigorous leap and twist, and fourteen little running steps again. But when the same children are asked to develop their skill in the leap first, the "unmasculine" running steps become incidental before-and-after approaches to the leap, and the dance goes better.

A first requirement for breaking with the traditional curriculum, then, is that the content to be made available to children must be examined for those facets that hold meaning in child terms. Undoubtedly, there will be anxious inquiries. "But won't something be left out—important dates, places, events?" The answer is yes. But that yes will mean something different from its face value when adults think back to their own elementary curriculum, which was built around the notion that everything could be covered, and ask themselves what they remember from it. What adult could pass a fifth-grade geography or history test?

Learning Must Be Significant

When children are invested in their learning, they remember more than when they learn by rote, even if they do not learn "everything." But it is also true that information significant to man cannot be avoided when learning is oriented to searching. In one way or another, at one time or another, the perpetual learner comes across the major people, findings, and events that altered the lives of men and women. In the middle years of childhood, it is more important to keep alive and glowing the interest in finding out and to support this interest with skills and techniques related to the process of finding out than to specify any particular piece of subject matter as inviolate. Any number of different aspects of human knowledge can serve the purposes we endorse if used well. But what does "used well" mean?

Each area of human knowledge revolves around internal laws which represent the different ways we have of defining the realities of man's life and understanding. These laws are the basic structure, principles, and concepts which are unique to a particular discipline. Each area of knowledge also has its wealth of detail, incorporating illustration, application, and specific skills. If, during their wonderfully formative, expanding middle years, we do not acquaint children with the basic principles which give meaning to important areas of human knowledge, but instead deluge them with unassociated facts, hoping the truth will appear at some time, they run the risk of becoming estranged from the discipline and possibly lost to it forever. This is true in content areas as different from each other as literature and mathematics, history and science. Using literature as an example, Bruner says its basic structure is tragedy and comedy, the stuff of life itself.[1] One could add life's malleability, as well as its subjection to chance, its universality, and

[1] Jerome Bruner, *The Process of Education* (Cambridge, Massachusetts: Harvard University Press, 1960).

uniqueness for individuals, all of which can be seen at any level of life, including childhood. But children in the elementary school are not generally introduced to this intrinsic character of literature at their own level of comprehension. Instead, they are processed through a series of readers for the major purpose of exercising their powers of deciphering print. They are tested on right answers in an area where there can be many answers; they are shielded from the reality of human joy, suffering, and fallibility in favor of a skewed emphasis on moralistic behavior so they will learn proper lessons. But they hardly come to grips with literature as literature. As a consequence, unless children pick up this taste from their parents, their reading is done as assignments only, and they welcome the day when they will no longer be held responsible for reading. They become lost to literature as a source of enjoyment and deepening.

On the other hand, if their study of a major content area is geared to basic principles from the beginning, details fall into place in relation to each other and in a way that allows for genuine expansion of knowledge and understanding. Should they have to learn and practice specific skills that are needed for deeper study, the tasks will at least make sense, even if the repetition and drill grow tiresome.

Since children learn best though concrete operation, and science and math concepts are easier to extract through concrete operations than are concepts in the social sciences, let us begin with math and science to clarify the way in which knowledge of underlying principles of a content area supports detail and, together with detail, merges into competency at a child's level.

Mathematics

The intrinsic character of mathematics has to do with patterns and relationships. Children take pleasure in figuring things out, and their growing power to deal with more than one variable at a time, plus their increased ability to perceive alternatives, now combine to make possible a truly mathematical kind of thinking. For example, the concept of patterning from a variety of base numbers makes problems in computation stemming from base 4, base 5, or base 6 a challenge to be mastered, although more traditionally trained adults cannot budge from the decimal system with nearly as much ease. In developing patterns with rubber bands on nail-studded boards, the relationships between and among forms are then translated into numerical equations.

Implicit in learning math is the concept of inverse relationships, and Piaget has shown that children of the middle years are ready to see that addition and subtraction nullify each other, and multiplication and division nullify each other. Children are intrigued by doing multiplication in a variety of forms, once they understand that multiplication is based on addition. For example, they can use the following pattern in which the figures within the slanted parallels are added to multiply 1374 by 23:

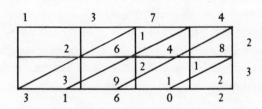

Or they can arrive at a result by doubling, as in the multiplication of 80 by 16:

$$
\begin{aligned}
80 \times 1 &= 80 \\
80 \times 2 &= 160 \\
80 \times 4 &= 320 \\
80 \times 8 &= 640 \\
80 \times 16 &= 1280
\end{aligned}
$$

Or by distribution:

$$104 \times 45 \text{ becomes } (104 \times 40) + (104 \times 5) =$$
$$4160 + 520 = 4680$$

The multiplication table becomes available as a short-cut which they can use without anxiety when their knowledge that multiplication is only addition after all allows them to find their way through a table, should they forget any part of it. By contrast, when children who learn their tables by rote and without this insight slip up, they cannot make the transition from, for example, $9 \times 5 = 45$ to $9 \times 6 = 54$, by simply adding the nine, because they do not grasp the pattern. Some children do figure this out by themselves and then feel guilty about using "a trick" when they have been told they should have remembered. Others are paralyzed with confusion and cannot help themselves out of their distress.

Earlier than was thought possible, children can tackle the concept of negative numbers with the fluidity with which they make the transition in play between the real and the unreal. The problem of $1 - (1 - 2)$ is not as unbelievable to them as it might seem when learned by formula and rote. In the new math, children play around with mathematical concepts, using different kinds of numbers to do it with, and the playing around aspects are precisely what make for mathematical thinking. Accuracy of computation, short-cuts, techniques, all become practical adjuncts instead of ends in themselves, as in the third-grade puzzle on page 264.

The learning in math does not happen by chance or by intuition alone. It takes careful planning by teachers, patience and effort by children. But when the learning is real, it leads to genuine pleasure, because of a sense of control of the operation. This is what is so strange a notion to adults brought up on the tradition of the "right answer." It need not all happen at the blackboard, either.

Children can learn math in application to an actual situation, as did a class in England, which made a survey of all the birds'

1		**2**	////	**3**	**4**
	////	**5**	**6**		
7	**8**	////	**9**		////
////	**10**	**11**	////	**12**	**13**
14			**15**	////	
16		////	**17**		

Across

1. $1000 - 2$
3. $4 + 4 + 4 + 4$
5. Ten hundred
7. 3×6
9. In 392 the 9 means
10. 4×7
12. $3 \times 67 = 2 \ \square\square$
14. Largest 4 digit no.
16. $7 \times \square = 70$
17. 300×3

Down

1. $(9 \times 100) + 1$
2. 9×9
3. 100 tens
4. 4×15
6. $999 - 90$
8. 1658×5
11. $88 + \square = 90$
13. 10 tens
14. One more than ninety
15. $100 - 1$

nests within a hundred yards of their school, identified the species, and kept a watch to see how many eggs were laid in each and what proportion of the young birds survived. (Math is here the tool of science.) Children can do their math learning in their seats or out of them as class lessons, as in answering the question, "How strong is string?" In that one, children had to think about and obtain the apparatus they needed, subject different samples of string to the same series of tests by attaching weights and noting at what point each string broke, repeat the tests for checking, and, finally, arrange samples in order of strength with breaking weight attached. At that point, they grasped the meaning of relative strength.[2]

Children can also learn math in the individual pursuit of problems laid out for them in cards graduated as to difficulty at the math center, or in their own notebooks, working individually or in small groups. In the latter case, discussion becomes as valuable a part of the learning experience as individual effort. But in any case, eights, nines, and many tens still need action-oriented experiences to perceive relationships before they can handle the paper and pencil formulations.

Because children respond so well to the flexibility of the newer approach to math learning, parents must become sensitive to new kinds of pitfalls. Whereas children formerly tended to tune out, because math was remote from their kind of reality, today's children may end up using "discovery" quite mechanically, as a drill, largely because adults fail to give them the time and encouragement that are necessary to develop active thinking and judgment about the problems they need to solve. Mathematical ideas do not reside in materials, but in the action undertaken with the materials; the symbols children use describe what they have abstracted from their manipulation of the materials. There is no formula by which children can be hurried through this kind of organic experience. Each must come to it in his own time, although the teacher can offer various approaches and organize the materials into manageable units that help the integration to occur. There are still, unfortunately, teachers who resist the newer approaches in mathematics, because they do not understand the fundamental changes involved in dealing with basic principles along with facts. To salve their consciences, such teachers offer the children two approaches labelled: "the way I was taught, which is still what you will need in life" and "modern math, which you

---

[2] John Blackie, *Primary Education* (London: Her Majesty's Stationery Office, 1967).

need to compete on tests." The children are then taught the "goesinter" method (How many twos go into eight?) side by side with "number stories" and discovery by rote. The children end up thoroughly confused and convinced of their inadequacy in math.

Science

Science, too, seeks patterns and relationships, but science seeks cause and effect relationships that are tied to the problems of survival, whereas mathematics only expresses them. Children normally have a burning curiosity about natural phenomena, and when this curiosity is honestly met, they welcome help in building an effective model for themselves of how the world works. The destruction of the earth's resources and the damage to the ecological chain are sufficiently advanced by now, however, to make necessary more than mere acquaintance with the names of birds, or the interesting fact that salmon swim upstream to spawn, or the demonstration that a lighted candle will be snuffed out when a glass is put over it. Principles of conservation based on ecological insights must be built into children's science study so that the pursuit of science does not lead to further disaster. In the growing distance between man and nature, we must affirm the relationship between the two for our children. We dare not move them into a technological world which repudiates this relationship by functioning to best nature, foil it, trick it, exploit it, but not acknowledge it as having any underlying relationship to man's existence. We do not know what the development of man will be in a milieu increasingly removed from contact with the earth, trees, animals, water. We know only that the history thus far of man's encounter with nature has shown him to be dependent on nature in his struggle to survive.

Children are natural scientists, but today's children must be deliberately taught to look respectfully at nature with an eye to differentiating ecological relationships from the greedy perceptions of the real estate developer. The old log which waits to be gotten rid of must be re-seen as organic matter returning to the earth, and the worm about whom childhood lore says it can be cut up into pieces and still survive, must be seen as a loosener of the earth and a helper of plants. Instead of being preached to about the interdependency of life, children must be helped to see how this life spreads into every corner of their world. One of the directors of a new Center for Environmental Studies in New York put it this way:

> Studying trees, animals, or insects separately is not relevant any more. We want these children to understand how important the relationship of one animal or plant is to another. So we take them right into our gardens and have them make charts and notes themselves on what is going on out there, guiding their attention to such phenomena as food chains between one species and another, nature's own method of "garbage disposal," and how man's upsetting of this balance is beginning to hurt him. Working with these plants and animals firsthand is a tremendous eye-opener to these city kids! [3]

The developmental characteristics of the middle years lend themselves well to such study. The concept of interdependence of all living organisms can be learned in the children's own concrete style through direct observation of woods, streams, swamps, backyards, and parks, as well as experimental situations set up in class. This means that children must be taken out of the classroom to allow them to read man's history along streams and lakes, up hills, through woods, and along layers of rock formation. They must see how a river is formed, what changes its flow, and what its capacities are for rejuvenation. Fossils, rock, and mineral specimens can be collected and exchanged with other schools in different parts of the country. Life in the ages before man appeared can be clarified through model-building, murals, and films.

Sources for the study of man's relation to the natural world

[3] "Tackling Pollution in the U.S.," *The Times Educational Supplement*, London, August 1970.

lie everywhere. The hill on which a suburban school stood was eroding, and the fifth-graders found, by talking with the construction engineers at the site, the landscape gardeners and the science consultants at their school, that planting is one way of preventing such erosion. Their interest broadened from there to floods and flood control. What might have been remote and dull when handled as preparation for a test became highly relevant when related to themselves and their future. For the urban child, camping trips involving sleeping away from home for brief periods may have to be planned at different times during his school years. Yet, even in a city classroom, months of serious study in the natural sciences can follow certain very common occurrences. A bee flies through the classroom window, a spider spins a web in the corner of the same window, the children carry pebbles and rocks into school in their pockets, and caterpillars attack the single tree in front of the school. In every case, children can be given time to observe and describe, to uncover the patterns leading to scientific law. The teacher need not rig up experiments; the children can design them.

Appreciation of nature's beauty is an important aspect of children's learning, but the study of the natural sciences need not bypass the realities of destruction in favor of the aesthetic. This is not to say that children should be left feeling helpless and frustrated, as restless groups of children do when their teacher drones on about the dangers of pollution, and the children mutter, "Kids can't do anything anyway." This is precisely an area where children's competencies can be applied in a larger social cause. There is something constructive about setting nature to rights again, perhaps because that brings aesthetics back into our lives. In the class of fifth-graders who had spent an hour discussing the Kent State killings and moved from that excitedly to other examples of violence in their more immediate lives, one child suddenly suggested, "Let's go out and clean up the woods around the school." The whole class agreed enthusiastically, and during their lunch hour that sad day the children took paper bags and collected rubbish from the floor of the wooded area near their school. They needed to feel that they could make an impact on the world that had let them down and physically cleaning it up helped.

The positives involved in realistic uses of the earth's resources and the strengths man has shown in coping with problems must be studied assiduously by children old enough to grasp the concept of alternatives. For example, air pollution has been controlled to a considerable degree in certain European countries, certain desert lands can still be reclaimed, and indeed some already have been in the Middle East. Undersea land is constantly being reclaimed by the Dutch, and new strains of wheat that increase the harvest to a spectacular degree are being grown in India, a country that has long known extreme poverty and even starvation. The World Health Organization controls epidemics and saves us the worldwide disasters of sickness so prevalent in the past. Almost-extinct birds have been coaxed back into multiplying, although we have still lost far too many species during this century.

We do not have to give children a soporific view of the world in order to give them the hope that man's intelligence and good will can cope with the problems of natural destruction. Increased knowledge for this generation must lead to respect for the natural world without losing faith in the power of man to live at peace with that natural world and with his fellow man. The earth is a single unit, and the effort to save it will call for the combined efforts of men and women of all nations, colors, and creeds. This perception must become a basic assumption to children growing up during a period when upheaval and transition exist on a world scale.

Science Learning Has Many Directions

Vital, realistic study of the natural sciences, combined with children's interest in current industrial and technological development, can lead to the physical sciences, to the study of electricity, optics, mechanics, and chemistry. Crossing magnetic lines of force with wire from a dry cell is the base for understanding the steam or water turbine; knowledge of images and lenses underlies the powerful Laser beam. Children of the middle years can learn to understand the development and function of electric motors, pumps, pendulums, water wheels, windmills, thermometers, barometers, compasses, and the many other instruments by which man has made his life more orderly as a consequence of his grasp of important laws of nature. In some instances, children of the middle years can go through the same steps of hypothesizing and testing that might have been pursued by early inventors and enjoy the satisfactions inherent in the processes of reasoning. Eight-year-olds can rediscover the wheel when small logs are made available to them as the only materials they may use in solving a problem of transporting something. Nines can "invent" a means of carrying water from one level to another. The concepts of latitude and longitude can be developed by ten- and eleven-year-old children, once they are given the knowledge about the fixed position of the North Star (available to navigators since antiquity) and the awareness which led Renaissance scholars to hypothesize that the earth was a globe—namely that ships disappear over the horizon. With this information, the very real questions—What, in an era of expansion and search, could people do to help themselves chart their way through unfamiliar waters? How could they keep their bearings and get home again without simply going on and on until they completed the circle?—can stimulate a lot of thinking. Contemporary children, brought up on traffic signals and street signs, can figure out a system of directional guides related to a fixed star, even if the guides are imaginary. The lines of latitude and longitude developed this way take on a meaning they never had for the majority of elementary teachers, who learned it by rote and taught it by rote for generations.

Social Science

The content of the social sciences is man's solution to basic problems he has always faced, and continues to face, in coping with his environment and with his fellow man. The complexity of the contemporary world makes it difficult, however, to establish a real and illuminating relationship with it, especially for children. While vicarious as well as direct material can begin to have meaning now, the depth and breadth of understanding that is potentially possible for young children can be realized only to the extent that their bodies and emotions are engaged along with their minds. They must feel that they are thinking, involved participants in the life of the world.

As children deal with material in the social sciences, it is important that the human situation be lifted for them a notch into the general and abstract without affecting their own spontaneity or subjective style. This is best accomplished when three dimensions of the learning process are considered: the nature of experience, from first-hand to vicarious; the conceptual level, from concrete to abstract; and the intellectual approach to the content, from cumulative to analytical. New material might be attacked in a familiar style—as when children study Indians by using the information in non-verbal and physical, as well as verbal, ways. New approaches might be applied to familiar material, as when sixth-graders return to a study of their community, which they first learned about in first grade, but this time to analyze its government and agencies of operation.

It is easier for children to deal with the physical organization of life and the feelings people have about them than with social and political organization, as has been indicated earlier. Clear and distinct terms of relationship to the environment, such as that between climate variation and plant and animal growth, or clear terms of relationship among people, as in kinship systems, are easier to perceive than such complex phenomena as religious movements or psychological motivation. When one considers the great speed of technological growth compared with the far slower development of social attitudes in mankind generally, then the unevenness in children's capacity to learn different kinds of content may be better appreciated.

Geography

Geography was described by Lucy Sprague Mitchell as "a matter of relationships between people and the earth." Looking at geography this way, children would examine a physical map to figure out which sites are practical as settlements in terms of needed facilities for life—food, shelter and transportation—rather than to routinely locate capitals, rivers, and mountains without knowing how these affect lives. Inevitably, children who seek such relationships select the same places for settling that men and women before them did, and they discover this when they compare maps. Of course, air travel and technology may seem to alter these perceptions for contemporary settlement, but the relation of technology to basic need becomes clearer when studied in this concrete way.

Basic relationships of the physical phenomena of the earth, as these affect man, lend themselves particularly well to the learning style of nine- and ten-year-olds. The relation of plains to mountains, of rivers to oceans, of elevation to rainfall, of valleys to mobility, can be worked out in three-dimensional models, some before and some after the children have grasped the mathematical concepts of ratio and scale. Such models form an excellent support for the more abstract two-dimensional maps which give us bearing in the global, as well as local, arena. Moreover, the importance of the three-dimensional background that must precede map-reading of the more conventional kind is valid even in the space age.

Before air travel, there was no question that children had no idea about the size, shape, or general characteristics of the geographic area they lived in, much less of a larger, more inclusive area. It is tempting to assume that that is no longer true about children who have seen the shape of their earth in pictures taken from the moon, and who have many times seen aerial photos of places in the news on television. Nevertheless, despite the impact of the objective, pictorial view, teachers find children no better able to visualize distant space and space relationships than before. A very recent study revealed a direct relationship between the degree of egocentrism in children and their capacity to develop accurate perceptions about their world.[4] The ability to read maps, which depends upon a grasp of spatial relationships and of scale ratios, is affected by the degree of subjectivity with which a child reacts to the external world. The pace of this kind of internal development apparently is not that easily altered. The transition to map-reading and map-making, therefore, continues to mark an important stage of progress in objective thinking. From earlier beginnings of a three-dimensional nature, as with blocks, children proceed to maps in chalk on the schoolroom or schoolyard floor to maps in crayon, paint and collage on paper on the classroom floor, depicting rivers and streets, highways and houses, boundaries and other topographical details as they perceive them.

Translating concrete phenomena into the more abstract symbolization of maps is not easy. Sybil Marshall described her effort to help ten-year-old children to an understanding of map representation of physical space and topography thus:

> I had been struggling to impart some knowledge of contour lines, without much success. . . . The trouble was that we lived in such a flat county that it was really very difficult to relate the lines on the map to the actual countryside. Somehow I had to demonstrate the meaning of all the curious squiggles on our maps. We had a hundredweight of potter's clay in an old bin outside, clay which had been used again and again and had got tired. We used it to create an island. We pinned white paper carefully to a table and then emptied the clay-bin bit by bit on to the paper, moulding the wet, sticky clay into hills and valleys and cliffs and beaches and promontories and harbours and peaks and estuaries (and learning all these geographical terms as we went along). When we had finished, we coloured the paper all

[4] John Towler, "Egocentrism and Map Reading Ability." Unpublished paper presented at American Educational Research Association, Minneapolis, Minnesota, 1970.

round blue, to represent the sea. Then with a mighty concerted effort, we heaved the whole island up just far enough for someone to pull out the paper from beneath. (I ought to have said that I had intended to do this, and had used very tough paper on purpose, and also that the clay had been allowed to dry considerably before attempting to pick the island up entire.) The paper showed very clearly the outline of the island at sea level: for the first time many children understood an outline map properly. We then made a wire cutter, exactly like a grocer's cheese cutter, from a piece of wire and two pieces of kindling, and proceeded to cut off layers of our clay island. Each time, as we cut it, we placed the lump we had cut off on to the original outline map and drew round it. When we had finished we had a complete contour map of our island which everyone understood. We created storms by raining on the island with a watering can with a rose on the end of the spout. We watched where the water ran between the hills, and marked out the course of the rivers. . . . Now rivers and peaks began to be claimed by the children, and when at last one of the more romantically minded boys invented a cove full of buried treasure, geography gave way at last to English and story writing in particular.[5]

History

The sense of time and space beyond the immediate that emerges during the middle years means that history-mindedness can begin to be a new mode of ordering the world. But for history to come alive, children must feel that they are living the past. This means that they must identify at other points in time with the repeated human experience of resolving basic problems. Naturally, the problems they look at must be comprehensible to their youth and inexperience.

For example, eight-year-olds studying old-time Indian life have long made Indian garments and headgear which they wear freely at school, taken on Indian names, made vegetable

[5] Sybil Marshall, *Experiment in Education* (London: Cambridge University Press, 1963), p. 56–57.

dyes, cooked Indian foods, built an Indian dwelling, and, by their activity, given life to the facts they have learned from their teacher, books, pictures, and slides.

To strengthen the sense of time as reaching back into the past and forward into the future, nines, tens, and elevens can profitably study their communities by tracking down the concrete evidence of how it changed, and is changing. They can examine old documents, such as letters, handbills, or posters; records and pictures that indicate the existence of prior buildings, streets, stores, and roads; the paintings, literature, and music of a period. They can interview people of several generations for their recollections of what stood on the site of the school before it was built, in what kinds of stores they shopped before there was a supermarket, or how they got about when cars were less plentiful. They can study changes over time in such commonplace items as cooking utensils—examining and using a mortar and pestle, wooden bowl and chopper, grater and strainer, meat grinder (hand and electric), and blender. Or they can follow patterns of food storage—from earth to cave to cold cellar to ice box to refrigerator; or garbage disposal—from the toss-over-the-shoulder method through truck cartage, incinerators, and compressors. If they are lucky, the neighborhood might even have possibilities for a dig that would allow them to uncover ruins for themselves.

They learn easily about heroes, such as pioneers, explorers, and space men, because their own aspirations for adventure and independent exploration allow them to identify with the actions of such heroes. Heroes are important to children, and it is the better part of wisdom to bring to their attention the heroes whose dramatic actions have social, as well as personal, implications.

There are many aspects of the study of man and his way of coping that children can understand and which will stretch them beyond where they are. It is not necessary, however, to force a higher order morality on the study of history and other cultures before the children are ready. If they repeat verbally, without a sense of involvement or comprehension, they will be estranged from history in the same way that they can be from math and literature, and this is precisely the effect of traditional schooling that must be overcome. Children need to develop a historical sense and study history for what can be learned from it; but they will use history most profitably if their burgeoning time sense is supported in ways that make sense also in those other aspects of living that matter to young and inexperienced children.

Children are not at all clear as to what binds men together across the ages and across the world. Because a technological society makes it so difficult to "see" people and their feelings, and because it is so easy to "miss" people in studying the past, the continuity of human endeavor and feeling must be consciously extended into the study of man and his social experience as children grow beyond the action-oriented learning style of their younger years.

Once past ten or eleven, most children can understand the universal incidence of fear, satisfaction, pleasure, generosity, greed, selfishness, indifference, and compassion in themselves and in others. They know the feelings associated with ingenuity, coping, and success, as well as with uncertainty, inadequacy, and failure. They must be helped to deal with multiple cause and effect relationships, both in the past and in the present, and to look at human dilemmas with greater attention to seeking out the factors involved in decision-making. To the extent that they, as adults, are less likely to sit in judgment on people, they are more likely to be concerned with changes in the conditions of life, and this they must come to by giving history a human dimension they can grasp. What were Rosa Parks' feelings the day she refused to sit in the back of a bus in Montgomery, Alabama? How did the men who conquered Peru feel about taking the belongings of a strange people and keeping them? How did the Indians feel when the skills by which they had always lived could no longer be applied to the living conditions imposed upon them by their white conquerors?

Of vital importance are the themes that heighten the awareness of one world and one humanity. A study of how explorers of the polar regions live, work, and study under rigorous conditions on past or present expeditions introduces experience that cuts across national boundaries. Making puppets in the style of the East as well as the West takes children a step out of our rootedness in Western civilization. Life in Africa, as well as the Black experience in America, must also be tapped in ways suitable to age and style of learning to expand children's recognition and acceptance of the varied modes of common human experience.

If children study people honestly, they and their teachers will come up against feelings that are still unresolved, such as those in Western cultures about birth and death; or they may begin to glimpse the future that will follow logically from present evasions. For example, it will be their generation which will face seriously the social and scientific contradictions involved in the battle between ecology and industry. Their searches may bring them back to the sciences again, because honest social studies programs cannot help but merge with the sciences, just as in life the need for new tools and skills for living leads to discovery and invention.

Study Themes and Sex Differences

Any discussion on content would be incomplete without a comment on the likenesses and differences in the tastes and responses of boys and girls. Both sexes are subject to stereotyped reactions that must be discouraged in the determination of content. Teachers do see differences, and studies support their experience, but these do not apply to every boy and girl. Boys are generally more interested in the less personalized content, girls are more social and drawn toward nurturing plants and animals. But there is a marked overlap, and it is important that classrooms be rich in variety and leave individual choice of activity to the individuals themselves.

It is easier for children to resist the pressure of sex stereotyping when the teacher does not categorize class work, status, or achievement along sex lines. Even so, children may need to try out activities normally associated with the other sex (cooking for boys, for example) in the safety of like-sex groups. One teacher helped her eight-year-olds over the hurdle by setting up a Friday Afternoon Trading Post, at which both boys and girls felt free to try each others' flipping cards, jacks, bead looms, and scout knives with impunity.

It is important that areas of study—the social sciences in particular—have leeway for boys and girls. The elementary curriculum has, in general, not catered to themes boys could find significant, such as whaling or polar exploration, which embody challenge to the physical self, to courage and daring. But when they have been suitable, as in the study of the Pioneers, not enough attention has been given to the female role. And this has also been true of the study of the Abolition movement. Studies of African life, in which women were often the active ones, or of the Amazons simply do not appear at all.

Girls are, on the whole, successful at school, and the criticism in this area focuses on the deprivation suffered by boys. But the fact that girls have been better able to conform to the demands for neatness and quiet must not be interpreted to mean that their intellectual lives have not suffered equally, or that a simple change to curriculum suitable to boys will automatically be good for them, too. As the concepts of masculinity and femininity undergo change, the school must allow for those children who accept the conventional male and female roles to stay within them in choice of parts in plays, themes of study, and so on, at the same time that it offers alternatives for those willing to try them. Large themes of study must be looked at for their type of psychological appeal in terms of boy-girl differences as well as stage of development. If the possibilities are embedded in the study, then individual boys and girls will be able to find themselves in their own way.

Here is a story written by a little girl in a class where this was done. Note how she is working out her feminine role through the content, but along lines of liberation.

Once there was a Eskimo girl named Pomiok. She loved to go seal hunting. Her father wouldn't let her go because he thought she would get scared from the dead seal and all the blood in the snow. But she didn't. So her father let her go. She was the *best* seal hunter in the whole family.

When they moved to a new camp she was the best seal hunter in the whole camp. When they were starving Pomiok caught more seal. And her family never starved again.

But one day her grandmother came to visit and Pomiok's father tole her that she could hunt seal. When the grandmother heard she said, "What? Eskimo women are not supposed to hunt seal." So she had to stop seal hunting. So they all starved again, and the grandmother too.

So she let her seal hunt. Pomiok was happy. So they never starved again.

When the carabou season came again she was able to hunt carabou by herself. So her family never starved again. They were proud of her.

Experience and Expression

What children experience must ultimately be dealt with in symbolic form, because to do so encourages observation and extends sensitivity by the sheer nature of its demand. With thought and feeling both at work, children must recreate their experiences symbolically in order to recognize the patterns inherent in them. However, many of the things they experience cannot be put into words, so that, although high priority must be given during the middle years to the relationship between experience and expression, the symbolic expression must be non-verbal as well as verbal. The arts thus take on a symbolizing potential that is as important as language during these years.

That children can perceive abstractions mainly through concrete operations and not as meaningfully through words alone is one side of the coin. The other side is the developmentally rooted difficulty involved in expressing abstraction through words. Beyond these is the objective reality that translating oral language into written form involves a lengthy period of technical training which constricts even further the possibilities for language as a total medium of expression during formative years of learning.

Art offers the ground experience in expressive activity that eventually leads to writing. Freedom and guidance, sensual experience, and the process of expressing are as inherent in art as they are in writing. As children use media which do not require a long apprenticeship to gain workable techniques, the experiences they understand and feel, but cannot put into words, are clarified by the transformation into paint, wood, clay, linoleum prints, fabric, and other unstructured materials. Since children are at a stage when it is as important for them to be productive as it is to enjoy the sensory aspects of materials and media, there is a heightening of self-imposed standards of workmanship and a pride in being productive which help to offset the unrewarding, slow acquisition of skill in writing.

To perceive the arts as something pleasant but inherently useless is to miss the point. Art is a means of giving coherence to a realm of human experience. To neglect it is to neglect the self. Those who speak of art as a frill tacked on to a serious curriculum would do well to remember that the skills of reading and writing appeared rather late in man's history, whereas the arts were always there. There is a whole range of human experience which only art can express and which we need to value at least as much as we value technical proficiency and skill. In this connection, reference must be made to two of the most beautiful and exciting accounts of work with children to have appeared in recent years—Sybil Marshall's already quoted *Experiment in Education* and Elwyn Richardson's *In the*

Early World.[6] Both of these gifted teachers, who began to work with children at school in the arts, describe in rich detail just how this led to verbal learning.

Words As Means of Expression

Expressing meaning through words must nevertheless proceed and be supported. It can take many more forms than the old question-and-answer or formal report of the traditional school. Discussion, for example, is a verbal experience that must become an inevitable, repeated aspect of a curriculum in which children are encouraged to grow. Children must speak to, and with, each other and the teacher about what they observe; they must exchange information; they must struggle to find words to describe the feelings with which they respond to their successes and failures; they must present evidence to support their generalizations and their hypotheses. They must think together and together determine the right questions to ask for further inquiry. Through discussion, children find words to share their predictions, their plans, and their appreciation of suitable and exciting words that best convey their feelings and thoughts.

Discussions of this kind are basically a way of probing experience. It is hard for middle years children to do this without help. It is easier for them to build a snowman together than to talk through ideas and concepts together. They require the skilled touch of a knowledgeable adult on a regular and ongoing basis in order to learn it. They are ready to begin using words for group thinking in this way, but if development in the skill is not consciously supported by their teachers during these years, they lose out. Few college students can conduct a serious discussion without help, and few teachers can lead one, primarily because most people throughout their schooling were not asked to think aloud with peers and arrive at solutions to

[6] Elwyn Richardson, *In The Early World* (New York: Pantheon Books, 1969).

problems together, the richer for having put several heads to a task instead of one.

Dramatization is another form of verbal expression which, combining words and action, is admirably suited to the middle years. When children are free to play outside of school, the making up of plays to show to adult and child audiences is a perennial favorite carried over from generation to generation. There is no reason why this natural bent should not serve to support the organization of ideas and actions in a sequential unfolding of newly learned information. Turning to their own understanding of the content studied, or to the universal in childhood feeling and fantasy, or in a combination of both, small groups of children struggling to make up a play learn more than meets the eye in their finished performance. In planning together, they must grope for words to make themselves clear to each other; they must use words to find agreement on the broad and specific themes to be embedded in their play; they must argue and determine the validity and accuracy of props, stage sets, backdrops, and costumes; individually or together they must probe the depth of characterization required for the parts. To act comes naturally to children. By combining their talent for drama with information, they are in the process of integrating, they are able to focus better on the weighing and sorting of relevant from irrelevant in a way that gives the content a special quality of reality.

Sometimes children prefer to use puppets instead of themselves to say the things within them that need saying, and this can lead not only to the projection of their own images of the puppet characters, but to a more objective study of puppet techniques in different countries, including the shadow puppets of Java, India, and China. They can taste the flavor of an Oriental culture and enhance their sense of the aesthetic, while fulfilling an internal need to use symbolic forms to express their thoughts and feelings.

Oral speech and written speech are sufficiently different from each other so that children require considerable help in expressing their ideas and feelings in written form. Oral language relies on facial expression, gestures, pauses, intonation, repetition, contradiction, and immediate feedback. But a word, a phrase, a sentence, once set down in writing, have a finality that must stand on its own. Children of the middle years need lots of practice in writing what they have to say and they need strong moral and practical support for writing with clarity and style. But such writing develops best when related to need and not put to death by interminable practice of the formalities of margins, capital letters, and sentence structure uncommitted to any content. The latter is what has actually been the focus of children's writing experience for generations, with the result that people at every educational level feel stymied and trapped by their anxiety over structure, when structure should become second nature to the message.

Children need to become masters of written form, not slaves to it. They are not likely to achieve such mastery during their elementary years, although some children can go quite far (See *Sammy Snake*, pp. 284–292.) Their lasting interest in writing must be safeguarded during the years when they are struggling with the frustration of form in combination with the frustrations of physically creating the writing on paper, as well as composing it mentally. There are proven techniques for this, which are periodically disregarded when parents and teachers grow too anxious to give children the time they need.

Children's writing at this stage, like art, ought not to be geared toward communication with someone removed in time and space, as is done in the hours devoted to proper form in the heading, salutation, and closing of formal and informal correspondence. Writing is best used to satisfy a personal need to relive an experience. Skills can be stressed to better advantage in the many realistic requirements for factual and objective reporting that eventuate from group life at school. As in all expressive media, form must serve meaning.

A curriculum concerned with meaning inevitably uses language to clarify meaning. A curriculum concerned with the children's learning will not overlook the importance to them of the skills and techniques that will give force and power to what

SAMMY SNAKE

Melissa Roche

Sammy The Snake

Chapter 1 Moved

There once was a snake. His name was Sammy. He lived under a doorstep. One day He was wiggling around. Suddenly a huge hand grabbed him! In a moment he found himself behind a big black fence. "Wow" said Sammy "that was a close one, better start looking around my new home" sighed Sammy.

Chapter 2 Looking Around

Well what Sammy didn't know was that a Mongoose owned these parts. He also didn't know that Mongoose's killed Snakes! Well one day Sammy was wiggling along when all of a sudden he came face to face Mr. Zonk the Mongoose. "Mmmmmmmm" said Mr. Zonk "You look very scrumptious" "Whaaat do you mean by scrumptios said Sammy "I mean that if you don't get out of here, in ten seconds I'm going to eat you!" said Mr. Zonk "yipes! I better get out of here and fast" said Sammy.

Sammy started wiggleing around and suddenly he found a big hole - without knowing what to do he quikly wiggled down.

All that time Mr. Zonk was scampering

around. He suddenly stopped short infront
of the hole. He looked around and sighed
"Oh, well I can't find him anywhere
but I don't really care I just better
not see him again on my property."
Mean while sammy was wondering which
way to turn because he had found
himself at the boddom of the hole.
And in a room full passages. "Oh boy
not again better find the way out of here and
fast.

3   Exploring the Hole

"Whooo! I must of been through a millian
tunnles" sighed sammy. After about an
hour of searching sammy stopped in a
passage that entered into a neat little
room. To his surprise it had a little
stove, and a very long bed about as long
as sammy! could it be a little
snake lived here just like sammy.
"Oh my! Oh myyy! I think another snake
lives here! well anyway I'm going to
stay here until he or she comes"
in about an hour or so sammy
heard somone huming "diddle dee aum
diddle dee dee dee dee" sammy said

②

"Oh boy! the snake's coming. I better hide."

♥ 4 A Girl Snake! ♥

"I think I'll hide behind the sofa said sammy. All of a sudden the snake came in. "Oh my goodness a girl snake! screamed sammy. "Who is it? said the girl snake "It's just me the sofa, whispered sammy. "I know there's somone in here now come out wherever you are, said the girl snake. "Ok, I'll come out said sammy. "Ahhhhhhhhhhh! screamed the girl snake. "Eeeeeeee! screamed sammy. "A boy "A girl they both screamed... "Hi, my names Serena, she said. "Hi my names sammy, said sammy. I was just wondering how you got here in the first place and how come you're in my house, said serena "Well it all began when.... "Oh never mind said serena. "You know said sammy I rather like you "I rather like you too said serena "Ooooo "I'm tired, I wish there was a bed for me yawned sammy "I'm sure we can fix up a nice bed for you".

5 The Big Shadow

Late that night while they were sleeping, serena woke up. Ohh, I think I'll get a drink of water from the 99th hole said serena sleepily. When serena was in the 99th hole which was the hole nearest the opening to the hole which was the nearest hole to the top. After she got her drink of water, serena decided to take a walk since it was such a pleasant evening. But, when she had wiggled only a foot a giant shadow crossed her path "So it's you I thought I told you to get out of here two years ago. It was Mr. Zonk! Iii know you did gracious sir shivered serena. Mean while, sammy felt sort of scared and alone. "Serena" wispered sammy. there was no answer "Serena!" this time sammy shouted, "Serena where are you! shouted sammy. Ahhhhh! it was serena!. "Dont worry serena, Im coming screamed sammy. Oh dear which way do I go Oh yea I remember. turn left at the th hole turn

right at the 32nd hole, Left 42nd, right 52nd, left 62nd, right 72nd, left 82nd, right 92nd.
When sammy got out side he hid behind a mulberry bush. Then he saw Mr. Lonk carrying off serena. "Come back here you snakenapper" screamed sammy. "Hey I thought I got rid of you yesterday" screamed Mr. Lonk.. But sammy did a very strange thing he turned around and went back down the hole! But he secretly followed Mr. Lonk underground the way he did it was he tunneled near the surface and listened to Mr. Lonks footsteps. "Let me down you beast!" screamed serena. ~~finally sighed sammy.~~

6 In Mr. Lonk's House

At last sammy tunneled into a dark room "Eeeeee!" screamed sammy. "Oh my goodness how horrible!" yelled sammy. There in the room was about a hundred dead snakes. Some in stocks with their heads off, some with knives in them and some with teeth marks. All of a sudden sammy realized

that the reason all those snakes
were dead Mr. Lonk had probobly
killed them all because they
wouldn't get off his land. Then sammy
heard footsteps coming down the
steps. "I better hide said sammy
"Ohhhh "sighed serena What happened
to all those poor snakes Mr. Lonk gave
a mean laugh, "Haeeeeee soon you and
the boy will be one of them". Sammy
couldn't stand it any longer and suddenly
jumped out from behind a dead
snake and shouted "Not it I can help it you
won't".

7 Escape

Mr. Lonk was so starteled that he
droped serena, "Oh sammy yelled serena
I thought youed never come. "Stay
where you are you little brats you
shouted Mr. Lonk, Mr. Lonk was holding
a knife and standing on a platform.
"Now Iv waited long enough serena
Im going to kill you both". "Hissssss
your wrong your the one who's leaving.
and with that sammy took a torch
from behind his back and set fire

Mr. Zonk's coat. "Owwwww" howled Mr. Zonk
Mr. Zonk turned around and started
running back up the stairs.

8 More Snakes

"Oh sammy my hero" serena went over
to sammy and gave him a big hug.
"Come on serena help me bury all these
snakes" said sammy. I was hard to dig
so many holes. finally sammy and serena
finished and went back through
the tunnle by then it was about
4 o'clock am. so they went to bed
in the morning around 9 o'clock
sammy woke up but serena was'nt
in her room she was in the 2nd
hole all around her were eggs "Oh
serena" that was all sammy could
say. Just then the egg's hatched
and all them said at one time
"Dada Mama". The End

turn page

The End.

they have to say. Provision for such learning must of course be made. But it must be made in a total setting in which what a child has to say is the central focus, and the form in which he says it is urged on to the greatest possible clarity, but not held as a whip over his head. It is important to recognize in this connection that the traditional piecemeal approach to language learning has not been effective. For example, fifty years of research on the teaching of grammar has shown that the children who know their grammar are those who speak well in any case and that children whose language is inadequate do not readily apply abstract rules to their own speech and writing.

Reading must be discussed within the same frame of reference, that is, as communication. Reading during the middle years should not be a separate subject learned at school, but a communication process underlying much of what is important and interesting at school. Reading is one way—and an increasingly important one as the years go by—in which to gain ideas and knowledge from people who are otherwise not accessible. It differs from some of the newer forms of communication in that it allows for a dimension of depth precisely because it is slower and therefore encourages thought and response as an ongoing aspect of the communication. Reading must permeate everything at school and be in constant use. It must not be isolated from the heart of the content by abstracting it as a subject to be attended to once a day.

This is not to say that children do not need to continue to strengthen their reading skills nor that they will not need scheduled help in doing so. During the middle years there is wide stratification in the levels of competency involved. While a number of children have begun by eight to be quite independent in their capacity to read effectively, many more have not. Even at ten, there are children who require special attention and help. Diagnosis at this stage must continue to be completely individual, because the causes of difficulty range from simple immaturity to neurological problems, from emotional complications to poor teaching.

For all children, the approach to reading at school must

stress its basic purposes and function, while the needed assistance in technicalities goes on in small groups or on an individual basis. During the middle years, attention must be drawn to
the perspective that reading serves for pleasure and enjoyment
of stories, for general information, or to answer specific questions raised by some research in which the children are involved. Children can read to follow newspaper stories as well
as to explore documents related to a topic of interest. They can
read to distinguish fact from fancy, or to become more critical
of literary style. (What did the author do that made you
laugh?)

Reading must be seen to make writing come alive, whether
it is a child's own, another child's, or an author's. It is truly a
matter of communicating, and children of the middle years
must be helped to sense this in full measure. The reader-text in
which a specified story is read in order to answer some specified question in the terminology of the text is a poor substitute for meaningful reading, even when it is supported by contests to see who reads the most books in a month. This kind of
competition does little to support a passion for reading of the
kind that causes a child to keep his flashlight on under the bed-
covers so he can finish a book. Children become readers by
reading everything in sight, not by being prescribed a limited
sample of print so that their errors can be corrected—after
which the book is closed for the day.

When reading is related to a purpose that children feel and
see, the most unexpected material might prove good reading.
In a sixth grade that was hotly excited about a presidential elec-
tion, the teacher suggested that the children conduct a straw
poll in the school. She obtained a voting booth for them, but in
order to set up the rules within the school, the children had to
read the voting regulations of their state and community.
Under ordinary conditions, no teacher would select that for
sharpening reading teeth; but the subject was voting, not reading, and the children went at the fine print and unfamiliar
words with earnestness and persistence.

A last word for two other non-subjects: music and movement. It is natural for man to use his body and his voice to express feeling, and all children begin life knowing this. By three, a child chants his made-up songs and moves easily on his knees, on his haunches, on his toes, or in leaps and jumps. By six, traditional schooling has put him into a seat for long hours each day and allowed him calculated breaks of carefully supervised movement and sound to take care of his deep need to run and leap, to shout and sing. In some countries, folk dancing and choral singing are common adult activities that continue the use of movement and music generated spontaneously in childhood. But most American children have no such model, and their parents and teachers must deliberately recapture for them the joy of movement and sound by making provision for these in their schooling. At first, among the youngest children, this would be largely self-directed activity in movement and song-making. As children grow ready for refinement of skills during the middle years, they can be helped to develop techniques in movement and music without sacrificing the basic satisfaction inherent in being a doer with one's own body and voice. In this area, too, technical skill must be a means and not an end. There are satisfactions here that go deep into the inner being, and schools must include movement, especially as academic studies grow more intense, to balance intellectual and physical effort. Children must be full human beings in body and spirit as well as mind.

Educational objectives that combine awareness of the stage of childhood, individual differences, and social need are well summed up by Barbara Biber of the Bank Street College of Education.

Schools must aim to develop competency at the highest possible levels in several areas: a literacy level in words and numbers that begins to be functionally rewarding; differentiated perceptions of natural phenomena, work processes, and social functioning of both past and present societies; abilities related to solving problems, acquiring and ordering information that stem from the strengthening of reasoning, of judging, of inferring; increasing the skills of doing and making in manipulative, as well as bodily, in mechanical, as well as creative, areas. . . . Diversity and change must become an intrinsic part of children's perception of the world they live in; curriculum must be sensitive to individual and sex differences in pace and style of mastery; to coexisting and conflicting drives, loyalties and behavioral patterns of all children; and to sub-cultural variations in family and cultural styles without denigration of any one of them.

To this, one might add the reminder of how it is done by the children themselves:

> I hear and I forget;
> I see and I remember;
> I do and I understand.
>
> (Old Chinese proverb)

Parent and Child
During the Intermediate Years

. . .

It is not easy to be the parent of a middle-years child. For the first time in the experience of parenthood, the children show the desire for special and private experiences of their own, do many things away from home, and are secretive about what they do. It becomes harder for parents to hold the reins, and some parents begin to doubt their capacity to do so.

The children do not want complete freedom and independence. They would be terrified if they had it. But they do want to slough off the taken-for-granted dependency of their baby-hood, while holding onto the cozy sense of affection and safety that went with it. Family life and family figures mean a great deal to children during their middle years, but studies show two persistent concerns about family ties during this stage. One is the fear that the important effort to achieve greater independence and close friendships outside the home will cost them the love and support of their parents. The other is the fear that, in the face of quarrels and conflict within the family, home might not remain stable and solid. As they learn to cope with the day-to-day emotions invested in new and independent realms of behavior, they continue, despite their bluster, to need understanding and supportive parents who will define limits for them, while giving them enough latitude for adventure. But they do not make the task easy.

To the children, growing up means the denial of any implication that the old relationship with parents holds in the same old ways. They resist parental control over their bodies ("Time for your bath." "Wash your hands."), their responsibilities ("Do your homework." "Hang up your clothes."), their tastes ("This is a more suitable book for you."), and their consciences ("Don't lie."). They want to decide by themselves when to go to school, what to spend their allowance on, what to wear, how many baths and haircuts to take, and when to come in out of the snow or rain. They want to choose their own friends, make their own plans for Saturday and Sunday, pick their own books and hobbies and decide how long to read before putting out the light.

Nor is that all. They are indifferent to coming home on time, neglect to brush their teeth, and resent, defy, or forget requests or demands for regularity or obedience of any kind. They leave home for school neatly turned out, scrubbed and combed, and return with shirt-tail out, buttons mismatched in their buttonholes, collars awry, and fingers and knees grimy. They move at different tempos into becoming boisterous, dirty, discourteous, and even antagonistic. Their language forms and enunciation become slovenly and vulgar, and they are careless about all manner of carefully taught refinements for social living. They may eat excessively or find it hard to sit through a meal; table manners can deteriorate to the level of infant behavior. And their time sense is unbelievable.

They ask to be treated as individuals with a sense of dignity, but they themselves are insolent and utterly tactless. They can be unfeeling about others to the point of cruelty. They fight any show of affection, and to be kissed in public is a humiliation of the first order. Children of eight and nine who love their mothers dearly will cross to the other side of the street when they see her coming, if they happen to be with friends, because to greet or be greeted by their mothers in the presence of peers is to acknowledge having been (and perhaps still being) a baby. They revert from time to time to the sweet old dependency in private and on their own terms, but they can stand back and evaluate adults with a critical eye that seems to say, "You grown-ups don't know everything. Us kids know plenty you don't know." Sometimes they even run away from home.

At the same time, they have a tendency to flit from one interest to another, giving up costly projects and hobbies with a fine carelessness that causes their parents to wonder whether they will ever learn to persist in anything. The typicalness of this behavior was readily identified by a group of eight- and nine-year-old children, whose teacher, while reading *The Wind in the Willows* to them, came to the part in which Rat and Otter comment on the activities of Toad:

> "Well, tell us, *who's* out on the river?"
> "Toad's out for one," replied the Otter. "In his brand-new wager-boat; new togs, new everything."
> The two animals looked at each other and laughed.
> "Once it was nothing but sailing," said the Rat. "Then he tired of that and took to punting. Nothing would please him but to punt all day and every day, and a nice mess he made of it. Last year it was houseboating, and we all had to pretend we liked it. He was going to spend the rest of his life in his houseboat. It's all the same, whatever he takes up, he gets tired of it, and starts something fresh."

When the teacher stopped at the end of the passage to ask, "Does anybody here know anyone like that?", the children burst eagerly into anecdotes about themselves. There was general agreement that they were all like that at some time, and some children said, "I'm like that *all* the time!"

They hate to be reminded of what they need to do and fall back on their peer alliances to argue rights. "Other kids don't have to call their mothers," they say. "Other kids can go alone." They like to be considered responsible, but they are completely inconsistent and unreliable in assuming responsibility, as the following story of two brothers, one eight and the other six, reveals. The children were allowed to keep a puppy offered the family by a neighbor. Their mother read them a simple dog manual to acquaint them with the procedures necessary for the puppy's well-being. The very first evening of the puppy's stay, the eight-year-old said he wanted to write a book about dogs, and his obliging mother wrote down his dictated work, which he called *Rules for Our Dog Ginger*. The message was clear and detailed.

1. *Feeding*

Ginger must be fed on time. In the morning, she may have a bowl of milk and 3 slices of bread or 4 milk bones. Sometimes she may have an egg. At noon she may have 1 or 2 milk-bones. At supper she may have one-half can Gaines Dog Food. She must have water in her bowl all the time.

2. *Playing*

When dog jumps and nips lightly at hand, you must grab nearby old stocking, or bone, for Ginger to bite on. Play tug-o-war with her, until tired. Then she will be calm later.

3. *Dog Enjoyments*

A dog likes to have her master's hand pat her on top of the head, or right on the back, where part in fur is. And she likes what's called a belly-scratch which is a kind of tickling scratch right in the middle of her stomach.

4. *Leash-holding*

When you hold dog by leash, when strangers approach, shorten leash. Then when a stranger passes, you unwind leash again.

5. *Nipping*

When dog nips, do not leave it pass by, or else dog will always do it. Instead, smack dog gently across mouth. If you smack hard, dog will grow vicious after a period.

6. *Exercise*

For dog exercising take to an opened area once a day. Make sure area has fence around. Let go leash and yell Indian war whoop. Run with dog so dog follows. (You will really exercise your own feet besides dog's.)

7. *Training*

Take dog out when she gives warning. Take her out 5 times a day to same place. Scold her when she dirties house.

8. *Cleaning up her Bowels and Urine*

When Ginger makes on rug, if bowel, do not just smear paper over it to clean up. That will spread it all over the place. Instead, close two ends of the paper against the bowel, and pick it up that way. Carry it to the main disposer can *outdoors.* If she makes urine, don't just put the paper on and take it off. Instead, put the paper on for a few minutes. The urine will soak into it. Then put your foot over it and rub it. Pick up the paper and throw it away in the main disposer garbage pail *outdoors.* Take a damp cloth and rub away the urine spot.

All during the dictation, the eight-year-old carried the weight of responsibility, but made sure the six-year-old was listening and learning. But the next morning, he was not at all willing to give up what he was doing in order to take the dog out! Once the statement had been made and understood, he settled into his usual indifference to chores, to which responsibility for the dog was now added.

There were many discussions in that family. Schedules were made, calendars drawn, rewards and punishments meted out, but the progress was uneven. Eventually, the adults had to share the responsibility with both children in order to keep the dog at all, which the parents felt was of value. Yet the same eight-year-old, at age ten, was so solicitous and conscientious about a little field mouse he had found and was trying to rear, that when his mother returned from a neighboring cottage after a visit one night, she found this poignant little note propped up on her kitchen table:

"Please, Mom, Milk my Mouse when you come home and when you wake up before me."

Taken by surprise at open, unexpected disregard or questioning of family customs and habits, some parents become frantic and rejecting. Others, accepting their children's obvious involvement in a life of their own, have the illusion that they are no longer needed. Yet the conflicts and contradiction the children experience, which frequently lead to such expressions of tension as tics, bed-wetting, compulsions, and day-dreaming, are more common in the middle years than the happy-go-lucky exteriors would suggest. This is a stage when delinquency can begin, too, but if it does, it is far more likely to be the result of parental rejection than the effect of school or society alone.

The saving grace for parents is that the unpleasantness they may have to endure is generally superficial. That is, character is not involved in the manifestations of resistance to parental guidance, nor is there yet a bid for genuine separation such as will come in adolescence. In many ways, these years of parenthood are deeply satisfying, because the children grow increasingly able to communicate on matters relevant to adults and draw closer to adult tastes and interests.

Despite the external show of resistance, there is a steady assimilation of parental views and high points of confirmation to show that parental influence is at work. It is true that most of the evidence occurs in other people's homes and in emergencies. Yet some children, quite unexpectedly, on a Sunday morning will prepare breakfast and serve a hard-working mother in bed, to her utter amazement, and others behave with complete charm to visitors after their parents have agonized about whether the children would embarrass them once again with their crude behavior. And at school, during the same period, teachers in conference with parents often describe a child as cooperative, responsible, agreeable, and mature, leaving a parent speechless or murmuring, "You can't be talking about my child."

Look at the following petition submitted to parents by a thirteen-year-old girl and her ten-year-old brother during a vacation trip. In the normal way of sibling interaction, the petition is heavily interlarded with resentment, rivalry, irritation, and anger. But shining through are the criteria for social behavior their parents stressed. Their parents might not yet see these petitioners as fully accountable, but the children were clearly committed to the social expectations of their parents as the yardstick by which to condemn their nuisancy seven-year-old sister.

Petition

We can't stand Sarah because she
1. is a spoiled brat
2. is a baby
3. thinks she's queen of the world
4. thinks she can have everything her way
5. thinks she knows everything
6. thinks others are stupid
7. *is inconsiderate of others*
8. *laughs at others when they make mistakes*
9. gets away with too much
10. gets away with things we get punished for
11. cries when touched
12. *has bad manners and doesn't care*
13. bothers us by doing things she knows we can't stand
14. *is a liar*
15. *bosses people including others*
16. *is a thief*
17. is a pig
18. *is revolting to look at*
19. plays innocent
20. plays little sweet, honey, adoring girl to get her way
21. *is mean to kids in neighborhood, and in her class*
22. *is mean to animals—*
    1. our pets
    2. doesn't care for own pets
23. *if she does something wrong, i.e., spills milk, etc., she laughs*
24. *disobeys parents and others*
25. *is a cross-patch*
26. *stares at us, etc.*
27. thinks we should do her big favors—acts as if we were her slaves
28. gets us in trouble—example—we hit her *very* lightly, she cries, we get it
29. makes corny jokes and laughs at them
30. thinks she's favored pet of family, which she's treated as
31. ruins trips and vacations
32. thinks she should do everything we do
33. is a big shot
34. *makes fun of us* (when we're sick, make mistakes)
35. *never does anything helpful*
36. *doesn't do work, and when she has dishes: pouts*
37. always wants presents, toys, clothes, etc.
38. when she wrecks something, she wants a replacement immediately
39. thinks she's smart, but she's stupid
40. *gets to wear her hair the way she wants even if it's messy*
41. if a parent finds something good, she thinks they should give it to her

42. tells us not to call her names, but calls us names—she said, "Don't call me names, dummy."
43. *uses rude, impudent voice*
44. *talks back and talks fresh*
45. when parent is with other child, she tries to get attention
46. is jealous when others get attention
47. *when we're doing something such as bird-watching she distracts and is a nuisance*
48. *always gets things from cereal boxes even if she doesn't eat them*
49. *is ungrateful*
50. *destroys others' things and doesn't care*
51. *is nosy and doesn't mind own business*
52. *is unfair*
53. calls us fatso and she's fat
54. is a copycat
55. *doesn't admit own mistakes*
    We think you should do something
    about this!   Signed,

P.S. 56. is impatient

The apparent breakdown in normal routines and niceties must be seen as symptomatic of the struggle of children to be persons in their own right. Apparently, they must do this by attacking the very core of their earliest, most prolonged relationship with their parents—the care of their physical persons. "We don't mind not having to do for them any more. It's a bit of a relief," say parents. "But why don't they take care of themselves and their own things? They don't, unless they're endlessly reminded. They protest our doing for them, but will not do for themselves either." And that's the rub. Children of the middle years are contradictory. They seem so capable and yet so unwilling to do the most obvious things within the adult scheme of orderliness and responsibility. Yet they are struggling with adult values, ideas, knowledge, and skills, and are, in fact, learning to be responsible, orderly, organized, and realistic—but among their friends and, to some extent, at school. Home is the last place where they will show this striving, because home, during the middle years, is where children must dispel their parents' illusion that they are babies. They do this by resisting all the old conformities.

It is natural for parents to want their children to look attractive, speak courteously, respect others, and help with necessary chores. More, they have the responsibility to set such standards for their children and even to add others—concern for their children's reading, handwriting, homework, school performance, allowances, use of public transportation, and a host of other new areas of socially necessary living. But, although parents must persist in requiring that the routines of daily life be attended to, it must be with full awareness that, for the moment, the children will often seem not to be taking much in, and for periods on end may give no sign that they have heard at all. It is nevertheless very important, during the frustrating course of teaching them social amenities and work habits in the face of their unconcealed indifference, that the parent-child relationship does not freeze into a battle for control over bodily care, appearance, and orderliness. These are the areas where parents feel their responsibility, and children resist the hardest. Yet if parents and children become locked in battle on this level, a generally open communication is forfeited, and matters far more subtle and serious than the routines of living may escape guidance.

Parenthood requires communicating a philosophy as well as habits. Parents and their children of the middle years need to talk to each other about questions of ethics, prejudice, and war; about sex roles and how boys and girls treat each other; about things learned, pondered, and enjoyed; about rights for self and responsibility to the family and to others. Parents must begin to discover their children as individuals of developing tastes and views and so help them be, and see, themselves as thinking, feeling people. It is far too easy for a middle-years child to absorb an over-simplified picture of himself as a sloppy, unreliable, careless, irresponsible, lazy creature and not much more—an attitude toward himself he will carry far beyond these years. Seeing himself thus, he is hardly likely to participate with his parents in discussions concerning matters of more subtle, far-reaching importance.

With a little thought and patience, this can be a successful period of relationships within a family and hopefully lay the groundwork for minimizing heartache during adolescence. But it can be this way only to the extent that parents cut down their emphasis on what used to be important when their children were little—that is, their physical welfare—and bring into the picture their emerging moral, social, and intellectual selves. Parents must of course continue to maintain a position on daily matters that they care about. But stubborn stands are better taken on issues which more seriously influence children's growth as whole people than on matters of immediate appearance or convenience. If a choice must be made, and intermittently it must, better dirty fingernails than an absence of discussions involving basic values.

It has become increasingly difficult for parents to pass on values at all to their children, and almost impossible beyond a certain stage of growth. In adolescence, for example, the nature of children's battle for adulthood in our society most often takes the form of total repudiation of parental values and beliefs. In our time, this is exacerbated by the general breakdown in values in the culture. Even though many young adults come full circle to regard certain of their parents' views as having merit, they must come to these views, or others, on their own and by virtue of their own judgment.

The ability to assess situations by using judgment, instead of relying on impulse as the guide to action, can be learned. It is generally learned the hard way, by experience, but the process can be helped along by deliberate teaching on the part of adults who support its possible applications in childhood. Parents can help children develop judgment by exploring with them, whenever they can and without prejudice, the pros and cons affecting choices and decisions in matters that the children perceive as important to themselves. To a large extent, these exist outside the home, especially in the areas of peer relationships and school, because these are the significant testing grounds at this stage for children's attitudes toward themselves and toward people in general. Children have far more occasions to exercise judgment among peers than is generally realized.

This can be a hard time for children. They are less apt than adults to value the power, status, and privileges of adulthood, and superficial characteristics of class, color, religion or national origin have little to do with the basic relationships among themselves. They are very sensitive to the values of childhood which offer status, however, and there is always the danger that subservience to the group will be at the expense of individuality. As one psychologist put it, "The super-ego melts like a Hershey bar in the sun under the impact of group psychological heat."

Parents expect their children to be involved outside the home, but they anticipate this involvement as an addendum to already existing patterns within the family. This is a simplistic view. Children fall into family membership by pure chance and from then on are simply in. They take for granted the steadfastness of their loyalty to their family and of their family to themselves. But there is no such certainty in the new relationship. Admission to peer groups entails much anxiety and uncertainty and takes conscious, deliberate effort to ensure membership. Contradictory pulls between peer and family allegiances are inevitable, and children will do valiant things to guarantee their admission and safeguard their membership. Out of fear that parents will not accept the gang values, children will lie to avoid a fuss or to protect their friends. And they conform unbelievably to group standards. Nothing could be worse to a child of the middle years than being "different" from other children. In Gertrude Lewis's study, children wrote, "Everyone is afraid someone is going to make fun of them. That's the trouble. Everyone is afraid of being different. New kids at school are scared to death, and especially if they're smart." They feel safer testing their growing individuality in rebellion against their parents while being totally nondiscriminating about the pattern of behavior of peers. Yet they need to learn how to discriminate among peers.

Within the peer group, they are confronted with all the many levels of maturity and functioning that one sees in the adult world. There are children who have already learned to manipulate people for their own ends, to dominate, seduce, and punish. They manage to find children who are self-effacing, needful of affection, or frightened, to be their foils. Many children are shy and wait for the overtures of others, suffering from feelings of rejection only because they find it hard to make the first welcoming moves. And there are those who have gotten by among adults on charm and verbalization as a cover-up for failure to perform. They face exposure to far more critical, even unkind, eyes than they might until now have known.

It can be very painful to parents to watch their children undergo humiliation, chagrin, and embarrassment in the process of learning how to find satisfaction and self-worth away from home, but, fortunately, the situation is still fluid. The same children who can be so cruelly appraising can also be compassionate and helpful when they sense sincerity. And children can unlearn self-deceptive skills and strengthen their capacities. But they need help.

If they can succeed in strengthening their individuality and sense of judgment within the confines of the family, they are far more likely later to apply critical and searching eyes to the behavior of their own generation when the time comes in adolescence to complete the passage to adulthood. It is thus extremely important that parents be aware, without prying, of how children perceive the relationships among friends, so that they can assess what a child is learning about himself, other people, and possible modes of interaction. Children at this stage of development find it hard to express their innermost feelings and personal meanings with objectivity. They need adults who can help them achieve perspective and an ethical code, while giving them moral support and safeguarding their privacy at the same time. No easy task!

When matters under discussion are more directly related to adult approval and permission rather than child concern alone, parents also owe it to their children to share with them the reasoning and weighing of alternatives that go into their decision-making and judgment. Even though parents hold the final word, and, from the vantage point of maturity, may even have to be arbitrary about asserting their authority at times, it is important that children be shown a mode of thinking and of formulating judgments that helps to draw them away from the complete subjection to feeling and impulse that are so characteristic of the earlier years of childhood. It goes without saying that when children's arguments are cogent they should be seriously considered in decisions. But it is in the process of thinking through dilemmas with adults, or watching and listening as adults do this, that children learn how decisions are made with the greatest soundness a person can muster.

The middle years are ones in which children increasingly face conflicts on their own, and this kind of knowledge is the greatest source of strength for the determinations they must frequently make in these years, including when to ask for help and when to struggle alone. One of the truths to be faced by parents during this period is that they cannot do the work of living and relating for their children. They can be sounding boards and they can probe with the children the consequences of alternative actions. But unless parents consciously recognize their positive role in guiding children toward skills for safe, independent functioning, and unless children feel that parents care about matters that concern *them* as well as adults, children may not turn to parents for the guidance that can really alter their lives, such as that called for in the knotty problems of sex, drugs, and racism. Given the susceptibility of young children to the impact of society's struggles, parents have greater need than ever to play an active role in children's attitudes toward them.

Sex

It is hard for parents to see their children as sexual beings. Yet, despite Freud's assessment of the middle years as a sexually latent period, the sex interest is there, expressed in symbolism and rhyme if nothing else. Games, jokes, sexual play, and talk are part of the peer group ideology. As it always has been, masturbation continues to be a childhood activity. But the children are no deeper in their understanding than they ever were. The ten-year-old boy who says, "I'm going to be 'gay' and not go out with girls," can still be measured against the child of the same age who asks, "Why can't you have a baby if you're not married?" Masculinity and femininity are taking shape in a period when guidelines for male and female behavior are fast moving away from stereotypes and traditional modes, but moving toward no one is quite sure what. Just about everything hitherto assumed concerning men and women in their outward behavior and behavior toward each other is under attack. Yet, in preparing children for future roles, it is interesting that historical attitudes persist in parents despite the intellectual acceptance of new modes ahead. For example, a father, his fifteen-year-old son, and his ten-year-old daughter were watching television when a commercial came on to advertise a chemistry set. Turning to his son, the father said, "If you were ten years old, that's something I would buy for you." When his daughter briskly retorted, "But *I'm* ten years old!" her father stopped short, suddenly recognizing the trap he had unconsciously fallen into. Yet there had never been a doubt in his mind that his daughter would receive as good an education as his son. This contradiction between the avowed and unconscious attitudes of adults means that parents caught in the transition from one era to another are not always clear about the guidelines their children need.

Children spend several years copying the stylized behavior projected by the conservative peer group—that is, boys on the ball field and girls jumping rope. In their play, they act out the traditional roles of males and females vis-à-vis each other. According to one eight-year-old informant, "The boys play football, hit the girls, play baseball, and shoot water guns at the girls. The girls roller skate, swing, jump rope, sit on the bench and talk, make rings out of beads, and do cooking and baking." By the end of the period, some may express interest in the new ideas, but their personal struggle to relate to the opposite sex is not clarified by this.

In addition to contemporary confusion about social sex roles, there is also the fact that, for all the sophisticated talk, adult feelings about body experience are mixed. Guilt and shame still exist, and the new sexual being is still in the making. Children pick up the tone of stress, the uncertainty, and the confusion. At the same time, they are tuned in to the open sexuality of the youth group now emerging.

Parents can work to strengthen certain basic attitudes to help offset the confusion attendant upon a dated morality stemming from the assumption of male superiority and the double standard. In looking to a future in which men and women are perceived as human beings first and a gender second, they can support the inherent talents and capacities of children of both sexes regardless of traditional classifications. This emphasis is timely, as it feeds into the beginning disappearance of job distinctions on the basis of sex. A concomitant focus must be on a quality of honesty in human relations which will operate within and across sex lines, because emotional involvement of people with each other is likely to remain an important human need regardless of the form of family and social organization. If children grow up knowing that both men and women are capable of love, consideration, responsibility, and respect for people, then the special male and female need for love, child-bearing and child-rearing can only be deepened by the common human base.

A third emphasis must be on safeguarding the legitimacy of sexuality for both sexes. Children must be allowed to know that their bodies can be sources of pleasure as well as pain. But for parents to break the almost intuitive, negative response to childhood sexuality, they must begin by acknowledging that each person's body is his own and that, unless an individual causes harm to another, his sexual activity is not a subject for public scrutiny or judgment. And they must find the strength to be unashamed of their own pleasure.

Drugs

The other area so difficult for parents to face and cope with—drugs—is perhaps even more serious, since life itself is involved. The way in which drugs permeate the consciousnesses of contemporary children is illustrated in the following anecdote, told by a teacher of a third-grade class. He was reading the story of *The Princess and the Pea* and referred to the princess as the heroine. All the children looked blank, and one child finally asked, "What do drugs have to do with the story?"

Young children know about drugs, and they are vulnerable in a special, childlike way. The eleven-year-old who says, "Are you going to bring 'stuff' back with you?" must be understood in the light of the confessions of older children that they try drugs, because it's "in." The need to conform is a source of danger even for children who are not seriously unhappy.

Dangers have always existed for children, and parents have always had to teach them what these were and how to cope with them. Just as one keeps matches at a safe height when children are little, so at this stage parents have to be alert to the possibilities in their medicine cabinets. And just as there is a time to teach little ones how to use matches safely, so the drug danger must be exposed and prepared for. Not to talk about it with children who may already have been approached by pushers, or who may have sniffed glue, is ostrich-like behavior. Without playing up the horror excessively, children need to know that people take drugs because they are frustrated, bored, or unhappy; that it is a good idea to escape from such feelings, but there are alternative ways that are safer; that people have always needed release and escape at moments in their lives, but there are ways to do this which allow a person to live and grow. Parents must be honest. The conflict about marijuana's harmfulness has to be spelled out as just that—a difference of opinion that is as much due to incomplete knowledge as to prejudice.

The compulsion to be like others that plays so large a role in the drug-taking of children, must be explored with the children in the same way that all other matters involving individual strength and judgment are explored. Even if a child has already been involved, it is better for parents to know that their children have been tainted than not to know and run the risk of losing them. Simultaneously, parents must join with others in the community to make the total environment safe from drugs, because a major factor in the destruction of children and adolescents is its sheer availability.

Racism

Racism, a third area of conflicted feeling, must also be faced openly and honestly. Few parents have stopped to consider that black and white children of today must live together as black and white adults in a very few years, that they are both on the seesaw of historical change, and both are victimized by the failure of adults, albeit in different ways. The insidious implication of inferiority that causes the black child to have to battle for feelings of self-worth is the more obvious hurt. But the subtle counter-assumption that the white child is superior is equally destructive. It is not only the bigot who passes on such feelings to children. The assumption is built into the structure of the social fabric to such an extent that even parents who consciously believe in the equality of rights and feel sympathy for the black child, do so out of a false belief that their own children are untainted. But they are not untainted. They are poisoned, as surely as the black children are hurt, by the subtle corruption implicit in the social endorsement of superiority based on superficial differences. Their self-evaluations are skewed too, in that their self-worth is not completely rooted in objective reality. Adults must consciously save children from remaining foils in this immoral dilemma by bringing it to an end.

In a society that has long segregated people by color and religion, despite its constitutional avowal of equal rights, feelings about others are determined more by socially prevalent attitudes than by contact. Parents may have to struggle with the negative feelings they learned in childhood before they can help their own children break old patterns. As in so many other areas of important learnings, children are sensitive not to the words, but to the tone and feeling that infuse their parents' own behavior. Loud protestations of equality colored with anger, meekness, or cynicism leave residues of anger, meekness, or cynicism, not unprejudiced attitudes. In all the subtle ways by which a people reveal their prejudice and fear of others without meaning to, children learn the truth. They need to understand, as they grow able to, the nature of the struggle to give up the attitudes of centuries. They need help in assessing, the meaning of prejudice, fear, and hate in those in whom it exists. There can be no pretense if there is to be growth.

By the middle years of childhood, attitudes toward race and religion become integrated into the life style, and children can learn either to play a hypocritical game or to accept the differences among people as enriching variations on the human theme. Group identification, as such, is important to children. They need to know and feel good about their own racial, ethnic, and religious membership. There is comfort to children in belonging; they enjoy the ceremonials, rituals, holidays, or historical antecedents associated with specific group membership. But, for themselves, and for the nation's future, they must learn to find interesting and worthwhile the variations in mankind revealed in a variety of group memberships.

The Effect of School

School and school responsibility offer that area of growth for children which parents perhaps see as the most important of all.

Certainly parents play a guiding role in their children's school success whether they do so deliberately or not. The Plowden Report points out that "parental attitudes have greater correlation with pupil achievement than material home circumstances or variations in school and classroom organization, instructional materials, and particular teaching practices." [1]

All efforts to estimate the relative effects of home and school point to the overwhelming influence of the home. Schools can be wonderful allies of a good home experience, or they can open possibilities for the first time to children whose homes are insufficiently stimulating. No matter what the schools are like, the quality of a child's mind is nurtured basically at home. School can support such nurturing and help extend a mind. It can also fail to involve a mind. When the latter is the case, children for whom neither school nor home offers a climate of intellectual stimulation are in trouble. But for children whose questions are answered, whose naïveté is not scorned, who are given the opportunity to explore and experiment with materials, and who are not pushed into achieving for status—for these children, a school experience that does not involve the mind can be a painful disillusionment, but it need not be a disaster.

There are many children who conform completely to the vapidity of a poor program because they love all the side benefits of going to school and therefore accept school as it is without too critical an attitude. One need not worry about such children, because they select what has meaning for themselves, and as long as their powers of inquiry and search are supported at home, they will lose only the extra richness that is potentially possible in a strong school program. They will not lose what they already have. Realistically, more than one elementary school conformist has turned into a rebel at college.

There are also children who adjust to a situation which is

[1] *Children and Their Primary Schools,* A Report by the Central Advisory Council for Education, commonly known as "The Plowden Report" (London: Her Majesty's Stationery Office, 1967), Vol. 1, Ch. 3, para. 89–100.

not as good as their parents would like by ignoring the school requirements and living a private life. They draw, doodle, smile at friends, shift in their seats, and wait patiently for the school day to be over, when they begin their real learning. They do not commit themselves to school and learn to get by without attracting attention one way or the other. This is a pity, but it could be worse, since they do go on learning, in their own way, at home.

The child to be concerned about is the one who is actively unhappy, who is afraid of what a teacher will say or do, who is overwhelmed by the demands, the competition, and/or the punishment of school, and who responds with failure, or excessive anxiety about performance or misbehavior. In the long run, a child's emotional development has a far greater impact on his life than his school performance or the curriculum's richness, so it is wise to do everything possible to change a situation in which a child is suffering excessively. The negative effects on a child's perception of himself as a learner and even as a person are far more serious than his academic progress during childhood. It is easier to "catch up" on skills and facts, at home or in later schooling, than it is to heal a badly hurt child. When a child suffers humiliation, guilt, bewilderment, and helpless anger in his school experience, parents must take up the cudgels for him by insisting on a change of teacher or arranging for a change of school.

Where the situation is dull and inadequate, but basically non-punitive, there are ways in which parents can encourage their children so that their minds remain open to learning. While a parent cannot consistently supply the quality of interaction with children that a school can offer, parents can help locate books that hold answers to a child's special interest, whether that is baseball, astronomy, ballet dancing, musical instruments, jokes, riddles, or snakes. They can arrange for their children to see documentary films within the scope of their understanding, such as television's *Birth of a Baby,* or an old documentary like *Nanook of the North.* And they can get into discussions at any time. But books and talk are not enough. Children need raw materials to carry out their understanding, such as cloth, paper, props for costumes and sets, wood, clay, cardboard, and paint. They need these at home as much as they do at school, and it is as hard for most children of the middle years to find freely available materials at home as it is at school. Books and pencils are clean and neat, they are rungs on the academic ladder, and they are easier for parents to concede. Yet, in our neat, civilized homes, places must be found where children can learn as children, by using raw materials to work out their ideas. For example, a child of nine, while on a summer visit to grandparents in New York City, reported with excitement that in one of the books in a popular children's adventure series he had read that a model of a particular dinosaur which had figured in the story could be seen at the Museum of Natural History. He and his father made a special trip to the museum, but it turned out that nobody there knew anything about the model. To ease the disappointment, father and son went into the museum bookshop to examine books about dinosaurs and bought a vividly illustrated soft-cover book on the subject. Back at his grandmother's, the child began to model the dinosaurs out of plasticine, and his grandmother offered him an old card table on which to work. Over several weeks of that summer, the child built a world of dinosaurs on the table, creating drawings and cutouts of the vegetation as a backdrop for his plasticine dinosaurs. No one could have foretold where this interest would go, but a little adult help in expediting resources and materials allowed this boy to pursue a topic that had captured his imagination to the point where he became much more knowledgeable about it than the adults who were offering guidance.

Helping children learn at a level of genuine intellectual inquiry takes imagination on the part of the adult. Even more, it takes the courage to become a resource in unfamiliar areas of knowledge and in ones for which one has no taste. But parents, no less than teachers, must respect a child's mind and not exploit it for their own vanity or ambition, or to soothe their own anxiety. There must be readiness to share openmindedness with children, but that sharing must be bounded by what is possible for a child to understand; verbalization is not the same as comprehension. One needs faith in children's power to learn and a willingness to be a learner oneself, but one must not be too easily impressed by words.

The Parents' Role in Reading Progress

Children also need support in the skill of reading, but not in the mechanics as such. The primary task of any parent in relation to reading is to build and develop a love of books in their children. Many parents are as literal as their six-year-olds in assuming that once a child begins to learn how to read at school, he is immediately a reader and able to enjoy books on his own. Nothing could be further from the truth. The laborious decoding of fairly simple story material is necessary training in the mechanics of reading, but satisfaction in the story is generally a subsidiary and even nonexistent accompaniment of reading lessons. By third grade, the entire sounding-out experience can become quite a bore, and it is easy for children to lose sight of the end goal—that is, the smooth, uninterrupted flow of words in a gripping, satisfying story. During the years when normal children struggle to get over the hump of sheer technical intricacy and make the leap into reading with pleasure and ease, they must continue to hear good literature they can grasp, even if it is too difficult to decode. This not only means reading to children from the time they are old enough to sit and look at a picture book, but continuing the process as late as the fourth grade. Parents can also read aloud an interesting news item or funny portion of a story they themselves are reading. Books can be used to find out about things, such as how to make a skirt, how astronauts survive in a capsule, what gerbils require in the way of care, or whatever else concerns the children.

Children can help select the books they will enjoy hearing

by accompanying their parents to the library on a regular basis and borrowing books that they can handle alone, as well as some which require adult help. The library experience in this age of mass media is a sensitive and touchy one for children and calls for tact on the part of parents. Because there is so much status associated with reading, the beginning first-grader wants to show greater prowess than he actually has, and the sophisticated fourth-grader has not quite gotten over the same anxious desire to show up well. Consequently, their pride must be protected, and they must be allowed to save face at the same time that attempts are made to encourage them to select reading material at the level they can manage.

As they learn to use the library themselves, children go through a period of impulsive grabbing of anything and everything, with no attention to such criteria as interest, difficulty, size of print, or size of book. It takes a lot of patience to bring them around to acknowledging that some books are not for them, whereas others are suitable. Often the librarian can be more helpful than the parent, because the children's battle with their parents to prove that they are not babies interferes with rationality and objective choice-making in a crisis. Once choices are made with more or less realism, a batch of books comes home that may then sit on a shelf untouched until they have to be returned. This is where the adult practicality must tread lightly. It is tempting to remind a child that, as long as he has brought books home, he might just as well read them; or scold a child about the uselessness of going back to the library if the books of two weeks ago are not all finished, or even opened. But going to the library must become a habit, as must reading, and young children can often do only one thing at a time. For a variety of reasons, the actual act of sitting down to read a book all by oneself looms very large for some children. Children do not like to struggle, and reading, even in third and fourth grade, may still be more of a struggle than they care to admit. With reading strongly associated with school and lessons, they have not yet developed the habit or the taste for reading by themselves, which is what parents must try to help them establish.

Children, therefore, have no idea what they are missing when they omit books from their choices for recreational activity. They may be engrossed in things which are too exciting to put aside; or they may have changed their minds about books which looked good at the library, but which, on second perusal, are not that appealing, or that turn out to be harder than they thought. The point is to get them into the library as a first step, and this may mean that, for months, children carry home six books with self-conscious delight and pride, only to carry back the six books with a slight edge of guilt over not having read them, but with no feeling of loss. Meanwhile, a patient parent tags along. This state of affairs gives way finally to one in which the children still insist on taking out the maximum number of books, but actually get to read one, or maybe they take out fat books to impress themselves and others, but read thin books to chalk up a sizeable reading list. They go through periods of single interests in reading and periods when no book pleases them. They will follow the lead of other children and take out books that are "in," sometimes enjoying them, sometimes not. Slowly and arduously, they will learn what books are for, provided parents do not lose heart and give up their ultimate objectives because it is taking so long.

The regular trek to the library must continue, despite all the back-tracking, because, if a parent gives up at this apparently fruitless point, the loss may be final. Children begin by playing a game of going to the library for books to read. For that game to become serious, it must be supported as long as is necessary for the reading virus to take effect. Since television offers adventure and spice for less effort, there is no special need that children can see at this early point in their skill. As the library habit, which starts as a stab at being grown up, changes slowly into something meaningful, the habit of enjoying books must be continuously reinforced. Meanwhile, at school, the slow process of learning the mechanics of the reading skill goes on at its own unpredictable pace.

As children grow older, they will turn to comic books, because comics allow them to enjoy a tale with relatively little effort and much speed. Picture stories can be of real help at this stage in increasing a child's reading speed. There is nothing wrong with comic book reading as such, although children have to be safeguarded against two negative possibilities. One involves the negative contents of some comics, which can readily enough be controlled, given the numbers of comics available. The other is the danger that children will not go beyond the superficial characterization and quick action of the comics into more serious literature. This can be negligible if, during the time when children are reading "quickie" material, they are also exposed regularly to literature of greater depth by hearing it read. The trail from the comics to the series books will lead to literature if a child's maturing tastes are fed on books of quality during the long haul when his skills are slowly strengthening. Children so exposed themselves begin to feel the difference between the shallow characterizations in the comics and the series books and the depth in literature; the comics and the series begin to pall in time, or else are put into their proper place as escape literature. The taste for the deeper qualities inherent in good children's books does not develop simply as a consequence of learning to read. Taste must be carefully nurtured, supported, and encouraged at home, until the child, with increasing total maturity, is able to make the transition as his technical skills permit. Skill-learning is aided when children are encouraged to move through each stage of the reading process with faith in themselves and without comparison with siblings or classmates. For the parent, this means transmitting to a child the absolute conviction that he has what it takes to learn to read.

When children read to their parents, it should be to share the story, and parents can allow them that pleasure without feeling that every bit of print has to be a lesson in struggle or that it is a wasted effort. The struggle is there all the time, but it is especially focused at school. At home, the pleasures of reading are better stressed. Encouragement is the key word, not pressure. Parents and children can share natural reading situations as these develop, such as reading a card from a friend or relative, a message from a parent or neighbor, or reading a joke in the newspaper. Testing children constantly by forcing them to perform turns reading into a source of discomfort to be dispensed with as soon as they are old enough. Older children can be encouraged to read simple books to younger children, and younger and older children may illustrate poems read to them which have sensory images, like this one for example:

Sleepy Fish

Down in the sea where the fishes sleep,
The water is wet
And the water is deep
And all the little fishes keep
Their eyes open while they sleep.[2]

Parents can leave notes for their children as frequently as practical, remembering to write clearly, make up crossword puzzles for a child or work together on puzzles in magazines. There are games to play, in which good sentences can be made out of scrambled ones, e.g., *came car the road down,* and recipes can be read for cooking or baking. It is fair to tell a child words he does not know as he reads and not make him struggle to the point where he cannot get any pleasure out of a story. If a child cannot cope with 75 per cent of the words in reading matter, it is obviously too hard for him. At 50 per cent, he will need steady help. Below that percentage of difficulty, he is at a level at which he can proceed with some speed and success, provided he gets the help he needs to achieve the flow he wants. At third grade and beyond, there are other reading tasks than sounding out. Getting the point of a story, differentiating between words that express opinion and words that represent fact, recognizing that reading can serve different purposes, appreciating style—these grow increasingly valuable in the process of strengthening reading skill.

[2] Margaret Wise Brown, *Nibble, Nibble* (New York: Young Scott Books, 1959).

There are tricks of support along the way, of course. One is, as has already been said, the continuity of the library trek. Another is to begin reading a mystery story to a child of eight or nine, and then, at a fascinating moment of suspense, discover an emergency task that needs attention, and leave the child to unravel the words alone—or sit in frustration until you return. With still older children, parents can begin the reading of a classic that warms up too slowly for modern taste, but is nevertheless a really good yarn for children. Once the action begins, children can go on by themselves until such time as the description or other transitional material gets heavy, and then parents can step in again. This is how a present-day eleven-year-old can get through a novel like *David Copperfield* and enjoy it. The entry into Dickens' world is far too slow for the image-minded child of our time, but the life experiences Dickens recounts are still gripping.

There need be no conflict of classics versus contemporary non-classics. There are excellent contemporary books that promise to become classics by their persistent popularity with readers over several generations, and, while many books of other eras are unsuitable for today's children and are losing their popularity as a result, others remain in favor. Choosing a book for a child simply because it is a classic is no guarantee of pleasure for a particular child. For example, boys and girls have different, as well as overlapping, tastes. Children have individual preferences of theme and style, and books should be chosen to please the particular individual. Some will be found among the classics, some among more recent publications.

Problems in Reading

The leap from decoding to reading comes somewhere near the third year of effort for most children, although teachers generally suspect potential difficulty earlier. Reading authorities with clinical experience tend to agree that if, despite instruction, children over eight do not recognize or figure out words, this is serious enough to call for professional diagnosis. Additional signs of poor functioning are often poorly coordinated movements, poor speech, and poor attention, generally in a combination of more than one such symptom.

The difficulties with reading in children over eight, if they do not stem from anxiety or pressure, are often related to problems of hearing or sight. These are difficult to diagnose and treat, because so little is known about the neurological connection-making between what is heard and what is seen. Katrina de Hirsch, who worked for years at the Neurological Institute of the Columbia-Presbyterian Medical Center in New York City with average and above-average youngsters with reading difficulties, believes that a total integration of growth within the child, basically related to neurological functioning, makes him ready or unready for the specific skill of reading. There is further danger that emotional overlay will complicate the matter. But while experienced teachers at the second- and third-grade levels recognize when a child's problems require more attention than they can give, diagnosis must be made by specially trained personnel. Teachers can do no more than indicate concern; they are not trained to diagnose or treat the less usual causes of difficulty, but when they recommend diagnosis, their advice is generally sound.

Sometimes, a simple battery of psychological tests will reveal that all a child needs is extra help along certain lines, and this can be handled by the teacher and/or parent. In other cases, it may take a total neurological checkup to ascertain just where the inadequacy lies. If there are signs that help is wanted, parents must be sure to check the qualifications of the tester or testing agency. Private commercial reading clinics and institutes have been known to take advantage of parents' anxiety over school success by charging excessive fees or extending the "treatment."

For reasons not clearly understood, boys show up in reading clinics more frequently than girls. Whether they tend toward slower maturation rates, whether they suffer more in female-dominated schools, or whether it is just harder to live up to the expectations demanded of males, is hard to say. But it is important to safeguard the self-image of boys which can easily be battered in the wrong kind of school. For example, eight-year-old boys write in unbelievably sloppy scrawls, in marked contrast to the larger number of girls of the same age who have neat, controlled handwriting. Far too few teachers or parents recognize this sex difference in maturation, and boys are unnecessarily shamed.

The School Situation

No matter what kind of school children attend, in the age-old manner of children, pleasure comes before duty, and, even when they enjoy school, there are chore aspects in the pursuit of learning that cause many of them to balk. By the time they are nine, children begin to worry about school. Long before then, they show genuine eagerness to learn what the adult world offers and they sense the meaning of accomplishment and achievement in academic areas. But there is a gap between a question and its answer, and closing that gap sometimes comes hard. The struggle with what is not understood, the repetitive practice of what must become automatic, the sufferance of ambiguity and confusion in the unknown are not cherished by children any more than by adults. But while adults have perspective to carry them, children do not. Their eyes hurt when they have to study, their hands hurt when they have to write, their stomachs hurt when they have to clean up after completing a project. In the traditional school organization, parents have felt obligated to step in and help in school tasks. Where marks are so tied in with success, many parents have helped to the point of doing the job for the children, and many others have offered bribes for higher marks. Still other parents have felt, and shown, exasperation and open contempt for the school's approach, making one or another compromise with the children's homework problems, all the while grumbling.

Parents can expect teachers in schools today to be as concerned with intrinsic learning as they are themselves, and the responsibility of the parent may then be somewhat eased, because, hopefully, assignments are neither irrelevant nor obtuse. But the relation of a child to a task assigned by his teacher still calls for a particular kind of relation between the child and his parents, especially when the task is taken home. In both traditional and freer schooling, children need to find their way into responsibility for their own learning and to face the realities of work and workmanship. They must receive the amount and kind of support that will allow them to build their self-respect and safeguard their autonomy as learners. In the end, it is the children who must accept responsibility for their spelling, for their social studies research, for the solutions to their math problems, or for remembering to bring fabric for a costume. Children are not all equally competent in the diverse range of skills and abilities called for in being autonomous in school tasks. Reading techniques, research techniques, the abstraction of generalizations from evidence, focusing without being distracted, organizing and scheduling abilities are unevenly distributed. So are such qualities as patience, persistence, and self-confidence, and all of these go into the completion of school tasks.

The day parents assign their children to the schools, the focus of their responsibility for their children's learning shifts. In their life at school, children build new and special relationships with adults, in which their own performance becomes a basic component in the relationship. Teachers know nothing of the early growth of a child, of his nightmares, illnesses, special food likes, or toileting problems. They relate freshly to the child before them as the person he now is, and children have the freedom to make their way into their teachers' hearts and minds without the weight of prior involvement to create bias. The promise of freedom to be oneself carries a burden of responsibility for self. It is toward that responsibility, asked by the teacher, that a child must stretch and grow.

If parents can believe that a child's effort is the line of communication between him and his teacher, is the heart of the teaching-learning process itself, then they can concern themselves less with the product out of fear of what the teacher will think of their child (and of them!). They can give themselves over to supporting the process by which a child learns to work, without interfering with his autonomy or with his equally real need to face reality in the form of his teacher's evaluation.

Parental Responsibility

Parents can help by being sure their children understand what they are expected to do. The best teacher can sometimes be unclear, and the brightest child can fail to grasp the meaning of a task even under optimal conditions. Parents can offer their help by suggesting and locating resources likely to be unfamiliar to children, such as people, books, and materials that can be useful. They can help by strengthening, and in some cases even teaching, the skills of finding out—for example, clarifying the use of a library catalogue, index, and table of contents, or the uses of the Yellow Pages of the telephone directory. They can help the children work out schedules for homework, play, and television that minimize the conflicts involved in what to do first. They can offer moral support and encouragement to persist, to try again, to struggle for understanding and mastery. And they can share a child's pleasure in mastery and accomplishment. But they must not do the job for the children. And they must not lose sight of the difference between the means and the ends.

Both the traditional school and the traditional home have too often valued work habits above content, and children have long known, in such settings, that a neat, properly paragraphed paper could go far in covering up inadequacies of thought. Understanding and the search for meaning are the hallmarks of a learner. While good habits of workmanship need not be abandoned in favor of understanding, they should not be considered the major goal of scholarship. During the middle years of childhood, parents must constantly strengthen their children's capacity to think clearly and encourage work habits and orderliness as allies of clear thinking and good communication, but no more than that.

Beyond the Home
to School and Community
• • •

Reports and Conferences

When a child goes off to school, he goes alone. His life at school is now a separate existence, and traditionally there has been minimal contact between a child's parents and his teachers. Parents eager to know how the children fare, have been reduced to the fruitless, "What did you do at school today?", which normally produces vague and unsatisfactory answers from children. When parents were called to school, it was because there was trouble: The child was either misbehaving or not learning. If the parent was not called, it could be safely assumed that all was going smoothly. When the report card came, it was either a confirmation or a letdown, and the child was made to feel proud or ashamed.

We have come to recognize that a set of numerical or letter grades does not tell us enough. I.Q. scores and test results say little about a child's motivation, attitudes toward success and failure, self-imposed or self-denied standards, feelings about authority, feelings about competition, position and status among peers, special interests, resistance to learning, or fears. Yet all these play a role in children's learning. Often, they are more significant than specific grade level or test scores, even when concern is focused on the academic process. Reporting confined to grades has the effect of setting up the school as an irreproachable arbiter of right and wrong that passes on to the parent the sole responsibility for doing something about the "misguided" child. Grades and scores must give way to, or at least be supplemented by, conferences, in which school and home can together evaluate a child's progress in greater depth than the judgmental grades and scores allow for.

Conferences in the truest educational sense and of most value to the child are built on a set of implicit assumptions: that home and school share the major time allotment in bringing up the child; that home and school are both deeply committed to the child; that each in its unique way affects the child. Out of this set of assumptions can come the continuing sharing of perspectives that unifies for the child the positive experiences available both at home and at school. Conferences with this in mind must begin before there is any sign of trouble. They exist as a matter of course for all parents and leave the way open for an ongoing interchange of mutual interest that, in the event of trouble, has home and school tackling the causes together, without blame or recrimination on either side. Where such relating does exist, parents grow in their understanding of the school's objectives, and the school grows in its understanding of children, thus leading to the possibility of shared thinking on change, should that be necessary. Where mutuality does not exist, and the school does not recognize its responsibility to initiate such relationships, it is in the best interests of the children that the parents do so.

In developing the cooperative relationships so essential for children, both parents and teachers face the task of defining their separate responsibilities for their children's education and well-being. Both must also recognize the feelings with which they approach each other—feelings that often overshadow their mutual concern.

Parents do not give up their children to strangers lightly. They wait in uncertain anticipation for an expression of awareness and interest in their children that is as genuine as their own. They are subject to ambivalent feelings of trust and competitiveness toward a teacher their child loves and to feelings of resentment and anger when their child suffers at her hands. They place high hopes in their children and struggle with themselves to cope with their children's failures. Parents have a tremendous investment in their children and want the best of everything for them.

At the same time, parents are themselves former pupils. Whatever feelings they had about school and teachers may color their perceptions of their children's school and teachers. Some are as frightened of teachers as the children are. Some hold teachers in awe. Some are cynical and see teachers as opportunistic, lazy, poorly educated, or indifferent. Some feel they are as good as, or better than, the teachers. Some are grateful that the teachers are kind and helpful, or firm and clear.

And the teachers? Every graduating class of young teachers is afraid of parents. They are sure they will not know all the answers. They worry that parents may find them inadequate, that they will not be able to deal with the aggressive parents, that they will be regarded as children themselves. But, as they become secure in their teaching, many grow able to offer assurance, help, and enlightenment to the best of their ability.

Among women who return to teaching after years out for parenthood, there is often a sympathetic recognition of the dependency of parents on the teachers' evaluations of their children. But there are older teachers who still retain some of their early feelings of anxiety and who react to parents defensively. Unhappily, in the present climate of criticism of the schools, all teachers have been put on the defensive. All of society's ills, plus the burdens of guilt for historical antecedents of educational practice that were once assumed by the entire community, are placed on their shoulders. Yet they, like parents, are also citizens of a country in transition; they, too, suffer from "the system," and they, too, are worried about the future. Any satisfaction they can achieve in their life's work is completely tied in with the success of the children, and when this is questioned, or they do not succeed, they feel baffled and uncertain. It is a rare school that deals with teachers' feelings about themselves and their work, and it is almost wishful thinking that they can be concerned about the feelings of parents and children when they themselves are not given the same consideration by administrators and the community.

Nevertheless, no school can work well for children if parents and teachers do not act in partnership on behalf of the children's best interests. Parents have every right to understand what is happening to their children at school, and teachers have the responsibility to share that information without prejudicial judgment. By the same token, teachers can plan better for a child the more they know about him, which sometimes means knowing factors that affect him at home. But, under the best conditions, there are problems. Even when both endorse the same philosophy and practice, parents and teachers may not find partnership easy. A parent and teacher may be at the same or different levels of maturity; they may be equally or unequally competent in the performance of their respective child-focused tasks. Either one may be beset with personal problems. Either may be shy, timid, brash, cocky, or anxious. Yet they must communicate, because they share the same child.

Such communication, which can only be in a child's interest, is not possible without mutual trust between parent and teacher. If at the least each could accept the hope the other has for the child, then their differences, if any, will not loom so large. Only when a teacher or a parent is harsh, while the other is not, or when both are stubbornly egocentric and defensive, is it not possible to find common ground. But most parents and teachers do not fall into such extremes, and most can reach each other in common concern. It should be a part of a teacher's professional training—which it is not at the moment—to understand the nature of this relationship.

Conferences between parent and teacher ought to be available, open, and as frequent as either finds necessary. Parents should be able to visit their children's school freely, though, when they do, they must respect the teacher's responsibility to her children and not divert her attention to themselves. Teachers, in turn, need to recognize that parental commitment to a child extends further in time and intensity than theirs and that they need not feel threatened by such visits. Parents need to see their children in a setting outside the home; they need to see the ups and downs of the learning process as the teacher views it, so as to be better able to guide their children at home. If school is recognized by both parents and teachers as a *working* situation, no one will expect it to be spruced up for company all the time, and the reality of what is happening to children will be better evaluated.

Many schools in communities all over the country work well with parents. It is hardest in large city schools, where the bureaucratic structure related to size makes all manner of inter-personal relating difficult. But it is not impossible even there, and what makes parent-school exchange work in the end is the fact that both parents and teachers can find comfort in having an ally with whom to share the responsibility for the child to whom both are committed.

Parents and the Public Sector

The individual relationship between parents and their children's teachers can occur in any kind of school, public or private, traditional or modern. But, while conferences put parents in touch with their children's individual school experiences, they do not give them the wherewithal to influence general school policy and practice if they should happen to feel the need to do so.

Parents want to have, and should have, an effect on the

schools that determine how and what their children learn. When they can afford to choose a private school for their children, they generally select one which is in accordance with their own views and aspirations, one in which a staff of similar persuasion theoretically offers unity around common goals. In these days of transition, many a private school has shifted from its long-held emphasis, and parents must then change schools, or not, as they agree. When parents choose to develop their own schools, they seek like-minded parents and teachers and go through a normal process of finding each other out in greater depth. This leads either to a strong group identification around the new school or to disillusionment and a shattered school. In both kinds of selection, the mirage of choice is there, although school policy as carried out by the teaching staff may not in either case satisfy every parent's conception of what that policy should be like in its entirety.

There have always been private, independent schools, and there should continue to be. But they are no longer an oasis for the hitherto favored child. Crime, violence, amorality, alienation, disheartenment, and cynicism exist everywhere, and no child is safe from them. Perhaps a lesson can be learned in this connection from the failure of middle-class parents to heed the pain of slum parents who wept silently for years while their children were being destroyed by drugs. The pusher is now in the schoolyard of the middle-class child, and so the alarm is sounding at last. It would have been more prudent to be concerned with the well-being of all children as protection for the individual child. Our public schools are where most of our children are. If we do not make them safe, healthy, and happy places for all children, it is likely that the handful who can momentarily be spared their inequities, will not ultimately have been spared. Already, children from the most carefully selected schools have been held up for money, or approached for drugs by children from their own or other schools on their way home.

The nation's health depends on the vigor of its public institutions, and it is especially the public schools that must be made to rise to contemporary challenges. It is that kind of reality that confronts us today, and all parents must face the task of transforming the public schools into places where all children can grow sturdily and learn well. It is a pity that the calls for completely individual choice of school that would lead to fragmentation of the public schools fall so neatly into the far from idealistic ambitions of the budget-slashers, as romantic and cynic meet on common ground. But, in spite of the criticism and attacks leveled against the schools, the country as a whole is not likely to give up its allegiance to free, public education as an institution of a democratic ideal. When the public schools work, they act to bring together children of all classes, races, and religions under an umbrella of commonly agreed-upon democratic principles. The fact that they do not always work is a reflection of society's unavowed but true aims and priorities, despite its lip-service to the common welfare and democratic principles. Yet these are the very issues which should bring parents and teachers together in a common struggle.

While parents of public school children in some communities have tried to effect change in their local situations, they have not, on the whole, been sufficiently conscious of their strength to overcome the bureaucratic structure that represses teacher participation in policy-making as well as their own. Yet parents and teachers are the two groups most directly involved. The times call for an alliance of parents and teachers to offset the authoritarian decision-making that stems from the offices of those within the public schools who are remote from the children. Just as important is the battle to wrest school financing from its low priority in the planning of legislative bodies that control public funds. The state of any nation's health and morality can be gauged by how it treats its children, and, for a wealthy nation, we have treated ours shabbily. Parents must build support for realistic school budgets. Teachers are entitled to be paid salaries commensurate with their requirements as professional people. Children are entitled to class sizes in which they do not get lost. Schools require physical facilities and services that make life constructive as well as bearable for the children and their teachers. The percentage of our national funds given to these priorities is not worthy of our national wealth. Worse, even when money was poured into education, as in recent years, its thrust was political, and the demand for quick and easy results led to further exploitation of children.

Parents should participate in the formulation of their schools' long-range plans and be involved in, or at least informed of, the reasoning behind the schools' major choices and decisions in carrying out its programs. But that involvement can only be as great as is compatible with the extent that professional competence and experience are required for the conduct of the school as an optimal learning environment. It is foolish for parents to reject the professional knowledge and experience of teachers, just as it is shortsighted of teachers to reject the life experience and knowledge of parents. Working together, they can act as a force to shape the social-political-legislative factors which impinge upon every local community, even as they carry out the specific realities of school and family interaction. If the school environment is to provide a healthy climate for children, then it must be healthy at the adult level, too. This means that it must be so organized that channels of communication are open among teachers, guidance workers, health personnel within the school, and with families, recreational facilities, and service organizations of the community outside the school.

Once united on behalf of all children, parents can turn their attention to two other overall influences which must be resolved for all children, or find themselves helpless when it comes to their own children. We refer to the right of children to space for play and to the responsibility of television for balance and sanity in their transmissions to children.

The Right of Children to Play

Children are asked to achieve competence on adult terms so overwhelmingly that something of their developmental growth is inevitably lost. Children need to test themselves and generally grow acquainted with the world on their own terms in experiences separate from their need for adult direction and guidance. There is little opportunity for legitimate exploration and experimentation in the manicured outdoors of suburbia or on the concrete playgrounds of the city. Neither gives much opportunity to children to achieve the deep conviction of competency that follows victory over self-chosen challenges. The drive for schools that allow action and movement has begun, but it remains a fact that large-scale urbanization has steadily decreased the number of places where children can play independently, even if the hours were available to them. Yet play is the birthright of childhood, and parents must take the initiative to protect the rights of their children to time and space in which they can play imaginatively and freely in the necessary way of childhood maturing. This means not only space and free time at home and action-oriented curricula at school, but parental action to force communities to set aside real estate for its children. The more crowded the cities become, the more serious is the problem of children's play. Space set aside for them must be of the kind that allows for challenge and exploration, manipulation of materials, and independent construction of all kinds. There may be no profit in this, and no observable, measurable gains. But the loss to children's physical and mental health when they do *not* play is something we are unfortunately able to see quite clearly when the opportunity is not there.

Childhood play is a bulwark of mental health. Within its self-imposed structure, children set up and resolve challenges and conflicts that are physical, intellectual, and social in nature. The emotional deepening that ensues as they become masters of themselves in these areas leads to important inner growth during the middle years. Very different types of competencies are equally satisfying to children, who do not as yet attach status value to one kind of learning over another.

Analysis of games children play during the middle years reveals the surprising comprehensiveness of their efforts. Beginning with a primary need to be physically skillful and able, they play games involving climbing, jumping, leaping, skating, swimming, biking, rope games, ball games, and many others, through which they test themselves and compare their skill with others. They gauge their striving by looking ahead to older children for standards and back to younger ones for a yardstick of their progress. So deep is the need for physical competencies of all kinds that the Opies, in their study of children's games, were able to classify some of the games children learn from each other over the generations as "contests mainly requiring strength," "contests requiring nerve and skill," "contests requiring fortitude," "games in which the qualities of most account are physical strength and stamina," and "games in which players incite each other to show their mettle." [1]

Some of this physical testing is individual, and muscular coordination is the goal. But much of it takes place in groups, and problems of cooperation and constructive competition are then tackled as well. Through games like hopscotch, hide 'n seek, giants, Johnny-on-the-Pony, and a host of others, children learn to cooperate and compete within a social framework of rules and timing. Children's play, unorganized and unsupervised by adults, allows them to be inventive, to use initiative and imagination, to be creative and social. Without adult evaluation or extrinsic reward, and truly at their own pace, they explore, experiment, test, err, and try again. They learn in many diverse areas without anything more threatening hanging over their heads than their own and their peers' estimation of how they are managing. That is serious, but it is not without balance. There is always the chance to try again and to practice some more. For there is no such thing as being "left back" in play.

The same kind of testing and stretching of self that appears in the physical and social realms appears in the intellectual

[1] Peter and Iona Opie, *Children's Games in Streets and Playground* (London: Oxford University Press, 1969).

realm also. The old standbys of Ghost and Geography are games which call for specific knowledge. Card games which children willingly play by the hour require and strengthen arithmetical adeptness. Through games of chance, such as Old Maid and Monopoly, children learn strategy as well as computational skills. They love the challenge to their memory, ingenuity, and imagination as they sharpen their minds in shrewd guessing on the basis of concealed clues. Games like Coffee Pot and Twenty Questions strengthen skills of abstract thinking. Collections of stones, butterflies, or car models give them experience in organizing, labeling, and classifying.

That children have for centuries helped each other in this way is a tribute to the natural urge to learn which is so basic a characteristic of childhood. The emotional equilibrium that follows constructive play involving body, mind, and psyche explains why adults recall this period in their own lives with such nostalgia. But today's children are being slowly compressed into a largely passive existence. They sit at school, sit through television, sit through after-school homework, lessons in music, art, crafts, religion, and foreign language. When they play, it is all too often under adult supervision and according to adult rules.

The opportunity for self-determined learning must be saved for this and future generations of children. The fact that the natural proclivity for learning through play has not been used well by adults as a guide to children's schooling is more serious than ever. For one thing, technology in education promises to be the instrument for denying individual initiative even further if it continues to be used for limited traditional goals. For another, cutbacks in space for play are proceeding at a rapid pace, as the fields everywhere give way to housing and roads. It is for parents to recognize their responsibility for their children's basic needs and to take action in the schools and in the community to guarantee their fulfillment. This will not be an easy job, but it must be done.

The Impact of Television

One cannot discuss the threat to children's self-directed play without also considering the negative aspects of television, which has, in large part, replaced play. It is beginning to look as though television, like the miraculous antibiotics and DDT, has hidden side-effects which only the Cassandras foresaw, but to which we must at last give attention. The most common complaint has long been with programming in which violence plays so large a part, or in which sex and violence are presented as interrelated, making the adult world appear to children to be as violent in reality as their most exaggerated fantasies. Such focus, without sufficient counterbalance of non-sadistic human reactions, supports an inexcusable distortion of children's awareness of reality. As far back as 1960, Selma **Fraiberg** warned in strong terms of the consequences of too much exposure to violence in the mass media:

> While all young children reveal pleasure in destruction and violence, we consider in our society—and in all civilized societies—that these aggresive and destructive urges must undergo a radical alteration in order for civilized values to survive. . . .
> In the civilized human being we expect to see disgust and revulsion against sadism. . . . This . . . is absolutely necessary for the survival of human values and today, one may add, it is absolutely necessary for the survival of the human race. . . .
> The danger to our children is self-evident. A child whose senses are flooded daily by the sights and sounds of brutality is in danger of losing the capacity to summon revulsion against brutality.[2]

The phenomenon of excessive violence is accepted as a fact of life by young children, just as drugs are. What relation this has to the increased incidence of children on tranquilizers or of

[2] Selma Fraiberg, "The Mass Media: New Schoolhouse for Children," *Child Study, 1960.*

drug-taking itself is anybody's guess. While TV alone is not responsible, it has played a major part in exaggerating the existence of sadism in human experience.

Selma Fraiberg speaks on this, too:

> Mass media have not created the appetite for violence; they have only discovered an appetite and expended their talents on increasing the market for it. And they have discovered that one of their steadfast and most loyal consumer groups can be found among children. They are not motivated by a desire to corrupt the young; their only motive is to build a market for a breakfast food or a soft drink. . . . If the average child spends only three hours a day before a television screen, we will have to admit that a substantial part of his education is in the hands of the manufacturer of breakfast foods, his script and ad writers. . . . Certain of the educational aims of the mass media are directly opposed to the educational objectives our society holds for children.[3]

Television programming for children need not be saccharine or insipid in order to give to violence its proper balance in the scheme of things. Violence has a legitimate place in children's stories, when its appearance is logical in the narrative. A part of life, it is a part of literature, too. But as an endless diet for the sake of excitement and sensation in stories whose plots are vehicles for killing and torture and little more, it is not healthy for young children. Unfamiliar as yet with the full story of human response, they are being misled when they are offered perversion before they have fully learned what is sound.

Even more serious in some ways is the attack television makes on children, which was discussed earlier, and that is the seduction of children into the consumer economy before they are old enough to have judgment and experience to help them make choices. It is remarkable that, although the commercial backers of the broadcasting industry have smugly and arrogantly rubbed their hands in glee over the "kiddy market," parents have not really fought back hard. They have been torn between the dentist's admonitions that children should not be

[3] *Ibid.*

eating too much sugar and their youngsters' demand for the sugar-coated cereals pushed by the commercials. They have struggled with their guilt about saying "no" to the children's endless requests for purchases suggested by children's programs, and they have had to cope with their chagrin when, after they have yielded, the purchases proved worthless.

Everybody has been "taken," but not until recently have the effects on children at last created some public alarm. For example, an article on children's television appearing in *The New York Times* of December 27, 1970, included the following statement: "It is not surprising that children who are exposed to 350,000 commercials by the time they finish high school grow up to be deeply suspicious of a society which systematically lies for profit." The same article went on to document the fact that some programs are so indifferent to anything but the "sell" that they ignore the guidelines for radiation safety by calling children up close to the screen, while others play on vanity, greed, competitiveness, and the whole range of lower level feeling to stir up an appetite for what is being sold.

On July 2, 1971, a *New York Times* report on a survey of children's programs in sixteen countries concluded that "American network programs for children were marked by a high degree of commercialization and a low level of informational content compared with other countries" and also found that there are more commercials on American children's programs than on adult evening programs, twice as much advertising as in any other country surveyed, and an undifferentiated pitch to children from age two to twelve.

Television has had another kind of influence, which falls into a different category altogether, one related more to the medium itself than to the message. This is described in an article addressed to teachers concerned about the growing distance between themselves and their high school students, a phenomenon that exists at the college level, too.

We are experiencing the children of the multimedia generation. Theirs is a world of images rather than sentences. Theirs is a

world of non-verbal symbols rather than words. Those born before the age of electronic media glimpsed briefly the picture images of movies. Certainly television did not play an important
part in our growing years. We are now experiencing the first
multimedia generation, a generation that has been bombarded
with the most beautiful and grotesque images man has created
for himself. . . . This generation . . . came to school aware
and armed with images. They came to school with images of action, of creativity, of destruction. They came to school, and we
gave, and continue to give them, what we understand best. We
give them words. It stems from our traditions: "In the beginning was the word . . . So let it be written, so let it be done."
We seem to be at odds with this generation at the most basic
level.[4]

The difference in thought responses that result from dependence on the oral or written word as against dependence
on visual images is sufficiently disruptive of the education still
rooted in books to warrant a brief analysis here.

The moving visual image is a timely answer to the need to
grasp the increasing complexity of life and its multiple cause
and effect relationships. Film can draw the mind beyond a literal, limited perception of reality by presenting a sweeping
panorama of many factors at once. Time can be hastened, distance shortened, and two or more people can be heard simultaneously. By allowing for focus on comparison and immediacy
of synthesis, film opens new dimensions of thought to the
viewer. It is an inevitable and appropriate form of communication for coping with the pace of change to which man is harnessed by virtue of his technology.

By contrast, the word, especially the printed word, is more
slowly paced, its images unfolding step by step over time
within the mind of the reader, and not before his eyes. But that
more leisurely speed allows him to pause and reflect, to question and think, to reread and clarify, as he responds to the ideas
embedded in the print. With TV, the immediate totality of

[4] Berman Leonard, "Rationale for a New Humanities," *The Humanities
Journal,* National Association for Humanities Education, November 1970,
pp. 20, 21.

the visual image in a continuous flow of simultaneity can be exciting and stimulating. But the rapid succession of excitement and stimulation leaves little time to think and almost no time to feel deeply.

It must be said that the struggle to attain depth in film is certainly going on, and new generations may well adapt to the increased pace of exposure to experience. But the loss of time for reflection and reaction has become a disturbing facet of our lives. At all levels of functioning, decision-making has been forced into superficiality, as haste and deadlines geared to technological functioning rule our lives. It may be that, in time, parents and children will meet again around common communication styles rooted in a joint experience with the visual media. But we are still in the transitional stage, when the human mind, capable of depth as well as breadth, is not coping well with the pace set by technology for breadth but not for depth. Even young parents have not experienced the full inundation by images that is so much a part of their children's lives.

This particular consequence of an image era described by Berman is being dealt with here in order to alert parents to possible effects of heavy doses of television viewing on children's reading. At the upper reaches of schooling, there is already a marked reluctance to use the more slowly paced linear mode of learning. We must therefore ask ourselves whether the price of superficiality is really necessary for the increased horizons opened by the world of images, or whether we can have the best of both worlds—using the word and the image for depth and breadth without injury to the one by the other. If we choose the latter path, then the parental role in relation to both television and reading becomes crucial to children, because the wielders of the mass media as they now exist for instant gratification and sensation are so powerful that the educational institution of the school cannot cope with their adverse effects alone. There must be parental involvement of a deliberate kind and combined action by parents and schools to right the imbalance.

Few are the parents who would have their children dependent on the visual image as the sole mode of learning. Parents want their children to read, to read well, and to read for pleasure. But the circumstances under which their children develop reading skills today are unfamiliar, not only because the television set is a competitor, although it need not be, but because the whole country has mobilized to pressure children into earlier and earlier academic achievement, making of reading a burden, not a source of satisfaction. The anxiety created among parents, teachers, and children is a serious enough block to reading progress. In combination with image orientation, it is costing children the loss of an important tool for learning in depth.

Admittedly, television has been a boon to busy mothers, but the price for the unselected, built-in baby-sitter comes too high under present conditions.

Only parents can protect their children from the greedy, the cynical, and the ignorant who make their way into children's lives with indifference to their needs. There are three positive steps parents can take to thwart the endless exposure to violence, sex with violence, and the continuous seduction of their children into helpless supporters of the economy. They can apply strict censorship of what their children may view when they themselves are not present; they can teach their children to be critical viewers, especially of commercials; and they can begin to tackle the big job of changing the fare offered to children. The first two involve a careful study of what the offerings actually are, which means time spent viewing programs to catch their tone and basic message. This is time well spent, because only as parents monitor programs will they themselves become the ones who determine whether the projected message is one they want fed to their children. If some inappropriate television programs cannot be kept from the children, as is sometimes inevitable, they can at least be viewed together, so that clarification, assurance, and other mediation can be supplied.

And for the third, parents will have to become involved in

346 THE LEARNING CHILD

the mass lobbying and action that are needed to effect the changes necessary to their children's well-being. Some organizations of parents and other interested citizens devoted to altering the nature of children's television already exist, such as Action for Children's Television Group (ACT), begun by four mothers in Newton, Massachusetts, the National Citizen's Committee on Broadcasting, and the Citizens' Communication Center in Washington, D.C. They must be supported by all who care about children's mental health.

Changing the Schools

Let us close with a final statement of what could make school satisfactory to children.

School and society are intertwined and it is our view that society's major problems are no longer complex scientific problems, but problems of values. In a changing world, changing family, and changing schools, we must help children to feel safe by affirming the values we believe to be enduring, even as we teach them to be open to knowledge that may change forms. Premature disillusionment with vacillating and uncommitted adults is unsettling for children and leads to feelings of helplessness. Parents must muster the conviction that people can control their lives and pass this conviction on to their children at home and at school.

When the society is stable, the main problem of education and child-rearing is the induction of children into the life and ways of the adult world. But when the society is in conflict, and the future uncertain, then the main problem is to help children achieve a sense of identity. The psychologist Robert Havighurst suggests that

> . . . the modern world needs people with a complex identity who are intellectually autonomous and prepared to cope with uncertainty; who are able to tolerate ambiguity and not be driven by fear into a rigid, single-solution approach to problems,

who are rational, foresightful and who look for facts; who can draw inferences and can control their behavior in the light of foreseen consequences, who are altruistic and enjoy doing for others, and who understand social forces and trends.[5]

Acknowledgment of such need must cause a dramatic shift in our educational focus.

Education has deteriorated into a pumping of information into persons without regard for the fact that a life satisfying to human beings is one shaped in terms of human relationships. The capacity to love and the capacity to work make more sense than ever in a push-button civilization so managed as to rob individuals of their deepest sense of self as men and women of dignity. To negate such effects, we must consciously support the slow pace of emotional maturing and avoid the false precocity that now replaces depth; we must encourage commitment to serious effort in childhood on childhood terms. The education of children at home and at school must be committed to goals of mental health such as these suggested below:

Positive feeling toward the self: a sense of safety, competence, mastery; enjoyment of one's own powers as a sensing, feeling, thinking being; expectation that one's own capacities will find approximate fulfillment.

Realistic perception of self and others: differentiated knowledge of self available to match the scope and content of wishes and ambitions; capacity to see others in terms of their motivations, opinions, and conditioning in life circumstances.

Relatedness to environment: a positive, motivated connectedness with the contemporary world of processes and ideas; the ability and drive to exercise capacities and skills in effective, responsible functioning; capacity to expand orbits of identification beyond the realm of personal encounter.

Relatedness to people: capacity to relate to others as individuals relatively free from group stereotyping; to develop and sustain relations of depth and warmth; to find a balanced, flexible way of interacting with others, while sustaining the core of one's own individuality.

[5] Robert Havighurst, Private correspondence with author.

Independence: freedom to undertake independent thinking, judging, acting; freedom from compulsion to submit or conform;
adaptation governed by objective evaluation of situational demands and ultimate individual goals; capacity to accept a position of dependence (take help), where insufficient knowledge, experience, and strength dictate it; balance between
adaptation and the need to sustain individual autonomy.

Curiosity and creativity: a sustained and deepened curiosity; a
drive to penetrate the unknown and to engage in directed
search for resolution; to keep imaginative processes in vital
condition and to be able to transform these into productive,
creative reorganization of experience.

Recovery and coping strength: the capacity to regain equilibrium
in the face of trauma, frustration and crisis; to corral and integrate available strength in the face of challenge and obstacle.[6]

Development of this kind is attainable through serious and
constructive learning. Knowledge and skills should be the outcome of any educational experience, but *how* children come to
content makes the significant difference in their lives as human
beings and as learners. Schools which do not offer children
solid content leave them unhappy and restless; but schools that
stress content without consideration for children's feelings and
social needs leave them unhappy and feeling inadequate.

Our schools are being challenged, and it is a time of change.
But the changes must reflect society's need for humanist values. There is a flood of interest in the informal, open school,
and the time is ripe for parents to find each other and join with
the teachers and administrators who are, or want to be, part of
that humanist stream. Together they can shape our schools in
ways that will give children the strength to make a good life
for themselves and their society.

Changes in schools must begin with adults. The hierarchy of
authoritarianism and compliance must give way to teacher and

[6] Adapted by Charlotte Winsor, Bank Street College of Education, from the
chapter by Barbara Biber titled "Integration of Mental Health Principles in
the School Setting," Chapter XV in *Prevention of Mental Disorders in Children,* by Gerald Caplin.

parent participation in policy-making and an ongoing evaluation of programs, innovations, and materials. Schools must become part of a network of child-support institutions that together deal with the total concerns of all children and families. Both in teacher education and within the schools, focus on developmental teaching must replace the adherence to skill-learning for its own sake. Competition and rewards and punishment within the status system of grades must give way to constructive evaluation of learning and growth. Mental health and child development specialists must become as familiar a part of school organization as books.

We must recognize that there are many ways in which a school can be a good school. If every staff were free to develop appropriate, specific curricula for its particular children within a generally agreed-upon set of mental health goals, we would enjoy a variety of programs such as we cannot now envision. Nor need we go on assuming that only adults care. Children gain satisfaction and ego strength from learning when their right to a childhood is protected.

Let us take our cue from a child of eleven who said it "like it is" for children:

> "You know, kids really like to learn; we just don't like being pushed around."

Index

. . .

Opie, Peter and Iona, 210–11; *Children's Games in Streets and Playground*, 210 *and n.*; *The Lore and Language of Childhood* 210 *and n.*

organization: *see* class; school

parents: childhood dependence, independence, 120–4, 298–300; and childhood feelings of competency, 53, 124, 310, 337–40; faith in children, 181–2, 186; help in reading, 180–1, 319–24; praise, 109–10; role in learning, 56–7, 79, 109–11, 193, 306, 316–24, 327–9; supportiveness, 52–4, 103–4, 217–19, 317–19; and TV, 346–7; *see also* achievement, pressure for; anxiety; home and school; home-school relations

parents and community action, 334–47

Pasamanick, B., and Knobloch, H., 85 *n.*

Pasamanick, B.: *see* Kawi

peers: *see* friendship

philosophies of education: *see* education

phonics: *see* reading

Piaget, Jean: abstract thinking (conservation), 142, 197–200; and British Infant Schools, 4; concepts of space, time, 139–41; education goals, 137, 147–8; ego-centricity, 139; inverse relationships, 262; mathematical learning, 74–5, 195–201; number, 197; stages of development, 70–1, 74, 77, 84, 195–6, 249; words and word meaning, 197–8

play: children's right to, 337–40; in curriculum, 72, 93–5, 96–7, 154–6, 206; and ego strength, 209–11, 337–40; ennui in children, 210; imitative, 68–9; impairment of, 206–7, 209, 210–11, 338; intermediate years, 205–6; kindergarten, 89–95; and mental health, 338; primary years, 135, 154–6; and productivity, 206; symbolization and learning through, 68–9, 90–5; time, excessive organization of, 211; *see also* games; materials

Plowden Report (*Children and Their Primary Schools*), 316 *and n.*

political awareness, in children, xii, xiii, 151, 222, 226–31, 249–51, 276, 306, 310

poverty, effects of, 85–6

praise, 109, 176, 294

Pratt, Carolyn, 19, 32; *I Learn from Children*, 32 *n.*

prenatal influences: *see* intelligence; reading difficulties

prejudice, 134–5, 306; *see also* racism

primary grades: anticipation, reality, 144–7; concrete experience in, 151–60; curriculum, intellectual nature of, 148–51, mathematics, 73–5, 195–204, natural science, 160–3; reading, 165–87; social studies, 151–63; urban life, 151–9; writing, 188–94; *see also* intellectual growth; learning; sixes and sevens

programmed instruction, 5–7

psychological measurement, inadequacies of, 87–8

questions children ask, 38, 69, 132–3, 154, 155, 160, 235, 236, 239

Rabinovitch, Ralph, 183 *and n.*
racism: effect on children, 228–31, 314–15; *see also* black children; children
reading: basal readers, purpose and limitations, 174–7; as communication, 294–5; critical, 294; developmental aspects, 170–3; early readers, 83–4; history of teaching of, 165–70; individual, group teaching, 177–80; and intellectual growth, 72–3; and I.Q., 79; intermediate grades, 165–87; kindergarten, 75–9; levels by age, grade, 174–7; methods, 167–9, normal time range, 173, 186; parental help, 180–1, 319–24; phonics vs. whole word, 167–73; pleasure in, 294; primary grades, 165–73; progress, 186; readiness, *see* reading readiness; reversals, 184; spelling and, 166–7; as symbol system, 75–7; time tables, 173–7, 186; *see also* anxiety, reading difficulties
reading difficulties: diagnosis, 186–7, 294, 324–6; dyslexia, 183; emotional, 185–7; environmental, 85–6; maturational lag, 184; neuro-physiological, 183–5; prenatal influence, 85
reading readiness, 77–89, 93; dramatic play and, 93; power to abstract, 84; power to differentiate, 80; as a proc-

ess, 77–9, 82–5; sex differences, 83
report cards, 330–1
research, educational, 85–9; limits of, 87–9
responsibility in childhood, 31–5, 211–12, 241, 300–2, 305; monitors, 35; school size as factor, 34–5
Richardson, Elwyn, 280–1; *In the Early World,* 281 *n.*
Rosenthal, Judith, 213 *n.*
rote learning, 8, 17, 23–4, 42–3, 84–5, 243; and comprehension, 196–200; and imitation, 196; letters, 87–8; mathematics, 74, 87–8, 196
rules: at six, seven, 44, 125–6; intermediate years, 223–4

school: administration, 28–9; British Infant School, 3, 4, 5, 19; as community, 28–31, 37; doubts, tensions about, 22–23, 146–7; effect of, on children, 315–19; efficiency approach to, 7–11, 17–18; goals, 14–17; and mental health, 24–6; open school, 19, 349; organization, size, 28, 31, 34–5; two philosophies concerning, 13–14; and childhood responsibility, 34–5; and society, 7–8, 13–14, 31–2, as social units, 28–31; and world outside, 28
science, 95, 148, 149, 151, 152, 160–3, 266–71
selfhood, 52–4, 57–8, 120–4, 217–19, 241–3, 314–15; effect of school, 24–5, 337–40; self-evaluation, 109–10; threat to, 209
sevens: *see* sixes and sevens

sex: attitudes toward and education in, 131–4, 234–9, 312; children's questions, 235; curriculum, 189, 277–9; fantasy, 133; sex difference and: intelligence, 243, writing, 189; masturbation, 235, 311; sex play, 131–2, 133; TV and, 234
sex role: school attitude, 277–8; stability and change in, 231–34, 311–12
sixes and sevens: cheating, 126; competency, 124; conscience, 127, 128; dependence-independence, 120–4; inflexibility, 124–5, 126; learning style, 149; resistance to temptation, 128–30; rules, 124–6; school, meaning of, 144–7; stealing, 128–31; tattling, 127–8; *see also* primary grades
skills, 16, 75–7, 147, 170–3, 179, 188–9, 202, 203–4, 244, 263, 281, 294
sloppiness, 299
Smith, R. P., *Where Did You Go, Out, What Did You Do, Nothing*, 205 *and n.*
social relations: *see* friendship, groups
social sciences: *see* social studies
social studies: geography, 272–4; history, 274–7; history of subject, 16–18; intermediate grades, 270–77; kindergarten, 32–4, 90, 91, 92, 94–5; learning style in, 271; morality in, 276–7; primary grades, 151–60; urban life, 151–9
space and time: *see* concept learning
Spiritual Milk for Boston Babes, 14–15

Spock, Benjamin, 216
standards: *see* achievement
stealing, 128–31
Suchman, J. R., 244 *n.*
symbolization: *see* concrete experience, intellectual development, math, Piaget, play, reading

TV: *see* television
tattling, 127–8
teachers: attitude toward, 21–3; children's dependence on, 98–9; deprofessionalization of, 21–3; in kindergarten, 98–100; male attitudes toward, 22; mental health of, 46–8; and parents, 21, 22–3, 99–100; qualifications: educational, 45–6, emotional, 46, training, 48; role of, 21–4, 39–40, 41–6, 47–8, 98–100, 107, 177; supervision of, 22–3
technology: children's awareness, 151; in education, 7–8, 12; effect of, 31–2, 57–8, 214–16; and social environment, 151
television: and book learning, 343–6; impact on children, xii, 113, 341–7; parents' role, 342, 346–7; and reality, 341; and violence, 341–2; *see also* consumer orientation, parents and community action, violence, war
tests: *see* anxiety
testing of intelligence, 9–10, 12; limits of, 8
time, space and: *see* concept learning
timetables: *see* reading
Torney, Judith V.: *see* Hess, Robert D.